P9-BJS-809

Playwrights for Tomorrow

VOLUME 4

*The World Tipped Over, and
Laying on Its Side*

BY MARY FELDHAUS-WEBER

Visions of Sugar Plums

BY BARRY PRITCHARD

The Strangler

BY ARNOLD POWELL

The Long War

BY KEVIN O'MORRISON

EDITED, WITH AN INTRODUCTION, BY ARTHUR H. BALLET

PLAYWRIGHTS FOR TOMORROW

A Collection of Plays, Volume 4

THE UNIVERSITY OF MINNESOTA PRESS · MINNEAPOLIS

© Copyright 1967 by the University of Minnesota

The World Tipped Over, and Laying on Its Side © Copyright 1966 as an unpublished work, 1967 by Mary Feldhaus-Weber. *Visions of Sugar Plums* © Copyright 1964 as an unpublished work, 1967 by Barry Pritchard. *The Strangler* © Copyright 1966 as an unpublished work, 1967 by Arnold Powell. *The Long War* © Copyright 1966 as an unpublished work, 1967 by Kevin O'Morrison.

Printed in the United States of America at the Lund Press, Minneapolis

Library of Congress Catalog Card Number: 66-19124

CAUTION: Professionals and amateurs are hereby warned that all plays in this volume, being fully protected under the copyright laws of the United States of America, the British Empire, the Dominion of Canada, and all other countries of the Berne and Universal Copyright Conventions, are subject to royalty arrangements. These plays are presented here for the reading public only, and all performance rights, including professional, amateur, motion picture, recitation, lecturing, public reading, and radio and television broadcasting, and the rights of translation into foreign languages are strictly reserved. Particular emphasis is laid on readings, permission for which must be secured in writing. All inquiries concerning these rights should be addressed to the author or his agent as named in the note appearing at the beginning of each play.

PUBLISHED IN GREAT BRITAIN, INDIA, AND PAKISTAN BY THE OXFORD UNIVERSITY PRESS, LONDON, BOMBAY, AND KARACHI, AND IN CANADA BY THE COPP CLARK PUBLISHING CO. LIMITED, TORONTO

812.08
B191p
v.4

192067

Mills College Library
Withdrawn

MILLS COLLEGE
LIBRARY

Playwrights for Tomorrow

VOLUME 4

INTRODUCTION

Arthur H. Ballet

In 1963, with financial aid and encouragement from the Rockefeller Foundation and with the blessings of the University of Minnesota, the Office for Advanced Drama Research (O.A.D.R.) was created. Our purpose has been to make the funds and talents of an active theatre community in Minneapolis–St. Paul and suburbs available to playwrights.

The assumptions under which this program has operated are basic: that living theatre must encourage new writers and must not depend solely on either "classics" on the one hand or the established "success" on the other; that between the smash hit and the disastrous failure of the professional theatre there should be room for the developmental and experimental so that the artists of the theatre have an opportunity for growth; and that a major university, in company with a body of active theatre groups, can provide writers with a testing ground for their skills, their ideas, and their talents.

In the four years that O.A.D.R. has operated we have had a reasonably good batting average. In Volumes 1 and 2 of *Playwrights for Tomorrow* were represented such writers as Maria Irene Fornés, Lee H. Kalcheim, Megan Terry, and Terrence McNally, all of whom went from their work with O.A.D.R. in its first year to Broadway and off-Broadway production. In the succeeding years of O.A.D.R., our playwrights have continued to move into the mainstream of the American theatre: Rochelle Owens, Sam Shepard, Jean-Claude van Itallie, Romeo Muller, Herbert Lieberman, and Philip Barber are only a few who built on their work under this program's aegis to achieve professional production.

The financial resources available for the program have not been great:

3

the seed grant from the Rockefeller Foundation, ticket sales for performances of plays presented under O.A.D.R. sponsorship, the university's support through released time for the staff, and, potentially, a share of royalties from the plays first developed here. But, with the dedicated cooperation of the theatres and writers involved, we have been able to use the money to greatest advantage. As Dolly Levi, in Thornton Wilder's *The Matchmaker*, says, "Money — pardon my expression — is like manure; it's not worth a thing unless it's spread about encouraging young things to grow."

Of the hundreds of playwrights considered each year, I try to select those writers who show the greatest promise. I have the aid and counsel of an Executive Committee appointed by University of Minnesota President O. Meredith Wilson. Members are Donald K. Smith, associate vice president of the university, chairman; Peter Zeisler, managing director of the Minnesota Theatre Company at the Tyrone Guthrie Theatre; Willard Thompson, dean of the university's General Extension Division; and Kenneth L. Graham, chairman of the speech, communication, and theatre arts department at the university. The playwrights are selected after careful reading of their work and, insofar as possible, personal interviews. The final decision on which playwrights to try to include in the program is mine, as director of the program; we learned early that committee selection invariably resulted in compromise and mediocrity.

Once a playwright is selected, a previously unproduced play he has submitted is circulated to a number of Twin City theatres, ranging from professional to community to educational. These producing groups are completely free to select those plays and writers in whom they find the greatest promise and with whom they'd like to work. Of perhaps twenty-five plays that I find of interest each year, only eight to twelve are finally produced.

Each playwright selected by a theatre (if he is available to that theatre during the time that it can work with him) is brought to the Twin Cities by O.A.D.R. He is given a modest honorarium (largely to replace salary which might otherwise be earned), a subsistence allowance, and, most important, developmental rehearsals and production before a discriminating and interested audience. We try, also, to bring to the Twin Cities one or more producers, critics, directors, or agents who have expressed interest in the playwright so that they may consult with him and see his work performed, which may lead to the play's being done elsewhere. We publish

4

some of the plays so that an even wider audience may judge them and perhaps bring about additional productions.

The O.A.D.R. underwrites the modest production budgets of the cooperating theatres, which in return share their profits on ticket sales for the new plays with the Office. More significant than any financial returns, the theatre offers the writer a laboratory, and the writer brings to the theatre the excitement and stimulus of working with a new script.

In Volumes 3 and 4 of *Playwrights for Tomorrow* are nine new writers. Four are in this volume and five are in Volume 3.

John Lewin's *Five Easy Payments* is both a sharp observation of and a hilarious satire on middle American mores. As playwright in residence at the Guthrie Theatre, Mr. Lewin wrote this play for a specific stage and company. He has since completed an adaptation of the *Oresteia*, published by the University of Minnesota Press under the title *The House of Atreus*. A production of this work, directed by Sir Tyrone Guthrie, was produced by the Minnesota Theatre Company in the 1967 season.

Jean-Claude van Itallie's *America Hurrah* was a much-discussed and highly praised off-Broadway production of the 1966–67 season. *Where Is de Queen?* is a brittle and wise blending of social comment and abiding compassion.

The Great Git-Away by Romeo Muller is fantasy based on frightening possibility. A collection of theatrical (and real) stereotypes (perhaps the more fashionable word would be "archetypes") face a new world in a highly moral comedy. This play was appropriately produced on the University of Minnesota Showboat and played to capacity most of the summer of 1966. Mr. Muller is a widely respected television writer, and he is in the process of adapting *The Great Git-Away* into a musical comedy.

A modern view of the smart set is wittily presented in John Stranack's *With Malice Aforethought*. The parallel between Restoration form and content and modern sophistication is brought off successfully in one of the jolliest high comedies our audiences have ever enjoyed. Mr. Stranack is South African by birth, American by adoption, and an international traveler by choice.

I, Elizabeth Otis, Being of Sound Mind by Philip Barber has been one of our most successful works, both with critics and with audiences. A mature, knowledgeable, and respected talent in the American theatre, Mr. Barber takes a view of small-town America that is honest and searing. At the same time his is an "old-fashioned" play in the best sense of that term.

Mary Feldhaus-Weber is a St. Paul poet who has chosen to work in the theatre, and in her *The World Tipped Over, and Laying on Its Side* she brings to the drama a keen and discerning ear and fresh insight. Her words and images shimmer brightly in a brief but penetrating theatre piece.

Visions of Sugar Plums by Barry Pritchard, who was playwright in residence at Theatre St. Paul, bears down unmercifully on the modern market place. Stifling routine and the easy laugh are the targets as Mr. Pritchard focuses sharply on a prevailing theme in modern drama. Mr. Pritchard is now in Hollywood writing for television and the films.

Theatre, drama, momism, identity, and Oedipus in reverse are startling-ly — and hilariously — welded together in *The Strangler* by Arnold Powell. The most pathetic of tragedies and the darkest of comedies, punctuated by the wildest of puns, this exciting theatrical piece is miraculously never a pastiche and always a moving experience. Mr. Powell is a teacher and theatre director at Birmingham-Southern College in Atlanta.

Kevin O'Morrison earns his keep as an actor in the Broadway theatre; in 1966 he appeared in *The Rose Tattoo*. His *The Long War*, which was worked with in Minneapolis under the title *Three Days before Yesterday*, is a major work which deals both bitterly and compassionately with questions of war and individual responsibility. The parallels to other eras, including our own, make a Greek heroic theme a modern commentary that is powerful and stirring.

A number of other writers, not included in these volumes for various reasons, also worked with our program. Mark Berman's *A Saxophone for America* was a workshop presentation of the Minnesota Theatre Company, and John Cromwell's *A Breezy Fourth* was given careful rehearsals and production by Theatre in the Round Players of Minneapolis. Sam Shepard's *Fourteen Hundred Thousand* was presented at the Firehouse Theatre, Minneapolis. Rochelle Owen's *Futz*, first presented by the Minnesota Theatre Company, Alfred Levinson's *Socrates Wounded*, produced by the University of Minnesota Theatre, and Herbert Lieberman's *Tigers in Red Weather*, also presented by the Minnesota Theatre Company, are all available in anthologies published by Hill and Wang, Inc.

And the program continues. Each day new scripts arrive, giving promise of an exciting discovery; almost every month a new play opens in the

Twin City area for an audience increasingly eager to make its own judgment of the work of playwrights; each year with pride we watch as "our" playwrights move on in the working world of the theatre. There are also problems and regrets: the struggle to make ends meet is often like something out of a nineteenth-century melodrama; critics are more often than not unsympathetic to new, unproved playwrights; audiences still want "hits" and are disinclined to buy tickets to see pigs in pokes; some of the best plays I read are not accepted by the cooperating theatres.

But over all the venture has been exciting, worthwhile, and, we hope, important. As theatres in the Twin Cities and throughout the country open their facilities to the playwright, there is increasing evidence that significant contributions can be made outside the commercial New York theatre, that amateurs and professionals and educators can join together effectively to work in the theatre, and that good drama can be nurtured. These volumes testify that such drama is not restricted to any one style, form, theme, or place: bouncing and vital and fresh, it is happening in many guises in all parts of the country.

MARY FELDHAUS-WEBER

The World Tipped Over, and Laying on Its Side

A PLAY IN ONE ACT

for Howard, South Dakota — in love and memory

Cast of Characters

AN OLD MAN
MUCK
ANOTHER MAN
A WOMAN

THE WORLD TIPPED OVER, AND LAYING ON ITS SIDE

OLD MAN

Think . . think . . think about the world tipped over and laying on its side. Think of all the pain since the world began . . the death of the white Christ . . the death of the black Christ . . the death of the black-and-blue Christ. That's why we're here, Muck. Because the world is laying on its side.

MUCK

I don't understand what you are saying. Say it again.

OLD MAN

We're here to build a concrete arch to hang the world on . . so it won't fall down. We're here to build a concrete beam to prop up the world so the world won't fall over. My God, it doesn't seem that it could fall much farther. There's no weight like the weight of blood and guts to pull something down. We're here to build a pair of concrete wings so the world can fly again . . great big beautiful white and gray wings, and we'll stick them onto the earth, and we'll make it stand up right, and we'll make it fly. What do you say, Muck?

MUCK

I say that it's time to pack up and go home. It's been a long day. Hot. And I'm tired.

OLD MAN

(*to audience*) You have just seen something that I would like to call

© Copyright 1966, 1967 by Mary Feldhaus-Weber. Address inquiries concerning performance or translation rights to Ellen Neuwald, Ashley Famous Agency, Inc., 1301 Avenue of the Americas, New York City.

Muck's emerging dignity . . or perhaps Muck's soul is lost and found, or perhaps . . Muck the Never Never, Well Hardly Ever. This is my problem. How to show a man he has a soul. Where do you start? Looking under a bushel basket? Or perhaps you get a grader and scoop up as much silt and chaff as you can, and see if there is a soul there under the pile. Souls are usually found under something, usually being held down. It's a rule of soul. So the problem is to find the little baby-fine fragile soul of Muck. Of course it's here. It's bound to be somewhere. If, in the time of time a god stood on his own feet and reached out into the heavens and pulled from the eye of the universe one small tear, and called it Muck, and cast it down on earth, a soul came too. Souls look like falling stars. Did you know that? So if there is a Muck, of course there is a soul too. Perhaps I don't have far to look, because once upon once, this man was a boy. And what happened then, Muck? You're eight years old. You're down by the river. You've been fishing. You're with your father. Tell us, Muck.

MUCK

(*slowly, as if hypnotized*) I'm . . small. (*A man appears from the side and enters the scene.*) My father is big and tall and strong. We've been out in the woods . . and by the river. We're going to catch our dinner. (*He wipes his hands on the sides of his pants and goes through the actions of trying to put a worm on a hook.*) Father? Father? You think it hurts the worm?

FATHER

(*laughs*) That's what worms are for.

MUCK

But look at it squirm, and wiggle, and it's going to drown because it can't get away to swim.

FATHER

Worms don't feel anything, boy. They just crawl on the ground and eat dirt. He won't even know when he's snapped up by a fish. Well, let's get to it. That's not the way. Wait till you smell the fish in the pan. Then you won't worry about any worm.

MUCK

You do it. Put the worm on.

FATHER

We should have named you Annabelle Lee after all. "We'll have a little girl," your mother said, "with long curls and we'll call her Annabelle Lee." But we got you instead, Muck. And you can't even bait a hook. You're no man at all! Come on, I'll show you, but you'll have to do it next time. My God, a worm. Boys *like* worms. Why, I used to have lots of worms and snakes and caterpillars. I'd hang up the old garter snakes at the end of the barn, put a nail right smart through old Mr. Snake's tail, and then I'd fire at them with a BB gun. See them squirm and jump. A snake doesn't die until the sun goes down. You can break its back, or split it down the center with a knife, but it just keeps moving around. There's a right time for a snake to die, and he won't go until it's the right time.

MUCK

Maybe the worm wants to wait too. See, it's like a snake. It's wiggling.

FATHER

Son, that's what worms and snakes are for. Throw your line in, Muck. Yes, sir, the Devil himself appeared as a snake and tempted a woman. A woman, and a snake, and an apple, and that's why man got thrown out of the Garden of Eden, and that's why I have to work for my bread. And you'll have to work someday too, until you die. Worms, snakes, they've got it coming to them.

MUCK

Mama won't even look at a snake. She wouldn't let a snake get her to do anything.

FATHER

Well, maybe that's what you think now, but you'll see. That's the way things are. Women get tempted by anything they hear. And lots that they see too. Come here. I'll show you how to skip stones across the water. See them bounce and jump? Just watch that one go.

MUCK

Why do mine always fall in the water?

FATHER

I guess you don't throw them hard enough.

MUCK

There! I did it. Look at the circles in the water where the stone hit it. Another circle and another circle.

FATHER

Come on, Muck, we've got to get to this fishing. (*a pause*)

OLD MAN

And then what happened, Muck?

MUCK

We went home . .

OLD MAN

Is that all? Nothing else?

MUCK

We . . uh . . we got a fish.

13

OLD MAN

Yes? What then?

MUCK

Well, we caught a fish, and two or three, and father got out his scaling knife . . sharp enough to shave with. "It cuts you so quick you hardly get a chance to bleed," he said. And then we put the fish in the water on a rope so they'd stay fresh . . and I got some wood for a fire . . and broke the big pieces over my knee so they'd fit the fire . . only dry old wood. And then he pulled the fish out of the water, and they were still alive. I could see them breathe.

OLD MAN

Yes? What then, Muck?

MUCK

(*This is very painful for him.*) Then he hit one on the head with a rock and it crunched . . and squished . . and the tail moved. And then he hit it again, and something broke. And he held it by the tail . . and the knife cut the scales off. But he's not dead, Papa! . . and the scales fell on the ground like mush. They were like rainbows on the fish, but when they were on the ground they were just junk and mush. And the fish still moved. He was still trying to breathe! And his body was all white and naked and his scales were lying on the ground and it smelled like the river. (*Muck talks more and more urgently and finally grasps his sides as if he were vomiting.*) He isn't dead, Papa. He isn't dead yet. And his skin is gone. And his eyes are open.

FATHER

That's what fish are for, son . . that's what fish are for. Why once I saw a man cut a fish in two with an axe and throw it back into the water and the front half just swam away. When that fish gets in the pan and you see him dancing in the grease, you won't worry about his skin then. (*Muck goes on watching the fish and once more grasps his sides. Muck looks at his father as if he doesn't understand. The man goes on about his business, not noticing Muck.*) Here it is. Piping hot. And you caught it yourself. Eat up now. You've got to have food if you're going to grow up to be a man.

OLD MAN

And did you grow up, Muck?

MUCK

Oh . . sure, sure. One day followed another . . some days it rained and some days it snowed . . and the sun shone and I went to school in the mornings. I got so I could read good enough to read the newspaper.

And I looked at things . . and walked and tasted and felt. In the summer I got so I could skip stones clear across the river. And I caught my own fish one day. And I got a lot taller . . and I could stand up for myself. Sure I grew.

OLD MAN

I heard people say that Muck became a chip off the old block. When you were twelve, people used to say you were his spitting image.

MUCK

(*simply*) Yeah. I guess so.

(*The father has now become Muck's twelve-year-old friend, young and awkward. He has on a hat and has his pants pulled up like knickers. Muck too is now a young gangling boy. While the action between the boys is going on a woman is sitting on one side of the stage. She plays a lyrical child of eight or nine years, just about the same age as we saw Muck in the river scene. She has long hair.*)

FRIEND

(*calling*) Hey, Muck!

MUCK

Hey, Weiner! How the hell are you? You brought your old man's pipe?

FRIEND

Yeah, yeah. And I've got the matches too.

MUCK

(*puts the unlit pipe in his mouth and takes a drag*) My God, that tastes bad!

FRIEND

Well, you're supposed to light it and put tobacco in it.

MUCK

It tastes like the pool hall smells, or the closet where Mother keeps the overshoes. (*They go through the process of stuffing the pipe and trying to light it. Muck also starts to roll a cigarette. They do these things while the little girl speaks. She is obviously not aware of their presence. It is almost as if there were a small wall between them.*)

WOMAN AS A SMALL GIRL

(*sits and hums to herself, her arms around her knees, then examines a scab on her knee*) Mama says if you pull the bandage real fast it won't hurt, but every day I lift it up a little bit and look to see what's happening. If she had a nickel for every time I fell down and a quarter for every time I lost a mitten, she says, she'd be rich. Rich enough to buy all the Band-Aids and mittens that I need. I don't know why I always lose the right one. It just happens. All those little ants living in a hole. They pile up little

15

pieces of sand like a volcano every time there's a crack in the sidewalk. (*She looks at them, then stands, seems bored.*) If you step on a crack you'll break your mother's . . back. Back. Back. Back. Here, ant lady, I'll put a leaf over your house so you don't get too much sun and it won't rot your good lace curtains. And then I'll put a flower by your house so you'll have a little garden. And a path for you out of sticks, so you can always find the way home. (*She gets up, gathers all these things from the surrounding area, and brings them back. She is bored, and at the same time seems used to playing games by herself. After some action of gathering the sticks, she stops and glances down, a look of surprise on her face.*) A bird. Lying on the ground. Come on now, get up and fly away. I won't hurt you. Are you tired and taking a nap maybe? (*She moves forward and touches it with one finger.*) Little thin orange toothpick legs. Fat stomach. Your feathers look sort of bad, Mr. Bird. They're all wet like you've been playing in the rain. Listen, Mr. Bird, I'll get you some water and you can have a drink and then maybe you'll feel like flying away. Mr. Johnson waters his grass every night, and he says that it makes it grow; and I'll get some water for you. (*She runs off and then returns.*) It's just a jar lid. It doesn't hold very much. But I don't want to spray the hose on you or anything because that would just make you cold. Now open your mouth. Hmmm. You don't want it. Well it's good for you. Now open your mouth. Maybe you're too sick to open your mouth. I'll get a stick and help you. (*She picks up a stick from the ant house and acts as if she were opening the bird's mouth.*) There now and I'll pour in the water. Pointy tongue. Wonder what your eyes look like. Like an old dead raisin. And now you're crying and you don't want the water and that's all I've got to help you. You're cold. You're cold all over and it's hot out today. I'll wrap you up in something and then when you feel warm, then it'll be nice again. Here's a doll dress. And I'll put it around you. (*She carefully wraps up the bird and sits back and hums . . and thinks. She looks at the ants, looks down at her shoes and finally back at the bird.*) I guess you're dead, aren't you. I guess you won't feel any better at all. Well, I don't know what else to do. I'll put you in a tree and maybe your mama will come and find you and she'll know what to do. Maybe you'll fly if I put you in a tree. (*She picks up the bird. All we see is the little rag or doll dress. She carries it carefully with her as she starts to walk away. She walks in front of the boys. They jump up when they see her. They are embarrassed that she has seen them smoking.*)

MUCK

What are you snooping around here for?

FRIEND

Your mother send you out to spy on what we're doing? Well, you'd better not.

GIRL

I'm not.

MUCK

(*beginning to tease her*) What you got there?

GIRL

Nothing. A doll dress.

MUCK

Since when do little girls go around killing little birds to play with?

FRIEND

How did you do it, Jill? Hit it with a stick? Or did you just stumble and fall on it?

GIRL

No. I just found it on the ground over there. It was laying there and I thought if maybe I gave it some water and it had a drink it would feel better. So I gave it some. A drink of water.

FRIEND

And it jumped up and down and said, chirp chirp. I'm Buster Brown, I live in your shoe! And my little dead smashed sparrow. He lives in there too!

MUCK

(*talking like the little girl*) So I gave it a little drink and then I hit it with a rock!

GIRL

NO! It didn't move. It just stayed there and the water ran down on its face . . like he was crying. So I got this dress. I wanted him to be warm.

FRIEND

(*in mocking tones*) So I got this little dress and I wrapped up the bird all nice and tight.

GIRL

And I thought I'd put it in a tree and the mama bird would come and . .

MUCK

What a dumb dumb dumb dumb dumb girl! It's DEAD. You DOPE.

FRIEND

It's deader than a doornail. (*Muck grabs the bird out of her hand.*)

GIRL

(*screams*) Give him to me!

17

MUCK

Hey, Weiner, you're the mama bird. (*He throws the dress to his friend. They run back and forth, playing catch, shouting, and laughing all the while.*)

GIRL

Give him to me!

FRIEND

(*still playing catch*) Come on, Muck. Throw it here! I've got a cat at home that eats baby birds, feathers and all.

GIRL

Please. (*Finally the dress is thrown high into the air. All three hold their pose as they watch it drift down to earth. The girl watches it fall, and cries. They all go off in slow motion.*)

OLD MAN

Time passes and time passed, time gone and time away. And God caused the fish to swim in the rivers and the birds to fly in the air. And he caused man to stand upright and walk on his two legs. You grew up then, Muck?

MUCK

What?

OLD MAN

You grew up? You walked upright? You reached your majority? What happened then, Muck? Tell me what happened.

MUCK

Oh, I don't know. I'm an ordinary sort of man. (*Muck stands simply. There seems to be sorrow in his voice.*) I thought about a lot of things when I was a boy, but they always used to say, "You'll get over that soon enough when you have to work for a living."

OLD MAN

And did you?

MUCK

Yeah. I got over all of it. One step at a time. I got over all of it. Funny, just like they said I would. Hey . . you think it hurts to die?

OLD MAN

What?

MUCK

You think that when you are laying there and you can't make anything move or do what you want it to, you think it hurts then?

OLD MAN

Oh, I suppose so. When you get older it always seems like there's pain to spare. Why do you ask?

18

MUCK

Well, you'll laugh if I tell you this . .

OLD MAN

No, I won't, Muck. I don't laugh very often. Really, Muck, when you think it's me laughing it's just things settling down into dust . . things that fly and swim and things that walk on the earth. That sound you think is laughing is just things going up, and things coming down.

MUCK

I see. (*He doesn't.*)

OLD MAN

What's this business about wondering if it hurts to die? You worried about that, Muck?

MUCK

I saw a dog die once.

OLD MAN

You a grown man then, Muck?

MUCK

Oh yeah. I'd gone to college and learned all of the songs. And I'd got married and I'd gone off to war.

OLD MAN

Who did you fight?

MUCK

Oh, I don't know. I never saw any of them up close. I just fired in the direction that they pointed me in. It wasn't so bad. A fellow had to do a lot of walking. But it wasn't too bad. Some gas got my lungs, but I got a little pension from the government. And we had a son when I got back home.

OLD MAN

Tell me.

MUCK

Well, see, we had this boy . . Ann and I. We waited a long time to be blessed with children, but finally we had a son. Tall and straight. He was a fine boy. He'd make airplanes in the backyard. Not models, you understand, but he'd get great big planks of wood and he'd put them together. The only thing he didn't have in one of them was an engine. The wife used to say that the boy made airplanes all the time because he wanted to be like a bird, so he could fly away from us. But I told her that boys need to have things to dream about. Well, see, I got the boy this dog. Nice strong dog. A boxer dog. I'd look out in the yard and there they'd be, the two of them. The boy making wings to fly with, and the dog, sitting watching him.

OLD MAN

Very pretty scene.

MUCK

Well, the dog used to fight a lot, and he'd come home all torn up and we'd patch him up . . he was a tough dog. And one time he came home with a great big gash in his neck.

(*The girl is now the mother, and the friend is a serious young boy, Muck's son. The three of them stand looking at something. Muck stands and faces the audience and reports this scene much as a sleepwalker might. This scene is most painful for him to tell.*)

MOTHER

Well, we can't afford to spend any more money on this dog. He's just a worthless dog. A tramp, coming home all chewed up like this again. There'd be some sense to it if he would stay at home and watch his own property like he's supposed to. Someone could come and steal us blind and he'd be out fighting.

SON

Father, we've got to get him to the doctor. His neck's all swollen and lumpy and he can't breathe.

MUCK

(*woodenly*) Money doesn't grow on trees, boy. You think I've got a money tree in the backyard to spend fifty or sixty dollars on a dog? I don't see you out working for a living. Everyone is sure quick to spend my money for me.

SON

He's stopped eating and he just lays there. His nose is hot. Come on, have a drink of water. Try to get up, boy. Try to get on your feet.

WOMAN

That animal has chewed my furniture and dug my flowers for the last time. Muck, I suppose you're just going to stand there and shell out sixty dollars for that dumb beast when I don't have a decent coat to wear that I can hold my head up in. You don't have the money, Muck. And you'll never have money to throw away. You see, boy, you treat the old man like he was the goose that laid the golden egg, but you'll see one day.

SON

He's all stiff and funny and he can't breathe. Please. Help. Please. Help me . . help me . . (*to dog*) I love you. I love you. Help me.

20

OLD MAN

What happened? Muck! What happened?

MUCK

(*as if coming out of a trance*) Well, let's see . . it's been a long time now. Well, we took the dog to the vet. Told him I couldn't afford to pay for an expensive operation like that . . but I'd leave the dog with him. Maybe he knew somebody that would want the animal . . they could pay for the operation, and have the dog.

OLD MAN

Well, that sounds like a good practical solution. How did it turn out?

MUCK

The dog died. I was there when it happened. I saw him. And my son saw him die too. I didn't mean for that to happen. But the vet said we got him there too late.

WOMAN

The Lord giveth and the Lord taketh away. (*At this time Muck hangs his head. The woman faces the audience and primly mouths the words. The son holds his sides and rocks to and fro. We remember Muck as a boy with the fish; the anguish is the same. All three people are drawn unto themselves. There can be no place where they will meet.*)

SON

Blessed be the name of the Lord.

MOTHER

There is a time to live . .

MUCK

And a time to die.

OLD MAN

And a time to rise up! And a time to fall back down. And a time to swim the oceans and a time to split the air with your wings, and a time to run faster than the wind . . a time to run so fast that not even death can catch you . . Time passes and time passed, time gone and time away. And Muck, remembering how he had been pushed over and how he too had tipped things over with his baby-fine black-and-blue soul, grew up to be a man . . like all men, I suppose. And he settled down like the concrete walk settles tightly to the ground: it runs up and down, and makes straight corners when it turns. And then Muck grew old. What happens to a man when he's down and out . . and when he's old, and when his skin is drawn so tightly over his bones that he looks more like a death's-head than a man . . with blue veins and dry parchment skin? He's always cold then, even though it's ninety-five out in the summer sun

. . the body is cold and has to be wrapped up in wool. And the curbs have gotten so high a man can hardly make it up over them. Even a block becomes a mile, and it's better to just sit and rest, and rock in the sun with the other old fogies, and tell each other a few lies . . I suppose there are better places to be than an old soldiers' home . . but if you don't have a home of your own to go to, it's better than a poor farm. And you can wear your soldier's hat and sit and rock and say, "They don't fight wars like that anymore" . . Yup . . It got my lungs . . I took my mask off for a minute, I felt like I had to sneeze, and it got to my lungs . . Doc said it's a wonder . .

MUCK

(*goes on with the old man's speech as he and the friend rock back and forth on chairs . . two old old men*) . . I'm here at all. "Must be a tough old buzzard," he said . . I've got lungs like an Army mule, he said.

FRIEND

Can't complain about that.

MUCK

Nope. Sure can't complain. (*a pause*)

FRIEND

It isn't like it was a man's home here . . a place where a man lived all his life . . where he knew all the folks and where he planted every tree and helped them get their growth.

MUCK

Well, three meals a day . . and a bed at night . . and a moving picture every Sunday . . and some young nurses to ask me how I feel and call me "Mister" . .

FRIEND

And "sir" and "the old gentleman" . .

MUCK

And some Legionnaires who come to call . .

FRIEND

And tell us that our country hasn't forgotten us . . (*a pause*)

MUCK

You know, those fellas smell kinda bad to me.

FRIEND

You old buzzard, you don't know what smells anymore. You're no rose yourself!

MUCK

Those Legion fellows smell of booze and sweat and mothballs. (*Woman as a girl, perhaps twelve or thirteen, lovely, innocent, enters.*)

FRIEND

Aw, come on now, Sergeant . . you remember back when you had to try to get into a uniform that wouldn't fit your shadow . . a uniform that the little lady put away in the cedar chest beside her wedding dress! . . That's what you smell on them . . *old*. When you've got mothballs and a tight fit like them fellas, it's *old*. That's all.

MUCK

They'll be here next . . sitting in the sun.

FRIEND

Old fogies like the rest of us. (*He looks off.*) Hey! There's old Shanty Bill's people again! Every Sunday, rain or shine, they get that old goat and take him for a little ride.

MUCK

Nothing wrong with that.

FRIEND

Maybe. Just maybe he don't want to go, that's all.

MUCK

Maybe so. Hadn't thought of it. (*His friend starts to doze and drops off to sleep. Muck continues to rock in his chair. The girl comes walking by. Muck smiles.*) You'd be some of old Bill's people, I betcha.

GIRL

I'm his granddaughter, sir.

MUCK

You're a lot prettier than he is . . What's your name?

GIRL

Angela.

MUCK

And how old might you be?

GIRL

Twelve. (*a pause*)

MUCK

(*finally*) Uh huh . . All right . .

GIRL

That's a funny hat you've got on.

MUCK

Wore that to the wars. You wouldn't think an old fella like me could even get out of this chair . . but once upon a time I was your age . . and once I went away to the wars. I was in the cavalry.

GIRL

(*interested*) Oh!

23

MUCK

You like that? You like horses? Do you? I guess all young folks do. I had a boy who used to. (*Muck is delighted at her interest.*)

GIRL

I've got horse pictures all over my room . . from calendars! And I've got thirty horse statues in my room! And I draw horse pictures all the time.

MUCK

You ever ride a horse?

GIRL

Once . . at the fair.

MUCK

Horses are a wonderful thing. A man's legs don't have to be strong if he's got a horse to ride on.

GIRL

I've only ridden once, but I know what it's like. I think about it all the time . . I dream about riding . . and he'd be running so fast that no one could catch me.

MUCK

What color is he?

GIRL

Black . . with a white star on his forehead!

MUCK

And what's his name?

GIRL

Diablo . . That's Spanish for "the Devil."

MUCK

Mighty spirited horse for a young girl to ride on. He might throw you.

GIRL

Oh, no! Of course, no one else can get near him, but he's very gentle with me . . I'm the *only one.*

MUCK

Was he hard for you to break?

GIRL

Oh, no! He was out running on the prairie and I called to him . . and he came over and I got on his back . . and we ran and ran and ran . .

MUCK

You ride him in parades?

GIRL

(*scornfully*) Of course not! He's not that kind of horse!

24

MUCK

Listen, Angela. I think maybe I can talk to somebody who might know where he is. (*as she looks at him doubtfully*) Well, these fellas around here have been all over the world and seen a lot of things!

GIRL

(*laughs*) I don't think so.

MUCK

Tell me again. Your name's Angela . . and he is Diablo . . and he's black and about . . oh, seventeen or eighteen hands high . . You home most of the time?

GIRL

I'm home all the time! Did you say you'd send him to me?

MUCK

Sure! I think I know a man who knows where he is . .

GIRL

(*shyly*) When . . when will he be coming?

MUCK

Any day, I think! But that won't matter . . You'll know how to take care of him when he gets there?

GIRL

Oh, yes! I know all about that!

MUCK

Well. He'll be coming!

GIRL

Really?

MUCK

Really! One day he'll be there! I think I can arrange something . . I just think I can . .

GIRL

I'll be there . . I'll be waiting . .

MUCK

Now you remember you've got to give him a rubdown after you ride him hard or he'll get stiff!

GIRL

Oh, yes! I know!

MUCK

And a carrot for him, and maybe a piece of sugar for him . .

GIRL

Oh, yes! Yes, I know! And . . well . . goodbye! And . . goodbye! I'll be waiting! (*She runs off.*)

25

FRIEND

Why did you go joshing a young girl like that?

MUCK

Go back to sleep, you old fool.

FRIEND

Why did you tell her that?

MUCK

Just go back to sleep . . it's nice here in the sun . . blue sky, the color of an old man's eyes . . watching the clouds bloom in the sky . . like a herd of a hundred chargers . . racing in the wind. (*a pause*)

OLD MAN

Muck? You asleep yet?

MUCK

Maybe. I can't tell anymore. Laying on my back this way . . looking up all the time . . it's like the world's laying on its side. From this view, it's like the world's laying on its side . . and I just lay here and watch it go on by . .

OLD MAN

Did you tip it over, Muck?

MUCK

I guess so . .

OLD MAN

Muck? . . Why didn't you tell that girl she was only fooling herself with that crazy dream about a horse called "the Devil"? Why didn't you "enlighten" her, Muck? . . Why didn't you kill off that horse?

MUCK

I'm tired. I'm going to sleep now. I'm just going to lay down beside the world here, and give it a little company, and go to sleep. (*sighs*) There . . There we be now . . (*Sighs. It is quiet. We hear taps in the background.*)

OLD MAN

(*walks slowly to the audience*) Here we be now . . Here we be . . to build a concrete arch to hang the world on. Here we be . . to build a concrete beam to prop up the world so the world won't fall down on us. But a man's arch is only three feet high, resting in the countryside, or just outside of the town . . a little piece of stone that's got his name on it, and the dates of the time when he ran from here (*gestures*) to here (*nod*) . . and then away . . (*A pause, a long one. Then he glances at Muck over his shoulder.*) Well, Muck? I guess we can pack up and go home

26

now! (*Then he addresses the audience again, significantly, but not without a sad humor.*) It's been a long day. Hot . . and you're tired . .

THE END

The World Tipped Over, and Laying on Its Side by Mary Feldhaus-Weber was presented November 27, 1966, at the Tyrone Guthrie Theatre, Minneapolis. It was directed by Michael Pierce.

Cast of Characters

THE MAN	Ken Ruta
THE WOMAN	Helen Carey
MUCK	Len Cariou

(Note. In this production the characters of the old man and the second man (father, friend, son) were combined. The play may thus be presented with a three-person cast. However, the playwright recommends that the fourth actor be used when possible.)

27

BARRY PRITCHARD

Visions of Sugar Plums

Cast of Characters

AL HUBBARD, mid-thirties
JOHN SHULTE, late twenties
ED COOGAN, sixty-two
PEACHES, late twenties
KETCHUM, mid-forties

VISIONS OF SUGAR PLUMS

ACT ONE

Scene 1

About 7:30 P.M. a week before Christmas. An editorial office where the company magazine, or "house organ," for a large Madison Avenue firm is written, designed, and edited. There are advertising posters and display signs about that indicate the name of the company: T.I.C. Two men, both well dressed but disheveled, are working busily on the upcoming issue of the magazine. One of them, Al Hubbard, sits at a long table talking to his wife on the telephone while making identifying marks on the backs of photographs to be used in the magazine. As he finishes marking each photo he hands it to the magazine's artist, who works nearby at a drawing board.

AL

(into phone) . . But it's not my fault — why get mad at me? . . You want me to lose my job? He doesn't care if it's your birthday, all he cares is I take pictures of the Christmas party . . *(hands picture to John as he reads information from back of it)* Mary Ann Matrango, Shipping Department.

JOHN

What?

AL

Bride's page. *(John looks at picture — makes face of annoyance. Al speaks*

© Copyright 1964 as an unpublished work, 1967 by Barry Pritchard. Address inquiries concerning performance or translation rights to Lucy Kroll Agency, 119 West 57th Street, New York City.

into phone, making certain no one is within earshot.) Look, Ketchum walks in here ten minutes ago and says, "Hubbard, bring your camera and plenty of film to the party — the photographer we hired got killed this afternoon on the Jersey Turnpike and can't make it tonight." So I'm supposed . . What? I don't know, I never even met him. He was just some photographer they hired to take pictures . . I don't know how many kids — maybe he wasn't even married. (*handing another picture to John*) Doris Cohen, Personnel, bride's page.

JOHN

(*taking picture, looking at it*) What an ox.

AL

(*into phone*) Anyway, I said to old rum-guts, "Look, this is my wife's birthday — we're all set to go out to dinner." He says, "Your wife can have her birthday anytime, we only have our Christmas party once a year." And he walks out.

(*Ed Coogan enters wearing the dark uniform of a night watchman. One of his arms is missing and the empty sleeve is pinned to the side of his jacket. With assumed nonchalance he crosses to John and, smiling, raises his hand in greeting which John acknowledges. He moves about uneasily for a moment as if waiting for something to happen, then goes to an ashtray near John, selects a long cigarette butt, and lights it. He continues to sort through the butts, depositing the more serviceable ones in his jacket pocket. Finished, he looks over John's shoulder, observing his work.*)

ED

Hey, not bad.

JOHN

Thanks.

ED

It'd look better though if ya'd arrange all those pictures in a circular fashion. A square arrangement looks . . (*Shrugs. John makes a face of controlled annoyance.*)

AL

(*into phone*) Sure I did . .

ED

(*to John*) Hey, lemme use your phone — I got an important call to make. (*John indifferently indicates consent. Ed goes to the phone on the desk behind John, gets an outside line, and dials a number.*)

AL

(*into phone*) I said, "Just a minute, Mr. Ketchum, my wife's birthday is a lot more important to me than any old . ." Well, actually, no, I didn't get a chance to say anything to him — he took right off . . Well what did you want me to do? . . I can't just . . It's part of the job! (*hands a picture to John*) Ketchum's niece — graduated business college.

JOHN

No room, no room.

AL

Ketchum's niece, make room.

JOHN

She doesn't even work here.

AL

(*shrugs*) Ketchum's niece.

ED

Hello, can I please speak to Mr. Cowan? . . Oh, is this him? (*familiarly*) Well, this is Ed, Ed Coogan . . from the other night . . Well, I was with a friend of yours you ran into at the White Rose on Third Avenue — Pete Jernigan . . As a matter of fact, you were sitting with him at the bar and I came up . . the White Rose . . Yeah, Pete Jernigan — he's an old friend of mine . . Coogan, Ed Coogan . . (*glances slightly at his empty sleeve*) Yeah, that's right, that was me.

AL

Hang on a minute, will ya, honey? (*He goes to another table and looks quickly through a pile of pictures.*)

ED

Well, so how are ya, Mr. Cowan? . . No, no, nothing in particular, just wanted to wish ya a Merry Christmas and all that . . Oh, not at all . . Oh, say, one other thing while we happen to be talkin' . . I couldn't help but overhearing when you were talkin' to Mr. Jernigan — Pete — the other night, you were saying you were lookin' for a man to open up a new territory in the Midwest for your arch-support company . . Oh, yes, I'm sure you said that — I was right there . . Well, I been thinkin' it over and . . (*with forced conviction*) I think I'm the man you're lookin' for! . . Yessir, I do!

AL

(*returning to phone*) Yeah, honey . .

ED

Yes, I was twenty-six years on the road as a salesman for T.I.C. . . . I'm still with 'em . . Well, not actively in sales, sort of behind-the-scene work. See, I had this hunting accident with my arm and I'm what you might call resting up a bit — between assignments . . Well, fifteen years ago . . Well, actually, if you were to describe it, it amounts to checking around here at night and making sure that everything's in order — just to keep my fingers in things, y'understand — a salesman has to . . Well, yeah, I guess you might call it that . .

ED

No, it's not a stag party, it's the *Christmas* party — it's just that only employees are invited . .

ED

I'm . . middle-aged . . Well, sixty-two, but you're only as old as ya feel. Heh, heh. The way I look at it, a man with my experience, age doesn't make that much . . Oh, I see, you already have . . Well, that's too bad, 'cause I'm available and lookin' for somethin' . . You know, nothing ventured, nothing gained. Heh heh . . Say, would ya do that, Mr. Cowan? I'd sure appreciate it. Let me give you a number, just in case . . Oh yeah, sure, of course — through Pete Jernigan . . Well, it sure has been nice talkin' to you again, Mr. Cowan, and . . Thank you, sir, same to you . . 'Bye . . (*starts to hang up, then as an afterthought*) And a happy . . (*phone is dead*) New Year . . (*looks at the phone and slowly hangs up*)

AL

Well, make yourself a sandwich until I get there . . You might starve by that time — I don't know how long I'll be . . As soon as I can . . I'll be there when I get there. All right, all right! G'bye! (*hangs up*)

ED

(*to John*) Very important friend of mine. Wanted me to open up a new territory for him but we couldn't get together. (*John butts a cigarette.*) Pays to keep up contacts though. (*crosses to ashtray, picks up butt*) You done with this? (*John sighs, nods.*) Couple of puffs left. (*lights up and examines layout over John's shoulder*) Comin' right along, ain't it?

JOHN

That wasn't the little woman, was it?

AL

Ya'd think it was the end of the world just because I get hung up on her birthday.

JOHN

Listen, if I was you I'd tell Ketchum to drop dead. Where does he get off makin' you go to the Christmas party at the last minute when you already got other plans?

AL

(*with determination*) By God, I got a notion to! You don't know how close I came to telling the old gas-bag where to head.

JOHN

You shoulda done it.

AL

If I didn't think I was goin' someplace in this job I would of.

JOHN

Aw, you ain't going anyplace; you shoulda done it.

AL

(*rise*) If you're so concerned about me getting stepped on, why don't you tell him for me?

JOHN

It's your battle, not mine.

AL

That just shows what a real yo-yo you are: I got a wife, and a kid on the way and you'd egg me into a fight with Ketchum where I might get fired just so you could get out of here and go to the Christmas party.

ED

Roll with the punches, boys, roll with the punches.

JOHN

Ah, you're sick. That's your trouble, you got a sick mind.

AL

Don't tell me. I know you. C'mon, wouldja? Get that stuff done so we can get out of here.

JOHN

Listen, I got an idea: why don't you go ahead to the party, take the pictures, and beat it. I'll just stay here and finish this up and when it's done I'll send it on to the printer. No use both of us stickin' around.

AL

Yeah, the last time I let you send something on to the printer without checkin' it, your layout looked like you threw up on it. C'mon, I know you, just get the work done.

JOHN

(*gesturing toward Al*) Ah, the editor of a crummy Madison Avenue company magazine. Steve Wilson of the *Illustrated Press*.

ED

Live and let live, live and let live. (*Chuckles. John glances at him with annoyance.*)

AL

Yeah, big trees from little acorns grow.

JOHN

That's you.

35

MILLS COLLEGE
LIBRARY

AL

Besides, the party hasn't hardly started yet. They're probably all still over at Longchamps.

JOHN

Christ, that's where I should be. But here I am, pasting up a bunch of mug shots. (*picks up a picture and holds it at arm's length*) "Jeannie Lee Radosovitch wed to James Jacobsen, December 2nd, Yonkers." James Jacobsen, what the hell's the matter with you? I don't know what kind of a dog you are, but you must be able to do better than Jeannie Lee Radosovitch. You don't know what you're getting into.

AL

How do you know?

JOHN

(*pause; puts picture down*) There's that lightning quick wit of yours again. (*pause*) Well, if we're stuck here, I'm gonna at least have a drink.

AL

You got something? (*Ed shows interest.*)

JOHN

(*reaches into desk drawer, takes out bottle of whiskey*) In case of snakebite.

AL

Do you think we should?

JOHN

Whatta ya mean "we"?

AL

What if Ketchum comes back, or Reardon?

JOHN

So what? Besides, nobody'll be back — they're all gone. Besides, everybody else is out having a good time, why shouldn't we at least have a drink? (*takes a drink from bottle, offers it to Al*)

AL

Yeah, what the hell. (*taking a drink*)

JOHN

That's what I like about you — the way you stand right up for yourself and make decisions.

AL

You gotta be careful if you're gonna get anyplace. Whew! That stuff is strong.

JOHN

That's why I drink it — it's the only way I can stand this job. (*takes bottle from Al and takes another drink*) Ah, that's what puts the roses in your cheeks. (*notices Ed — with an effort*) Have a drink, Ed?

ED

(*enthusiastically*) Well, I don't mind if I do.

JOHN

(*starts to hand him the bottle, then stops*) Let's see, there ought to be something around here you can drink out of. (*finds a paint cup, shakes it into a wastebasket, and wipes it out carelessly with a cloth*) Here we go. Had a little paint in it but that won't kill ya. (*pours a small drink, gives it to Ed*) Not too much; don't want to get you started.

ED

Aw, I don't have that problem anymore, John.

AL

Hey, be careful, that stuff might be dangerous.

JOHN

Naw, just a little tempera water paint. I got most of it out anyway.

ED

(*sips cautiously — tasting*) Not bad. (*sips again*) Tastes pretty good.

AL

Couldn't taste any worse than it does straight.

JOHN

Don't drink it if it tastes so bad. It gets ya where you're goin'.

ED

Yeah, it's not bad at all. (*to Al*) Here, try some. (*Al declines.*) What'd ya say was in here?

JOHN

Tempera water color. Indigo blue, I think.

ED

Indigo blue, eh? I'll remember that.

AL

C'mon, would ya get that done. My wife is waitin' for me to take her out to dinner.

JOHN

Yeah, yeah, yeah. (*going back to work, looking at pictures*) What a bunch of sows. (*takes another drink from bottle*) So how come you're not at the Christmas party, Ed? I mean, night watchman and all, you're officially an employee of this company even if you don't work the same hours as the rest of us.

ED

Oh yeah, well, ya know, somebody's got to watch the store.

JOHN

How d'ya like that? Old Ed here's worked for the company for over forty years, and they won't even let him go to the Christmas party, that's gratitude.

AL

Oh yeah, it's a pretty raw deal all right, but somebody's got to be here. Think of the people who work for the telephone company. They even have to work on Christmas. It's probably their busiest day of the year.

ED

Aw, it's not much fun unless ya know everybody. Workin' nights, bein' the only one here, I don't know none of the other people — except you, I mean, and Mr. Winkle who hired me . . arranged the job for me.

JOHN

Well, they could have at least gotten somebody from Temporary Manpower so old Ed here could go to the Christmas party.

ED

Aw well, you know. (*shrugs — drinks*) Say, where's this party at?

AL

At the Plaza, in one of the main ballrooms.

ED

(*impressed*) The Plaza, no kiddin'! Oh boy, that must really be somethin'. You should take your wives. That'd be somethin' they'd never forget.

AL

(*sourly*) No wives invited. Nobody invited but employees.

ED

Say, that's too bad.

JOHN

That's the best part about it.

AL

For you, maybe, not for me.

JOHN

You only been married a year. Wait awhile — you'll see.

AL

No sir, boy.

JOHN

(*working*) Tell me that this time next year — if ya haven't been fired already for hiding in the women's can.

AL

That's the difference between you and me: you can hang around some bar in the Village until you pick up some broad old enough to be your grandmother, spend half the night with her, then go home, look your wife in the eye, and tell her you love her . .

JOHN

I don't tell her I love her.

AL

. . but not me. If I ever stepped out of line I could never look my wife in the face again. (*smiles ironically*) Hell, if I ever *did* step out of line, she'd probably be the first one I'd tell about it. That's just the kind of relationship we've got.

JOHN

(*as he works*) Sounds swell.

AL

Who cares what you think. Actually, I feel sorry for you. You're missing one of the greatest things in life if you don't try to make something meaningful out of your marriage.

JOHN

Don't tell me, I've got the picture. You sit in front of the television, holding hands, looking into each other's eyes; then when *Ben Casey* is over, you go to bed and do the beautiful thing.

AL

(*slightly embarrassed — tossing it off*) Sure, that's how it is.

JOHN

Ah ha, a little too close for comfort, wasn't I?

AL

Listen, we got other things to do besides listen to you talk about my sex life. Get this stuff done so we can get out of here. (*He goes to a cabinet, removes some photography equipment, and begins to put it in order. Pause.*)

ED

Ah, your friend's right, John. Put your house in order. Even if everything else goes wrong, you've still got that.

JOHN

(*pause — as he works*) You were married, weren't you, Ed?

ED

Oh yeah, still am. Been married for thirty-two years. Me and the old lady haven't been livin' together for the last couple years, though.

JOHN

Yeah? Gettin' divorced?

ED

Naw, we're both too old for that sort of thing. We talk on the phone all the time — probably get back together one of these days. Two people together that long, ya just get tired of lookin' at each other. Does ya good to split up for a while.

JOHN

(*to Al*) Now there's your meaningful relationship.

AL

(*ignoring him*) You seen my light meter anyplace?

JOHN

Yeah, I know what you mean, Ed. My wife and I are tired of looking at each other and we've only been married three years.

AL

At least I had the sense to wait until I was old enough to know what I was doing before I took the plunge. You get out of marriage what you put into it — same as a job.

JOHN

That's the way to look at things. (*continues working — silence*)

ED

You fellas talk about makin' time with the ladies — they're all amateurs compared to a guy I had for a roommate down in Florida.

AL

(*taking light reading with a meter*) This damn thing doesn't work.

ED

Jake Wallace was his name. Dead ringer for Rudolph Valentino.

AL

I wish people would quit screwing around with my equipment.

JOHN

Don't look at me. I'm an artist, not a photographer.

ED

This was when I first started working for T.I.C. — before I was married even — just a young sprout, like you fellas. Boy, let me tell ya, we really had a time of it. There was more women comin' in and out of that house than you could count. We practically had to make up a time schedule, there was that many of them.

JOHN

There just ain't enough room on this page to get all these pictures in.

AL

We'll just have to crop 'em smaller then.

ED

It wasn't me that was the big attraction, y'understand — although I didn't

40

do so bad neither by normal standards. But it was this Jake Wallace I'm tellin' ya about. Man, he could do no wrong where the women were concerned. They'd do anything to get next to him — follow him down the streets, call him up, sit all night on the doorstep waitin' for him to come home — they were wild about him! Me, hell, I just sat around and handled the overflow. (*chuckles*) And at that I had to call for help a couple of times. Everybody in town knew about our place — we were actually kind of famous. And don't think it hurt business any, neither. Why, I'd call on accounts and when they found out who I was they'd sign up for big orders just to make sure I'd come back and tell 'em more stories about me and Jake. (*laughs*) 'Course we had to be careful we weren't telling 'em about their own wives or daughters. (*pause*) By God, those were wonderful times. I had the world by the tail then. Never thought once about . . Ah . . (*shrugs; pause*) I wonder whatever happened to Jake Wallace.

JOHN

(*working*) Probably died of exhaustion.

ED

(*laughs*) Died? Naw, not Jake. Why hell, I can't even imagine Jake ever gettin' old. Why I bet he doesn't look any different than he did . . (*dawns on him*) forty years ago. (*stunned*) Has it been that long? Christ, I guess it has. (*softly*) Holy smoke, maybe he *is* dead! (*pause*) I wonder if I'll ever see Jake again.

JOHN

Sure you will, Ed. You'll see them all again — all the fond friends and memories from the past — we'll all be together again in the big T.I.C. office in the sky . .

ED

Uh . .

JOHN

(*working*) Yessir, Ed, don't you despair, there's a great day a-comin' for all T.I.C.'s chillun. Don't think for one moment they'd let a man serve 'em as long and faithfully as you have, first as a salesman and now as a night watchman, and then just forget about him just because he dies. Not old T.I.C. No, sir! Would you believe it, Ed, they went and bought a special section of heaven where they send all former . .

AL

Aw, for chrissakes, shut up, will ya?

JOHN

Aw, what's eatin' you?

41

AL

You're always making fun of things other people take seriously. It wears a little thin.

JOHN

Aw, I was only kiddin', for chrissakes, where's your sense of humor?

AL

Sit back and laugh; that's the easy way out.

ED

He was only kiddin'. Me and John here, we understand each other, don't we?

JOHN

Sure, I didn't mean anything.

AL

Some things aren't funny, that's all.

ED

I just didn't realize how long . .

AL

All the same, and I only tell you this for your own good — you'd have a lot better personality if you were more considerate of other people's feelings!

JOHN

What is this, some sort of charm course?

AL

Take it or leave it.

JOHN

It's nice to know I've got a choice.

ED

Jeez, I didn't mean to start anything between you two.

JOHN

It's all right, Ed, don't worry about it.

ED

No kiddin', I'm sorry.

AL

Yeah, forget it. (*silence*)

JOHN

That's a terrific sense of humor you've got there, Al. (*silence*)

ED

(*finally*) Anyway, this Jake Wallace I'm tellin' you about — I'll never forget one time in Tallahassee . .

JOHN

Just to show ya there's no hard feelings, have another drink if ya want.

ED

Well . . thanks a lot, but to tell ya the truth, that last one didn't taste so hot in this paint tin. Didn't seem so bad at first, but the closer I got to the bottom the worse it tasted.

AL

Lucky if you're not poisoned.

JOHN

I'll tell ya what — you got a key to the cafeteria, why don't you go down there and get us some glasses and ice?

ED

Say, that's a good idea. You don't think they'd mind?

AL

C'mon, let's finish this up so we can get out of here.

JOHN

Ah, don't get so nervous. Hey, and here . . (*grabs a vase, empties flowers into wastebasket*) rinse this out and fill it with water. I don't like to drink it straight.

ED

Christ, I only got one arm.

JOHN

You can manage it.

ED

(*taking vase and going out*) Boy, we got a regular little party goin' here. (*Exits. John goes back to work.*)

AL

Where'd you pick him up?

JOHN

Ed? He's just the night watchman. Sometimes when I'm working late he comes in and chews the rag.

AL

Charming.

JOHN

Aw, he's all right. Besides, it's better than talkin' to yourself when you're here all alone.

AL

When you get time and a half for overtime, it's not to keep the night watchman company.

JOHN

Christ, you're the most corps-happy bastard I've met since I got kicked out of the Boy Scouts.

AL

If you stopped having three martinis for lunch you wouldn't have to work overtime so much. Besides, I don't like the idea of you takin' advantage of the company. What if everybody acted that way?

JOHN

So turn me in; maybe you'll get a promotion.

AL

I should bother — you'll cook your own goose. One of these nights Ketchum or Reardon's gonna walk in here and catch you playing gin rummy with Archie the cockroach and that'll be all for you.

JOHN

I can't believe you exist.

AL

Never mind the philosophy — it just doesn't look good, an old bum like that hangin' around.

JOHN

The thing about you is, you're all heart.

AL

Sure, the old guy's got problems, but we're not in the sympathy business. This is a respectable firm, not a soup kitchen.

JOHN

All right, all right. When he comes back I'll poison his drink. (*silence*)

AL

How much longer?

JOHN

(*attempting to discourage Al*) A couple hours, at least.

AL

A couple hours! I can't wait that long. This is my wife's birthday. We were going to hear the Mantovani Strings concert at eight thirty and we were *supposed* to go out to dinner before that. Christ, we won't even make the concert, even if she meets me at the door.

JOHN

Mantovani Strings! (*snorts with contempt*) I'm workin', ain't I?

AL

You shoulda been done a half hour ago.

JOHN

I can't concentrate.

AL

Well . . concentrate!

JOHN

I can't — I'm thinkin' about somethin' else.

AL

What?

JOHN

Look, ya know that new secretary they hired in Expediting last week?

AL

No, I don't think so.

JOHN

Don't kid me. The one with the sweater full of goodies. I saw you watching her.

AL

All right, so I know who you mean.

JOHN

Anyway, for the last couple days I been sittin' with her at lunch in the cafeteria. Dumb! Ask her how she is she's stuck for an answer. But is she ready for action! Honest to God, I could've knocked her over in the lunch lineup if there hadn't been so many people around.

AL

No kiddin'.

JOHN

Yeah, see, so I'm sort of set up for tonight at the Christmas party. I mean we didn't exactly put it in writing but it's just sort of understood that after the ball is over, we go find someplace to play leapfrog.

AL

Doesn't your conscience ever bother you?

JOHN

Not now, wouldja? Just let me get to the party so I can meet this chick.

AL

If she's all that crazy about you, she'll keep.

JOHN

Look, you don't understand. If she gets through the first dance and she's still perpendicular, there's something wrong somewhere.

AL

No, we gotta get this stuff done before we leave.

JOHN

What for? In the first place, do you really think you're gonna get this issue out by Christmas?

AL

We got to — it's the Christmas edition.

JOHN

Look, let's quit kidding ourselves. We both know that even if we got this to the printers five minutes from now, it wouldn't come out till the first week in January.

AL

What good is a Christmas issue the first week in January?

JOHN

Exactly the question I been asking myself: why break our necks when it doesn't make any difference anyhow? In the second place, let's just go to the party long enough for you to take pictures while I arrange things with Peaches. Then we can come back here and I bet I can finish up while you're putting away the camera equipment. Hey, maybe I'll even bring her back here. Sure, if I knew she was safe from those lecherous bastards at the party, I could finish up in no time.

AL

Well, we're not gettin' anywhere here. At least I could get the pictures out of the way. And the Santy Claus is going to be there early.

JOHN

(rolling down sleeves) Sure, c'mon, let's go.

AL

Listen, since I'm lettin' us go . . I mean, don't get me wrong or anything . . I'm not interested in this sort of thing myself; if you want to fool around, that's your business.

JOHN

Al, when they told me you weren't fit to eat with the pigs . .

AL

What I mean is . . I'd be sort of interested — just curiosity — to hear how you made out.

JOHN

Oh, you're one of those, eh?

AL

What're ya talkin' about? One of what? I'm just curious is all.

JOHN

Christ, if it doesn't bother her, you can watch for all I care. Only let's go before I have to stand in line.

AL

All right, but remember, we only stay long enough for me to get pictures, then we come back here. If you haven't arranged things by then, that's your tough luck. (*They get their coats from the rack and put them on. Al gathers equipment.*)

JOHN

All I need is five minutes. Three minutes!

AL

(*as they go*) If you're trying to pull a fast one . .

JOHN

Don't worry so much — you'll get an ulcer. (*They go. There is a pause, then Ed is heard approaching, talking before he enters.*)

ED

Hey, I only got one arm. One of you guys help me before it falls off. (*enters carrying vase, ice bowl, and three plastic cups, all in one arm*) Christ, a guy needs *three* arms to . . (*sees they are gone*) Hey, where'd ya go? (*unloads on table, looks around, notices coatrack is empty*) Well of all the . . (*slumps — softly*) Ahhh, for chrissakes. (*He stands motionless for a moment, then picks up an ice cube and licks it. He goes to John's drawing board, inspects the layout and grunts. He looks around as if expecting to find something of interest on the walls, then starts out. He stops, frowns, and turns to look at the bottle of whiskey still sitting on John's desk. He goes to the bottle and moves around it nervously for a few moments.*) They offered me a drink. (*He starts to pour a drink, stops, takes a pencil and marks the level on the bottle label, then pours himself a drink. He fills the bottle back up to the level with water from the vase and shakes the contents. He moves about the room drinking and comes back to John's layout.*) No, that won't do at all. Make it in a circular fashion, don't ya see, circular. That's the idea, boy. You listen to old Ed. He knows what they like . . (*begins moving about the room again*) Yessir, he knows what they . . (*stops*) like. (*goes back to the bottle and begins to pour himself another drink*)

FADE TO BLACK

Scene 2

About midnight. Ed is asleep at a table, his head resting on his arm. Nearby, the whiskey is still at the same level in the bottle, but is diluted and much lighter in color. A moment, then Al and John are heard approaching down the hall, laughing a little drunkenly.

JOHN

(*off*) C'mon, quit kiddin' around. (*laughing*) Listen you, if I don't get that picture, I'll smash that goddamn camera to bits.

AL

(*laughing*) Go ahead — it's your job. I'll just show Ketchum this little old picture and you're on your way to Siberia.

JOHN

(*uproariously*) You rotten bastard!

AL

The same to you . . double! (*At this point Peaches enters while the other two continue off. She conveys a sense of vacuousness and pretty much fits John's earlier description of her. She seems a little annoyed at the other two and wanders about the room aimlessly. She notices Ed but doesn't seem to find his presence unusual. Finally, she sits at one of the desks, removes a woman's magazine from her purse, and begins reading it.*) Hey, just a minute . . hold on a sec.

JOHN

What? Hey, Peaches.

AL

Well stop . . so we can talk.

JOHN

Let's just go sit down first.

AL

No, I'll forget.

JOHN

Must be pretty important.

AL

(*irritated*) Goddamn important, buddy, so let's just stop and listen, shall we?

JOHN

Jesus Christ, what?

AL

Don't get the idea this is the booze talkin' just because I want to get serious for a minute. I mean, I'm not drunk or anything.

JOHN

Neither am I. I mean, I've been drinking but I'm not drunk or anything like that.

AL

Neither am I. I mean, just every once in a while, the time comes to set things straight.

JOHN

Pick 'em up an' lay 'em straight, old buddy.

AL

The moment of truth, as ol' what's 'is name said.

JOHN

Eisenhower.

AL

Right. The thing I want to tell ya is this: I know that a lot of times I give ya a pretty rough goin' over, but see, it's nothin' personal. I mean, you know, I just got a job to do, sort of an executive responsibility.

JOHN

Sure, I know that. Don't you think I know that? You're not really a bastard, it's just part of the job.

AL

Sure, that's it. I mean, I realize that sometimes I'm a little gung-ho, but I don't *like* bein' that way. I mean, that's not my *real* personality.

JOHN

That's all right — I understand.

AL

Well, I thought ya did, but I wanted to make sure because sometimes I get the feelin' — I mean underneath all the clownin' around we do — that you really don't like me.

JOHN

That I really don't like you?

AL

(*laughing*) Yeah.

JOHN

Y'know, I never thought about it before, but I think you're right.

AL

How's that?

JOHN

Underneath it all, I really *don't* like you very much.

AL

(*not what he had expected*) Whatta ya mean ya don't like me?

JOHN

I don't know what it is exactly; maybe you're just not my cup of tea.

AL

Well, that's a hell of a thing to say!

JOHN

Well, ya asked me; I thought we were being objective.

AL

Objective hell.

JOHN

Aw, for chrissake, I didn't mean to hurt your feelings — I thought you were askin'.

AL

(*entering, followed by John*) It's too late for that kind of soft soap now. Don't come crawling to me with your crummy apologies!

JOHN

Aw, c'mon . . (*notices Ed at table*)

AL

(*going to phone*) I'm gonna call my goddamn wife and then if you can find time enough between your stupid remarks to finish that layout, I can get out of here. (*jiggling the phone, trying to get a line*)

JOHN

(*dancing a tango in Peaches' direction*) Peaches baby.

PEACHES

Who's that? (*pointing to Ed*)

JOHN

Hey, get a load of old Ed. (*shakes Ed, trying to wake him*)

AL

(*impatiently, into phone*) C'mon.

JOHN

Hey, I think maybe something's wrong with old Ed.

AL

Fine, that's all we need is some of your derelict friends dying in our office. (*into phone*) Gimme a line!

JOHN

You can't get a line this time of night — nobody's at the switchboard.

AL

(*slamming down receiver*) What a crummy outfit!

JOHN

Hey, c'mere a minute.

AL

(*Goes to table, still smarting. Although he occasionally becomes involved, there is something reserved about him from this point on.*) He's not really *dead* or anything, is he?

JOHN

I don't know — I can't tell. I think I can see him breathing every once in a while.

AL

That's a good sign. (*notices bottle — picks it up*) If he's dead, here's the poison.

JOHN

(*taking bottle*) Christ, it's half water! The old bastard drank my whiskey and watered the bottle.

AL

Jeez — he must really have a bag on.

JOHN

It cost six bucks a quart.

AL

Maybe too much alcohol got into his system and he died.

JOHN

Naw, he's just passed out. He used to do this all the time, that's why he quit drinkin'. He told me about it. He's okay so long as he doesn't have more than a couple drinks — after that he just keeps throwin' it down until he blacks out.

AL

People who can't handle their liquor give me a pain.

JOHN

Let's stretch him out on the table.

AL

Whatta ya mean? That's the layout table.

JOHN

Well, we're just gonna lay him out, for chrissake. Whatta ya suggest we do, throw him out the window?

AL

All right, all right. (*They clear a place for him on the table and stretch him out.*) Christ, he's really out.

JOHN

Yeah.

AL

What the hell, we can't leave him here all night.

JOHN

Yeah — well, let him sleep it off until we're done. That'll help some.

AL

All right, let's get this thing done.

JOHN

Yeah, yeah, yeah. (*He fairly prances now, humming gaily to himself, a sort of mating dance of the preening rooster full of anticipation. He ca-*

resses Peaches familiarly. Al watches, a combination of digust and admiration.) Hello, gorgeous.

PEACHES

(*looking up from her reading*) Hi there.

JOHN

(*going eagerly to his board and starting to work quickly*) What're you doing?

PEACHES

Reading. (*holds up magazine*)

JOHN

(*examining the magazine*) The Woman's Friend.

PEACHES

They have this marriage counselor writes this monthly column called "On the Rocks." It's taken from actual cases.

JOHN

No kiddin'.

PEACHES

You should read it sometime — it's very revealing. (*crossing up to John's board, leaning on it distractingly*)

JOHN

Maybe I could borrow your copy when you're done.

PEACHES

Sure. This month he's writin' about this couple named Mary and Frank L. Boy, have they got troubles.

JOHN

L?

PEACHES

Yeah, you know, like L M N X Y Z. They only use the initial of the last name, otherwise everybody knows all your problems.

JOHN

That figures.

PEACHES

They give both sides of the story, but in this case it looks like this Frank is really a loser. I mean, he treats poor Mary like a prisoner. Get this: he won't give her any money, won't buy her any new clothes, and he's so suspicious that when he goes to work he padlocks the door so she can't get out.

JOHN

The man's unbalanced.

PEACHES

And when he ever does let her out, he follows her.

JOHN

He needs a psychiatrist.

PEACHES

Well, that's what they suggest here. But if you ask me, it's hopeless. Boy, it really goes to prove that marriage isn't the bed of roses that everybody thinks it is. All these kids runnin' off and marryin' the first guy that asks 'em. Where do they end up? (*indicates the magazine*) No sir, boy, not for me.

JOHN

Thatta girl.

PEACHES

No sour grapes. I've had plenty of chances. Heavens.

JOHN

No sense rushing into things.

PEACHES

Exactly. (*long pause*) It's not that I haven't had chances.

AL

(*being suave*) Obviously a girl as attractive as you are isn't going to go wanting for admirers.

PEACHES

Thank you.

AL

I mean, just because a girl is approaching thirty and unmarried certainly doesn't mean she's an old maid.

PEACHES

(*abruptly changing the subject*) That was a swell party. How come we had to leave?

JOHN

I told ya. I had to get this work done.

AL

Then get it done.

JOHN

(*humming with anticipation, works quickly and with great flourish*) I'm working, I'm working.

PEACHES

Why didn't we leave me at the party while you did this and then you could meet me after?

JOHN

The heart hath reasons that reason knows not of.

PEACHES

(*nodding*) Oh.

JOHN

(*working quickly*) This'll only take a little while, then we'll get out of here and have our own party.

PEACHES

Gee, I sure was havin' a good time. Dancin' with all those executives.

JOHN

Yeah, I saw ya out there dancin' with Ketchum after he cut in on me. You watch out for that guy, he's up to no good.

PEACHES

He's a very good dancer.

JOHN

I'm tellin' ya, he's a dirty old man.

PEACHES

And all that good food. Didja ever see so much? All that shrimp and rice dish and artichoke hearts and turkey slices with stuffing and ham and wild rice and salad and pickled herring and meatballs and rolls . . (*sighs, remembering*) I had seconds on everything. (*John glances at her apprehensively.*)

AL

God, you sure can eat.

JOHN

She burns up a lot of energy.

PEACHES

I'm very active.

AL

(*suavely*) You must be, to eat that much and still keep a figure like yours.

JOHN

Ah, you smooth-talkin' dog, you.

PEACHES

Thank you. A lot of people have commented that they think I have an attractive figure.

AL

Oh, you do. It's very . . uh . . *enchanté.* (*crosses to John, looks at layout*)

PEACHES

Thank you.

JOHN

Hey, Errol Flynn, don't you have something you should be doing?

PEACHES

How long is this gonna take?

JOHN

Just a few minutes. Half an hour maybe.

PEACHES

Half an hour! That party isn't gonna go on forever.

JOHN

Patience, patience.

AL

Hey, you're two pictures short on this page. You only have twelve, you're supposed to have fourteen.

JOHN

What?

AL

We got fourteen pictures on this page — your layout only shows room for twelve.

JOHN

Oh no! (*slaps his head in despair*) Hey look, can't we do this tomorrow?

AL

Get it done tonight.

PEACHES

Dull, dull, dull.

JOHN

(*a little apprehensive about losing Peaches*) Yeah, well . .

AL

Christ, my wife will never speak to me again. Not that I particularly give a damn.

JOHN

Ah, now it starts.

AL

Ah, now what starts?

JOHN

The wolf gets his first taste of blood.

AL

What're ya talkin' about?

JOHN

You know what I'm talkin' about. I saw you off in a corner there dancing with Louella what's 'er name.

AL

So I was dancin' with Louella what's 'er name—big deal! So what? There's nothing wrong with dancing. A lot of civilized people do it.

JOHN

Not like *that*, they don't.

AL

That just shows how much you know about it. It so happens, that was the dance everybody was doing all night at the Halloween party our co-op apartment threw.

JOHN

Well, I can imagine how *that* ended up.

AL

You can imagine all you want — you're depraved, is all.

JOHN

You're just kiddin' yourself into thinkin' everything you do is all right. You're out there crawlin' all over each other but put a label on it — call it dancin' — and that makes it respectable. *She* knows what it really is and *you* know what it really is, but just so long as you don't admit it to each other, it's respectable.

AL

If you're as sick as you are, you can find something degrading in just about anything.

JOHN

Ah, don't kid me. (*drinks*) There's somethin' here. (*offers bottle to Al*)

AL

(*disdainfully*) I thought you said it was all water.

JOHN

Not all water — just not full strength — enough to keep the old fire lit.

AL

(*takes a drink*) Christ, what am I doin'? I don't need any more to drink. (*hands bottle back to John who takes a drink*)

JOHN

Yessir, that old Louella, she thinks you're pretty hot stuff.

AL

Ahhh . . (*turns away feigning disgust*)

JOHN

What's wrong with that? You could do a lot worse.

AL

Aw, she's just a kid. Besides, I'm married — I'm not interested.

JOHN

You coulda fooled me.

AL

So I gave the kid a tumble. That's harmless enough. Probably made the whole evening for her. I don't mean to sound conceited, but for a kid like that, her first job right out of high school, it's a pretty big deal when a junior executive pays some attention to her.

JOHN

Sure, if you offered to go to bed with her, she'd be so thrilled she'd probably explode.

AL

There's no talking any sense to you.

JOHN

No, keep goin' — it'll probably turn out to be an act of Christian charity.

AL

There's nothing wrong with an occasional flirtation. If a marriage is strong to begin with it's a healthy stimulant.

JOHN

I bet you used to be a real hound before you got married, didn't you?

AL

(*shrugs modestly*) Oh, I didn't do so bad.

JOHN

C'mon now, tell the truth and shame the devil, you were just a regular old dog, weren't you?

AL

(*trying to suppress a pleased smile*) Oh, I guess I did a little better than the average. What makes you think that?

JOHN

It's obvious — the women go for ya.

AL

Aw . .

JOHN

No kiddin', haven't you ever noticed the way the women light up when you walk into a room?

AL

Naw.

JOHN

Sure, you knock 'em dead, kid. Ain't that right, Peaches?

PEACHES

What?

57

JOHN

Old Al here, from a woman's point of view, wouldn't you say he was a very attractive man?

PEACHES

Enchanté.

JOHN

Y'see?

AL

(*embarrassed but pleased*) Aw, c'mon . .

JOHN

No, no kiddin'. (*back to Peaches*) On a scale of one hundred, where would you rate old Al on sex appeal?

PEACHES

(*not getting it*) What?

JOHN

On a scale of one hundred. (*She looks blank.*) Look, here's zero, here's one hundred. What score would he make on a basis of sex appeal.

PEACHES

Like . . Harvard twenty-eight, Yale nothin'?

JOHN

No, no . . like . . (*can't think of any parallel*)

PEACHES

Like in arithmetic period in grade school?

JOHN

Yeah, that's it.

PEACHES

Oh. (*appraises Al*) Approximately . . eighty-seven.

JOHN

Y'see?

PEACHES

B plus.

JOHN

B plus in anybody's league, baby.

AL

Aw, forget it.

JOHN

Who ya kiddin'? That's something to be proud of.

AL

I guess I haven't been paying much attention to what effect I have since I got married.

JOHN

Ah, you're right; that's the way to be. It's no good this steppin' out on your wife all the time.

AL

But it's nice to know I haven't lost my sex appeal.

JOHN

Sure. This way ya know it's there any time ya want it.

AL

And yet, right down the line, I'm faithful as an old bird dog.

JOHN

The best of both worlds.

AL

It helps the old confidence.

JOHN

That's the important thing.

AL

It's sort of like religion . . it gives ya somethin' to lean on.

PEACHES

Boy, it's like this guy whom we'll call Duane. Thinks he's irresistible.

JOHN

(*offering bottle to Peaches*) Drink?

PEACHES

No thanks. Thinks he's something special because he goes to night school at Fordham. (*John offers bottle to Al.*)

AL

Well, why not. (*takes drink*) Say, that's still pretty strong stuff.

JOHN

It's deceiving.

AL

Boy, I've really been putting away the old ointment.

JOHN

Aw, it does ya good to unwind once in a while.

AL

Yeah, I guess so.

PEACHES

I told him not to hold his breath waitin' for me to marry him. He takes me to the wrestling matches.

AL

Some people have no taste.

59

PEACHES

Ah well, it's not so bad. (*pointedly*) At least it's exciting. (*Ed moans loudly.*)

JOHN

Hey, maybe old Ed's comin' around.

AL

He's alive anyway. (*They go and stand over him.*)

JOHN

(*shaking him*) Hey, Ed. C'mon, ya can't stay here all night. C'mon.

AL

Aw, he's still out of it. Are ya sure he's all right?

JOHN

Yeah, just drunker than hell, is all.

AL

I mean, if somethin's the matter with him, maybe we should take him to a doctor. How'd it look if he dies right in the office or somethin'? (*Ed moans again.*)

JOHN

Naw, quit worryin'! I told ya, once he starts drinkin' he just keeps goin' until he gets like this. (*takes a drink from the bottle, hands it to Al*)

AL

He shouldn't drink if he can't drink. (*takes a drink*) Christ, I was startin' to sober up, but this stuff is gettin' me drunk again. C'mon, wouldja? Let's get this thing done so we can get out of here. Christ, what time is it anyway?

JOHN

Who cares?

PEACHES

Let's face it — you'll be here forever. I'm goin' back to the party.

JOHN

What're ya talkin' about?

PEACHES

By the time we get outta here I'll be eligible for social security.

JOHN

So what's at the party we don't have here?

PEACHES

Are you kiddin'? In the first place, all that food . .

JOHN

(*moves quickly back to board, takes candy bar from drawer, comes back to Peaches*) Listen, how about a Nutty Buddy?

60

PEACHES

(*looks at candy with contempt*) Besides, they're gonna start the games and the prizes.

JOHN

(*out of desperation*) Hey, I got a great idea. (*begins to move about excitedly, laughs at the thought of it*) Let's take old Ed and put 'im in one of the stalls in the women's can.

AL

Eh?

JOHN

C'mon, you know.

AL

(*starting to laugh*) Hey, that's a pretty good idea.

JOHN

When he wakes up he'll wonder what the hell he had in mind when he went in there. (*both laughing*)

AL

Or, hey, better yet — first let's go down to the cafeteria and get a tablecloth and wrap him up in it like a shroud, *then* lay him out in the women's can . .

JOHN

When he comes to, he won't know what the hell's going on, or where he is . .

AL

He'll think he's dead . . !

JOHN

Or what if some woman comes in there before he wakes up . . ! (*They are practically overwhelmed with laughter at the prospect of this. As an added touch, John takes one of the discarded flowers he had earlier put in the wastebasket and places it in Ed's hand so that he looks like the comic figure of a corpse. They laugh all the harder at this.*)

AL

Oh, Christ . . !

PEACHES

Are you kiddin'?

JOHN

(*wanting to capitalize on the enthusiasm of the moment*) C'mon, c'mon . . (*He motions to Al and, still laughing uncontrollably, they begin to lift Ed off the table but they lose their grip on him and he falls heavily to the floor.*)

PEACHES

What're ya doing?

ED

(*coming to abruptly — clutching his shoulder where ordinarily his arm would begin*) My arm, my arm! . . God, you hurt my arm!

PEACHES

(*going to Ed*) For God's sake!

JOHN

(*laughing*) Ya dropped him . .

AL

Not me, it was you . . you dropped your end . .

JOHN

Clumsy idiot . . !

ED

Whazis? Whazis? Wha's goin' on? What the . .

AL

(*still laughing, pointing at John*) He did it — it was his idea in the first place.

ED

Oh Christ, I fell on my arm!

JOHN

I couldn't help it. Damnit, that shoots the whole thing. (*still laughing*) Here. (*helps Ed to his feet*)

ED

(*still clutching his shoulder, almost falls*) I can't stand up.

JOHN

Are you all right?

PEACHES

Well, help him up for goodness' sake.

AL

He's still drunk. (*And he is. John seats him back at the table.*)

ED

God, I fell ri' on my arm.

JOHN

You're okay, aren't ya?

ED

What in the hell's up?

AL

Nothin'.

ED

I fall down or sumpin'? Wha's goin' on?

JOHN

Nothin'. We were just gonna play a little joke is all.

ED

Joke? What kinda joke?

AL

(*giggling*) Well, see . . we were gonna get a tablecloth, you know, from the lunchroom, and wrap you up in it . .

ED

(*confused*) Wrap me up in't? Wha' ya do thin' li' tha' for?

JOHN

(*also giggling*) No, see . . we were gonna . . wrap ya in this tablecloth, like a shroud, see? Then we were gonna lay ya out in the women's can . .

ED

Women's can! Wha's goin' on?

AL

Then see, when ya woke up, ya wouldn't know where ya were or how ya got there . .

JOHN

Or ya might even think ya was dead . . (*Both of them are convulsed.*)

ED

(*pause — puzzled*) I don't get it.

AL

Or maybe somebody would have come in before you came to . .

JOHN

Imagine the look on her face . . !

AL

Here, right in the middle of the floor . . in the women's can . .

JOHN

Is a corpse . . !

AL

(*doubled over*) I can't stand it . . ! (*They continue laughing. Ed, puzzled, frowns as he thinks over their joke as if there were something about it that he has not understood.*)

PEACHES

(*coming up to them*) Whatja do that for? (*John, still convulsed, can only point at her, speechlessly. John shakes his head. She looks at him for a moment.*) You know what? You guys bore me. (*John shakes his head at*

63

her.) At least the apes I go out with got other things to do than play jokes on old drunks. (*starts out*)

JOHN

(*starting to get control*) Hey . . hey . . where . . where ya . . going?

PEACHES

Back to the party. I'm missing too many social opportunities sittin' around here.

JOHN

(*follows her*) Hey . . wait a minute . . (*stopping her*) Hey, hold on . . listen I'll be done here in a few minutes . .

PEACHES

Kindly take your hand off my arm.

JOHN

Listen I'm sorry . . We'll go out and . .

PEACHES

I should point out . . I took karate at the YMCA.

JOHN

What's botherin' you all of a sudden?

PEACHES

I should sit around while you an' your girl friend in there play crummy jokes on that poor old man? There's somethin' wrong with you guys.

JOHN

Aw it was just a joke.

PEACHES

Some joke. Let me go, I'm going back to the party.

JOHN

What's at the party? Only that old lecher, Ketchum.

PEACHES

At least he's a gentleman.

JOHN

Aw, c'mon.

PEACHES

Once I've made up my mind I never change it and I have decided that you are no longer my type.

JOHN

(*intimately*) Whatta ya mean, you're nuts about me.

PEACHES

(*With a traditional jump and shout, she delivers a karate chop to his midsection, doubling him over.*) Yeah? (*She exits.*)

AL

(*laughing*) Boy, she sure is nuts about you!

JOHN

(*gasping*) Who needs her?

AL

Can't win 'em all.

JOHN

(*really mad*) Yeah, well everything would've been fine if Ketchum hadn't horned in, pullin' rank on me! Can ya imagine that? I had her all lined up, then he dives in. (*mimicking*) "Heh, heh, this is man's work, sonny." (*Bronx cheer*)

AL

Well, she didn't have to go with him. I mean, if she was really that solid on you, she could've told him to shove off.

JOHN

Are you kiddin'? When a second vice president asks one of those kids to jump, the only thing they ask is how far. (*pacing*) He's too old for that sort of thing. She'll kill 'im.

AL

I wonder where they'll go. I can just see 'em in an hour or so, old Ketchum . .

JOHN

(*in a frustrated rage*) AUGGH! The thought of it makes me sick! (*moving about anxiously*) I got a notion to write his wife an anonymous letter. Hey, whatta ya think of that idea?

AL

That's blackmail or something.

JOHN

Ah, the hell it is. Probably doing him a favor. He'll die of heart failure if he keeps fooling around with stuff like that. (*composing orally*) "Dear Mrs. Ketchum: Last night at the T.I.C. Christmas party, your husband was making an ass . . was *publicly* making an ass out of himself with one Miss . ." what the hell's her name?

AL

I dunno. Don't you even know her name?

JOHN

I just always call her Peaches. It doesn't make any difference, I can find out.

AL

Forget it — you'll wind up in jail.

JOHN

Ahhh . .

ED

You just leave me there, in the middle of the floor . . wrap' in a sheet, huh? (*They both nod, helpless.*)

JOHN

Listen Ed, I'm sorry — it was a stupid idea.

ED

That's a hell of a thing to do to an ol' man who on'y got one arm. Y'know what'd happen t'me? Get fired, is what! Ri' out on my ear.

JOHN

Ed, I apologize — I don't know what I was thinkin' of.

AL

Anyway, you'd be off duty.

ED

Well, that's a hellava joke play on an ol' man.

AL

Don't be such a poor sport. After all, it's your own fault for getting so drunk.

ED

(*protesting*) No . . jus' little bit.

JOHN

Aw c'mon, ya watered the whole bottle. (*holds up bottle*) Look at it, three shades lighter.

ED

No . . I didn' . . I . . I . . wha' I did was . . (*flounders hopelessly*) Aw Chris', ya offer' me a drink, didn' ya?

JOHN

Well a drink doesn't mean the whole bottle.

ED

Well, wha' kin' a trick is that t'play on a guy, anyway? Here we was, up here, talkin' an' tellin' stories an' havin' a good time, an' "Have a drink, Ed," an' . . sure, we're gonna have our own li'l party. An' what happens? I go outta room for a secon' an' everybody runs out on me. Swell trick t'play. Jus' fulla tricks.

JOHN

Well Christ, Ed, we had to get over to the Christmas party. Al had to take pictures.

ED

Jus' all of a sudden? Why didn' ya say sumpin'?

JOHN

Well . . we had a last-minute change of plans. We didn't realize how late it was and . . and we had to get over there to take pictures before the Santy Claus left.

ED

Santy Claus! Whazzat?

JOHN

You know, the Santy Claus. Every year at the Christmas party, the president of the board dresses up like Santy Claus and he poses for pictures with the secretaries sittin' on his lap. That sort of thing.

ED

Santy Claus! Pretty goddamn important, I guess.

AL

(*controlled anger*) You're damn right it's important. It may not mean much to you, but there's a lot of people that work for this company that look forward to this Christmas party all year long. And the Santy Claus is a traditional part of it. Hell, to some of these people, Santy Claus *is* the Christmas party!

ED

Huh?

JOHN

(*applauding*) Buy War Bonds!

AL

And that goes for you too, smart guy.

JOHN

Oh God, spare me the patriotism, will ya?

AL

You might be better off if you came up with a little of it yourself.

JOHN

Why jump on Ed? He didn't do anything.

AL

That's right, he doesn't do *anything*. Except get in our way and stop us from doin' what we're here for.

ED

(*weakly*) 'Zat a fac'?

AL

Yeah, that's a fact. Look, I don't mean to be a bastard, but try to think of it from my point of view. Look at yourself; middle of the night and here you sit, all drunked up. Think of the way it reflects on us if somebody walks in here right now. How do you think it makes us look?

67

JOHN

At this particular point do you really honest-to-God care?

AL

You bet I do. (*John shakes his head.*) And don't shake your head at me. It's easy enough to be a do-nothing cynic like you. Just sit back and laugh at everybody who's got guts or brains enough to try to accomplish something! Now, clean up your friend here or get rid of him or something, but quit screwing around and get that goddamn layout finished!

JOHN

(*looks at Al with unmasked disgust, then goes to where Ed is sitting*) C'mon, ol' buddy, why don't ya call it a night and go home.

ED

Can't go home — gotta keep watch . .

AL

(*laughs*) Oh Christ, we can all rest easy — old Ed's on the job.

JOHN

Lay off, wouldja.

ED

'Time is it?

JOHN

(*looks at his watch*) About five after twelve.

ED

Can't go home.

AL

Why not?

ED

Can't get outta the building.

AL

Whatta ya mean, ya can't get out of the building?

ED

'S a time lock — goes on a' midnight, don't go off 'till six A.M. Ain't nobody can get in an' nobody can get out. (*John smiles.*)

AL

How did what's 'er name get out?

ED

Musta just made it.

AL

(*concerned*) But there's gotta be some way to get out.

ED

Used to have a key could use to let me out. 'Bout a month ago, I was in

68

here one night — pretty drunk, I guess — hid it someplace so I wouldn't lose it. (*shakes his head*) Been tryin' to think ever since where the hell it was I put it.

AL

(*throws up hands in frustration*) Well think, man, think!

ED

'S no use. I been tryin' an' tryin' but I can't remember what I did with it. (*John begins to laugh, softly.*)

AL

Well for . . ! Why the hell didn't ya report it lost and get another one?

ED

I dunno — guess I shoulda. 'S a dangerous thing — lose that key. 'S afraid if I told 'em, I'd get fired. Just keep hopin' it'll turn up.

AL

The phones don't work; ya can't get outta the building — what would ya do in case of fire?

ED

Pull the fire alarm.

AL

What if burglers broke in?

ED

(*elementary*) Pull the burgler alarm. (*John laughs loudly.*)

AL

Aw, for chrissake! You mean to tell me I can't get out of here until tomorrow morning?

ED

Tha's ri' — six A.M.

AL

The hell with that noise. There's gotta be some way to get out of here. You probably never even looked. (*goes out quickly to investigate*)

ED

(*weakly, after him*) I looked . . Awww . .

JOHN

Oh Christ, that kills me. I can just see his wife, probably got J. Edgar Hoover outta bed — 'fraid somebody murdered her little Ally-Wally.

ED

Someb'dy oughta.

JOHN

Not him — he's too dumb to get killed.

69

ED

'Least ya oughta tell 'm go t'hell.

JOHN

Ah, what's the use?

ED

Make ya feel better.

JOHN

Naw — I dunno. Besides, ya gotta be careful with people like that. He got some super image of himself up here someplace like he was John Wayne or somebody. You shake that image, he'll get back at ya. Maybe not right then, but don't turn your back.

ED

Tha' kin', huh?

JOHN

You bet he is. He got a Polaroid picture tonight at the Christmas party of me standin' behind Ketchum's back makin' faces at him. All I need to do is give him half a reason and that picture'll end up on Ketchum's desk.

ED

Quit, whyncha?

JOHN

Ahhh . . it's easy to say. I got bills, things are goin' bad with my wife — I don't need any more troubles. Besides, I got canned from the last job I had; it looks bad to keep jumpin' around job to job.

ED

Tell ya sumpin' — tell that bastard go t'hell an' clear out while there's still time.

JOHN

Sure, Ed, sure.

ED

"Sure Ed, sure." No foolin' — 'fore 's too late. Wan' know sumpin'? We 'lot alike, you'n me.

JOHN

Flattery'll get ya nowhere.

ED

'S truth. Let people push ya 'roun', jus' like I did. An' this's how you're gonna end up! (*indicates himself*)

JOHN

Acch.

ED

Went huntin' with a buncha guys—drinkin'—trip' over a log, gun wen' off, blew my goddamn arm off. Said it wouldn' make no difference — just give 'em twice as much personality. Not easy thing, losin' 'narm. Don't think much about it, take it for granted while it's there but when it's gone . . (*takes his empty sleeve in his hand, waves it at John*) Started hittin' the ol' booze, got so I was no good to nobody. Finally Bill Winkle calls me in, tells me gotta cut back in sales force an' since my volume's lowes' I gotta get laid off temporary. But in meantime, they can gimme a job, night watchman. After twenty-six years! They figure it's easy way out for ever'body — that I got too much pride to step down that far — tell 'em all t'go t'hell an' quit. Well, tha's what they figured, but I didn't. I need' a job an' it was easier than pullin' myself back together. I tol' myself that this would gimme time t'straighten myself out. Well, it gimme time, all ri'; that was fifteen years ago. But tha's not so bad — bein' a night watchman ain't so bad, but it's what they think of ya for acceptin' it the way I did. I run into 'em ever' once in a while, the old salesmen I use t'know. Aw, you know, they all preten' everythin's the same (*shakes his head*), but I can tell the way they look at me, way they talk t'me it ain't the same. Couple years ago I caught myself callin' one of 'em mister! An' this is one o' the guys was on the huntin' trip I shot myself!

JOHN

Christ!

ED

Been better I shot myself through the head 'stead the arm. Least they'd still respect me. An' the young ones, 'bout your age, didn' know me in the old days, didn' know I was any good . . try t'tell 'em I really *was* good — they say, "Sure Ed, sure ya were." (*pause — looks at John*) You believe me?

JOHN

Sure, Ed, sure I . . (*realizes*) I mean . .

ED

Sure ya do. Tha's jus' it. I wouldn' min' so much if only they knew I really *was* good once — that I could B.S. an' hustle with the best of 'em an' not take a back seat t'nobody. But the harder I try to convince 'em, the less they believe me.

JOHN

Well, maybe ya shouldn't try so hard.

ED

Yeah, tha's what I keep tellin' myself. But then I see a chance to let somebody know, an' before I even know it . . When you're on the bottom o' the heap ya do anythin' t'try get a li'l respec', 'specially if ya had it once.

71

JOHN

Yeah, I guess that's right.

ED

Nope, where I made my mistake was in takin' this job inna firs' place. Shoulda starved firs'. (*pause*) Funny though, I wouldn' have starve'. I woulda made myself pull together. But this was easier. (*pause*) Now I got no choice. (*pause*) Maybe one other. (*John takes a deep breath. Silence. Gloom. Al re-enters — not as quickly as he went out, but fast enough to break the rhythm Ed and John have set.*)

AL

What's my wife gonna think, stayin' out all night? She'll probably think I've been murdered or something. She's mad enough at me as it is.

JOHN

What a break. Now we can spend the night together and continue our exchange of intellectual ideas.

AL

Shut up, you! If it wasn't for you all this wouldn't have happened in the first place.

JOHN

Sure, I planned the whole thing.

AL

Since we're stuck here, use the time to finish the goddamn layout.

JOHN

(*taking a drink*) Can I count all this as overtime?

AL

You won't have to worry about counting *any* time if you don't have this thing finished damn quick. I'm about ready to go to Ketchum about you.

JOHN

(*exhilarated — goes to drawing board, picks up pictures, scrambles them all up, and spreads them out carelessly over the layout sheet*) Listen, I got it! Our worries are over. Christ, what an inspiration, why didn't I think of this before?

AL

What the hell are you doin'? You're ruinin' everything we already got.

JOHN

No, no, don't ya get it? We take all these lovely young brides and throw 'em all together. (*continues scrambling pictures*) And we scramble 'em all up . . see, a sort of a collage effect.

AL

But nobody'll know which is which.

JOHN

That's half the beauty of it. Besides that we avoid the ordinary, dull, square or crossed kind of layout. It's different.

AL

Say, maybe you've got something. (*admiring the layout*) I think you've hit on something there — it's different.

JOHN

Goddamn right. Listen, we need a title for this.

AL

That's right, something like this needs a title. All we need is a title, then we're done.

JOHN

Okay. How about . . "Pot Luck"?

AL

Ahhh . . not quite right.

JOHN

Uhhh . . "Pig Pot."

AL

Naw, c'mon.

JOHN

"Pack of Pigs."

AL

Aw, for chrissakes.

JOHN

"Pick Your Pig."

AL

C'mon, get serious.

JOHN

Well, *you* think of something. You're supposed to write this damn thing, not me.

AL

It was your idea.

JOHN

Well, I can't do everything. Besides, I only meant it as a joke.

AL

A joke, whatta ya mean, a joke?

JOHN

This layout, it's a lousy idea. I was only pullin' your leg.

AL

Whatta ya mean, a joke. That's a good layout — it's different.

73

JOHN

It's different all right — it stinks.

AL

Yeah, well it so happens that your little joke backfired this time — this happens to be a damn good idea.

JOHN

That's all you know. Go ahead and print it — it's your job. Just don't blame me when the complaints start pourin' in from all those broads who expect to see their names and pictures in the company magazine.

AL

(*without confidence*) Well, it gets printed . . and I'll take the credit for it too.

JOHN

It's all yours.

AL

You bet it is.

JOHN

If you want to tell the world that all your taste is in your mouth, that's your business.

AL

Listen, you, insult my taste and you insult the taste of ninety-nine percent of the people that work for this company.

JOHN

That's the trouble with places like this: ninety-nine percent of the people that work here have got taste exactly like yours!

AL

Then why the hell don't ya quit if this is so far beneath you?

JOHN

Because I need the money, is why. Believe me, if I didn't I wouldn't stick around here for five minutes on a bet.

AL

Yeah, well that's not good enough for me. If you haven't got the guts and honesty to quit, I'll do it for ya.

JOHN

Ah, what're ya talkin' about?

AL

Consider yourself fired!

JOHN

Who the hell d'ya . . You got delusions of grandeur, sonny! You can't fire anybody.

AL

That's right — I can't, but Ketchum can and you can bet he will when he gets a load of this picture. (*pats his pocket*)

JOHN

Boy, that's really your little ace in the hole, isn't it?

AL

You bet it is.

JOHN

Well, if you can pull something like that and still look at yourself in the mirror every morning, go ahead. Personally, I couldn't stand livin' with myself.

AL

You'd manage.

JOHN

If you're gonna dangle that over my head from now on, I don't want the job anyway!

AL

I'm glad ya feel that way, because that's the way it is.

JOHN

Swell.

AL

Good.

JOHN

You don't hafta tell Ketchum anything. I resign as of right now.

AL

That's just fine.

JOHN

I'd leave right now and never come back, if I could just get out of the goddamn building.

ED

Can't get out till six A.M.

JOHN

Yeah, I know, I know. (*looks at his watch*) Christ, almost six hours.

AL

Well six more hours, then goodbye to you.

ED

(*congenial*) Goodbye, old John!

JOHN

Well, it can't pass soon enough for me.

75

AL

That goes double for me. (*pause*) It'll go fast enough for me — there's plenty of ways *I* can put six hours to use around here. (*goes to his desk and typewriter, quickly inserts a piece of paper, and begins typing furiously*)

JOHN

Idle hands are the devil's workshop. (*He takes his bottle, goes to his chair, sits, puts his feet up on the desk and takes a long drink. Ed continues to sit in a half-stupor. The lights go down.*)

END OF ACT ONE

ACT TWO

Scene 1

When the lights come back up they are all in the same positions; however, Ed now dozes lightly, John is thumbing through a magazine, and Al stares blankly at the typewriter before him, occasionally pecking out a few letters. John glances anxiously at Al from time to time, his mind obviously not on his magazine. After a few moments of this he seems to come to some kind of a decision. He puts down his magazine, rises, crosses behind Al and looks, unnoticed, over his shoulder.

JOHN

(*reading*) "The quick red fox jumps over the lazy brown dog."

AL

(*slumps*) Aw for . . Whatta ya creeping around for?

JOHN

That's very inspiring. Do you get paid for that?

AL

What do you care. My watch stopped. What time is it?

JOHN

(*looks at his watch*) Almost three.

AL

Three more hours. I wish there was some way to pass the time — I'm goin' nuts.

JOHN

We could play post office. (*Silly smile. Ed laughs loudly. Al ignores him. Pause. John speaks uneasily.*) Look . . in a little more than three hours I walk out of here and that's it — we may never see each other again.

76

AL

So?

JOHN

So we've been together for over eight months now and I hate to see it end like this. I mean, let's face it, it hasn't been a bed of roses — we've had our ups and downs. I guess we're just basically different types of people. But we've had a lot of laughs too and we've had some pretty good times together. So I hate to think that there's any hard feelin's between us after all this time. So whatta ya say we forget the unpleasantness and part as friends. (*offering his hand*)

AL

(*looks at the hand, then slowly*) I may have a great many shortcomings but hypocrisy is not one of them.

JOHN

Look, you're just sore over that little misunderstanding we had when we got back from the party.

AL

(*very formally — not looking at John*) A few hours ago, without any provocation on my part, while I was actually in the midst of making a gesture of friendship, you calmly told me that you didn't like me . .

JOHN

(*shrugging it off*) Ahhhh . .

AL

(*surmounting*) . . which means, I assume, that any moments of congeniality that have passed between us during the past eight months have been false, on your part that is, and that working in the same office with me has been a trying and unpleasant experience for you. Now when a man tells me that, it strikes me at the very source of my being because all my life I have tried to combine following what I believed to be right along with a pleasant personality and an attempt to get along with everybody I come into contact with. It hasn't been easy and it hasn't always worked, but I have honestly given it everything I have and it is to this end that the greater part of my conscious thoughts are occupied. So when a man tells me that he doesn't like me, I can't take it casually because in saying so he is criticizing everything I stand for.

JOHN

But if ya . .

AL

Not only that, but when he then comes to me a few hours later with a lot of this "let's bury the hatchet" tripe, that man, to my way of thinking, is an out-and-out hypocrite!

JOHN

But that's what I've been tryin' to explain to ya all night, only ya won't give me a chance.

AL

(*wearily*) All right, go ahead, explain away. But I warn you it won't do any good because I won't believe a word you say anyway.

JOHN

Well then, what's the point?

AL

You're the one begging for a chance to explain — go ahead.

JOHN

(*about to say something — checks himself — takes a deep breath*) Well . . I know I *said* there were some . . points . . that is to say . . basic outlooks . . on life on which we differ.

AL

No, no, no. What you said was that underneath everything, you really didn't like me very well. That was what you said.

JOHN

Did I say that?

AL

That was exactly what you said.

JOHN

I can't imagine saying a thing like that. After all, I'd been drinking.

AL

So had I, but I heard you correctly. Besides, "In Vino Veritas." I believe that.

JOHN

Oh, so do I. Definitely. It's just that you misunderstood me.

AL

When someone tells you they don't really like you very well, there's not too many ways you can take it.

JOHN

Exactly — you're absolutely right.

AL

Well then?

JOHN

Well then . . you see . . (*obviously floundering*)

AL

You're just making this up as you go along. You don't have any explanation. (*rises as if to go away*)

JOHN

(*stopping him*) No, no, yes I do . . please, just sit down and . . give me a chance to explain. Here, have another drink. (*Warily, Al takes another drink.*) Y'see, it's just that these things aren't very easy for me . . You know how I am — it's just hard for me to open up, especially in a serious situation like this one. (*Al sighs.*) But . . when I say I don't like ya, I don't really mean that I don't like ya, but actually . . I mean just the opposite.

AL

Talk sense.

JOHN

Because what I really feel is that I like ya a lot. Too much. See, it's a sort of resentment inside me because I like ya more than I can tell ya . .

AL

What ya, gone fruity on me or somethin'?

JOHN

No, no — Christ, nothin' like that. I'm no good with words, but . . what I'm tryin' to tell you is that I *admire* you . . as a *person* . . I . .

AL

What're you tryin' to hand me? You admire me!

JOHN

Honest to God. It's true.

AL

Don't feed me that. I know what you think of me. You don't hafta say anything — I can tell by the way you act towards me.

JOHN

But that's just it, don't ya see? The reason I act that way, it's not the way I really feel . . it's . . a . . a . . defense! (*Up to this point John has been grasping at straws, but now he finds a clear line of argument and develops it smoothly.*)

AL

What?

JOHN

Aw c'mon, don't play dumb — you must have sensed it plenty of times.

AL

What?

79

JOHN
That I'm . . Ah, I can't say it.

AL
What, for pete's sake.

JOHN
I'm jealous of ya.

AL
Get out of here!

JOHN
I'm tellin' ya, it's the truth.

AL
Who ya tryin' to kid. It's like Hitler being jealous of Albert Schweitzer.

JOHN
But I'm tryin' to tell ya — that's just it: you're all the things I'm not.

AL
Well I know that, but . .

ED
(*who has been following this*) Uh . . tha's right . . tha's just what he said.

AL
How do you know?

ED
Well . . uh . . some nights, when John here was workin' late, an' I come by an' we sit around and chew the rag . . you know how it is, late at night, ya start tellin' each other thin's tha' maybe ya wouldn't say other times . . he always said you was a prince of a fella.

JOHN
See, what did I tell ya?

AL
(*wavering, but not convinced*) Ahhh . .

ED
An' that he *admired* ya a great deal . .

JOHN
Yeah.

ED
An' that he *loved* ya like a brother . .

JOHN
(*sensing progress*) See?

ED
An' . . an' . . uh . . an' that you was a *prince* of a fella!

JOHN

Yeah, Ed, thanks. Now see, I'm tellin' ya the truth — otherwise why would I say those things to old Ed?

AL

(*wanting now to believe*) I don't get it . . Then why the hell would you say that you don't like me?

JOHN

Don't ya see? I see in you all the things I want to be — that I should be. You're honest, ya work hard, you're intelligent, ya got principles, you fight for what you believe in . . a real straight shooter . .

AL

(*gotten to*) Well . .

JOHN

But I don't have it in me to be all these things. So when I see all these things in you that I should be, it eats away at me and I resent it.

AL

Gee, ya shouldn't feel that way.

JOHN

And that's why I say things like I did. Hell, it isn't *you* I don't like — it's myself. I know what a real phony I am.

AL

Ahh, you're not so bad.

JOHN

You don't have to kid me — I know. So ya see, to me you've always been somethin' of . . ahh . . (*shrugs*)

AL

What? Go ahead.

JOHN

Well, sort of an idol — somethin' to shoot for. This may sound a little funny, but if I'd of had my choice, you're the kind of guy I'd have chosen to be my father.

AL

(*moved*) I take that as a real compliment.

JOHN

If I'd of had a father like you, maybe things would have turned out different.

AL

Well, it's no good thinking about things like that now.

JOHN

(*resigned*) Yeah, I guess not.

81

ED

You boys gonna patch things up?

AL

Hell, just a little misunderstanding, that's all. (*extending his hand to John*) Put 'er there!

JOHN

A real pleasure! (*They shake hands warmly.*)

AL

It was damn big of ya to make the effort to straighten things out after the way I'd been acting. Y'know, I get a little . . sensitive sometimes.

JOHN

(*an afterthought*) That's another thing — you're very sensitive.

AL

Well, I get my sights set on something, you know how it is, then something like that happens and everything gets out of whack for me. It's a shortcoming of mine, I guess.

JOHN

Not at all; it's an attribute.

AL

I dunno — you know how it is: you know you're doin' everything the way you're supposed to do it, yet every once in a while ya get the feelin' that . . well, that people are only humorin' ya or that they're makin' jokes about ya behind your back. You know what I mean?

JOHN

(*looks at him blankly, then as if suddenly coming to*) Oh . . sure, I know what ya mean.

AL

Sure, I guess everybody goes through it from time to time. Ah, that's what I mean. I'm too sensitive. I let things like that get in my way. I know goddamn well I'm right all along, yet I let these stupid doubts get in my way. I'm just too sensitive — I gotta overcome it.

JOHN

Sure — ya got to.

AL

Boy, I know it. Don't think I don't keep tellin' myself. Oh, I know it. But see, that's what I like about workin' for an outfit like this: they have a certain way in which they expect ya to do things, in which they expect ya to behave — it's almost like a rule book. Not that anything's written down or anything, but it's sorta like . . well, a third ear in here that's tuned in on a special frequency or somethin', that tells ya what they think is right and what they think is wrong. And for a guy like me, that really comes in handy because anytime I got any personal doubts about what's right and what's wrong, I just go to the old rule book and that zeros me right smack in on the old target.

JOHN

(*making the whistling sound of a falling bomb*) Boom!

AL

Bombs away and let's go home, baby!

JOHN

(*nodding*) Yessir, that's the real beauty of workin' for a place like this.

AL

Don't get me wrong — it's not that I lack confidence. I got plenty of confidence. It's just that sometimes . . I'm not quite sure what to be confident about.

JOHN

Well, you're in the right place.

AL

Y'know, once I almost decided to chuck the whole thing. After I'd been working here a couple years I went on one of those winter cruises to Bermuda. Well, after the first couple days things began to go stale. I did the usual — lay around the beaches during the day and hang around the bars during the nights. One of the last nights I'm there I'm sitting in this bar listening to a steel band — I strike up a conversation with this couple, both about fifty, I guess. We shoot the breeze for a while and I find out he runs this little ad agency down there — local merchants, travel brochures, you know. So we're in the same business. After a few more drinks he starts tellin' me I should move down to Bermuda and go to work for him. Well, I figure it's the sauce talkin'. But the next day he calls me at the hotel — says to come over and bring some samples of my work, if I got any with me. It so happens I got a few things I'm working on along with me. Get this: before the afternoon is over, he's shown me the whole setup and offered me a partnership!

JOHN

No kiddin'.

AL

See, he's got this heart condition and doesn't expect to last much longer. All of his customers know this and he figures if he's going to keep people doing business with him he's got to give some sign there's going to be somebody around to handle the load should he drop dead.

JOHN

Figures.

AL

So I got the choice. At first I'm ready to jump at it. I mean, on the outside it looks like it's got a lot of advantages: no regular hours as long as you get the work done, no pressure — you only take on as much as you need. You don't even have to wear a tie if you don't want to.

JOHN

Why didn't you take it?

AL

Well, it's like the rule book I'm tellin' you about. In a setup like that it doesn't exist; you got no sense of direction. How ya ever supposed to know where ya are?

JOHN

What difference does it make?

AL

Ahh, maybe none to some people, but it does to me. I believe in playing it by the book. That way you know what's expected of you and what you can expect from other people. Knock it all you want — it works.

JOHN

Ahhhhh . .

AL

Besides, a man maintains his self-respect out of what other people think of his work and who's down in Bermuda?

JOHN

Well, there're *people* down there, aren't there?

AL

Yeah, but they're not *my* people, that's the whole point. You gotta make it in your own backyard or it doesn't matter.

JOHN

(*without conviction*) Yeah . . yeah, I guess so . .

AL

Get your fingers burned a couple times, you learn not to go running off with a lot of half-cocked, schoolboy ideas.

JOHN

Yeah, it's best not to go too much against the grain, if ya want to stay alive around here.

AL

Yeah, it's dog eat dog.

JOHN

(*weakly*) Arf, arf.

AL

(*laughs shortly*) Anyway, I just wanted to explain about this . . sensitive chink I got in my armor.

JOHN

Al, it opens up a whole new side to your personality that I never even realized existed. I'm glad ya told me.

AL

Yeah, well I don't exactly wear these things on my sleeve.

JOHN

Still waters run deep, buddy.

AL

And I want to tell ya that I was very moved by what you said. I have to admit I've had some doubts about ya, but now I think I understand ya a lot better.

JOHN

Well I feel a lot better, getting things off my chest.

AL

And listen, let's keep in touch. Maybe we can get together sometime for a drink or something. Or hey, better yet — we'll have you and your wife over for dinner some night.

JOHN

(*caught off guard*) What? How do ya mean?

AL

Well, I sort of hate to see ya go and I think we ought to stay in touch.

JOHN

Oh . . yeah, sure . .

AL

You know, get together every once in a while. Go on picnics maybe, or bicycle through the park. Jeez, it's funny we didn't think of —

JOHN

(*weakly*) Yeah . . But y'know, it just occurred to me, now that we've straightened out our differences, I really don't have to quit.

AL

Well, yeah, I guess we could continue the way we have; maybe a little better understanding than before. But y'know, somehow I don't think that would be the best idea. I mean let's face it, you're not happy here; this is the time for you to make a break. Burn your bridges behind you. Make it clean.

JOHN

(*hedging*) I don't know . .

AL

Sure, I believe very strongly in never looking back. Once you've made a decision, stick with it. As a general rule it's always the best policy.

JOHN

Y'think so?

AL

Definitely. Besides, maybe . . well, after the things you said, you know, the way you feel about things between you and me, maybe it'd be better if you found something else — another job. After all, it could be pretty frustrating for you being around a guy like me all the time.

JOHN

(*stuck with it*) Yeah . . I see what you mean.

AL

Sure you do. (*giving him a friendly pat*) You think it over, you'll see I'm right.

JOHN

But . . (*Can't come up with anything — sinks. Pause. Al looks at his watch, goes back to work.*)

ED

How about it, boys, everything hunky-dory?

AL

(*smiling confidently*) Hunky-dory, Ed, hunky-dory.

ED

That's what I like to hear. Does my heart good. Just like me and Jake Wallace.

JOHN

(*pause — looks at Ed, an idea beginning to form*) What did you just say?

ED

I said just like me and Jake Wallace.

JOHN

By God, Al, you're right. I gotta put all this behind me — move on to new things . .

AL

Glad ya see it that way.

JOHN

Yes, sir, I can hardly wait to get started!

AL

That's the old spirit.

ED

Give 'em hell, boy, you got what it takes.

JOHN

But ya know, even more than I believe in making a clean break, I believe in not leaving loose ends.

AL

Good point.

ED

'Atta boy.

JOHN

And there's somethin' about this company that's been buggin' me for some time now.

AL

What's that?

JOHN

The way they treat old employees like Ed here. It's a crime and an outrage and by God, I'm not quitting until we do something about it! (*pounds table dramatically*)

ED

Who, me?

JOHN

You bet, you. It's a disgrace the way they treat people like you who serve the company loyally for so many years. We just can't stand by anymore and watch this go on.

ED

Aw hell, don't go makin' any trouble on my account. I ain't important.

JOHN

Well, if you're not important, I'd like to know who is. It's people like you who are the backbone of this outfit. Or of the whole country for that matter. Hell, as far as that goes, of the entire world!

ED

Aw, I ain't the backbone of nothin' — Christ, I only got one arm.

AL

What're ya gettin' at?

JOHN

Ed, how long have you worked for T.I.C.?

ED

All told, oh, a little over forty years. Over twenty-six as a salesman until I lost my arm. Damn good salesman too. Look up the records. Since then I been doin' this.

AL

How come you had to quit selling just because you lost your arm?

ED

Oh you know — thing like that — I sorta went to pieces — started hittin' the old bottle. This job was just until I could pull myself back together. You know. (*shrugs*)

JOHN

How much do ya get a week?

ED

Seventy-seven fifty, before taxes.

JOHN

Seventy-seven fifty a week! After forty years of loyal service, seventy-seven fifty a week! I ask ya!

ED

It ain't so bad.

JOHN

After wringing every last ounce of use out of him during his productive years, they cast him away like an old shoe.

AL

(*reluctantly*) Yeah, I admit it's pretty terrible, but . . well, *he* doesn't seem to mind.

ED

Well . . it ain't so bad — the work ain't hard . . it's just the idea . . of endin' up this way. I mean, I got nothin' to look forward to.

JOHN

That's it exactly. Whatta ya got to show for all these years of loyal service: nothin' to look forward to.

AL

But what the hell can *you* do about it?

JOHN

Not *me*, old buddy, *us*!

AL

Us?

JOHN

You bet, sweetheart! An editorial campaign in the magazine: an exposé of the whole rotten business . .

AL

C'mon, get serious.

JOHN

I *am* serious. The power of the press. We blow the whole thing wide open.

You write the editorials, I draw the cartoons — you know, just like those political cartoons in the downtown papers.

AL

That's exactly it, this stuff is for the downtown papers, not a company magazine. Besides, it's against the magazine's policy; we're supposed to promote the idea that if the employees are conscientious and loyal and keep plugging, things'll keep gettin' better and better and they'll end up in fat city.

JOHN

Sure, the pot of gold at the end of the rainbow. The only trouble is, it's not there.

AL

(*a little defensively*) I'm not so sure about that.

ED

Uh . . listen, I'd rather ya didn't involve me in anything like this. They'd only think I was makin' trouble and I'd end up gettin' fired.

AL

Yeah, what if we got fired? Right out in the street, talkin' to ourselves. (*takes a drink*)

JOHN

But that's the beauty of it — they *couldn't* fire us! Once this got out we'd be too hot to fire. If they canned us they'd look like a bunch of cowards. Hell, we'd be heroes!

AL

You really think so?

JOHN

We can't miss! Christ, the opportunity's just sittin' there waitin' for somebody to come along and pick it up. This is an ill that needs to be cured. The employees want it, they just don't *know* they want it. They need somebody like us to lead the way.

AL

(*takes another drink*) I got to admit, it sounds exciting.

JOHN

Pull off something like this and you can write your own ticket around here. Hell, make your reputation on something like this and the sky's the limit. Maybe you'd even get hired by *Time* magazine.

AL

(*growing excited*) By God, this has got real possibilities!

JOHN

Unlimited! Then you're more than just another house magazine editor.

89

Something like this's got national implications. Hell, ya'd be a goddamn social reformer!

AL

(*smacks his fist into his palm enthusiastically*) Son of a bitch!

JOHN

Ya'd be another Lenin. (*Al frowns and begins to slow down.*) Uh . . Luce!

AL

(*that's better*) Yeah! (*takes another drink, pacing with excitement*) We'll do it! By God, the people will be heard around here. This kind of corruption has been going on long enough.

JOHN

That's the stuff.

ED

I still don't think ya'd better count on me, fellas. I'm gettin' on and this sort of thing . .

AL

Listen, Ed, look at it this way: this is your chance, maybe your *last* chance, to do something significant with your life.

ED

How zat?

AL

You're a perfect example of this sort of thing that's been goin' on and if we conduct our . . exposé around you, you'll become a national symbol to thousands of people.

ED

Symbol? What kinda symbol?

AL

A symbol of . . of . . (*stuck*)

JOHN

A symbol of the gross injustice being done to people like you all over the country.

ED

(*impressed*) Gee!

AL

And not only that, Ed, but when this situation is brought to light, it'll put ya on easy street.

ED

No kiddin'!

AL

Sure. A pension, retirement, maybe even a little place of your own down in Florida someplace. What the hell, maybe you can even get together again with your old friend Jake Williams.

ED

Wallace.

AL

Wallace. (*inspired*) Hey, there's an idea for a feature story: maybe we can dig up this other old guy, Jake Wallace, and stage a reunion. You know, "former employees separated forty years, reunited by T.I.C.," that sort of thing.

JOHN

Great idea.

ED

Ya think so?

AL

Why not? This thing's got all sorts of possibilities.

ED

Gee, me and Jake together again, just like the old days. Christ, I hope he ain't dead.

AL

Naw, not a chance. Hey listen, how's this for a lead-in on the editorial: (*takes a drink, paces as he composes orally*) "The *travesty* of big business attitudes toward older employees was dramatically demonstrated by the discovery of the pathetic plight of Ed . ." What the hell's your last name?

ED

Coogan.

AL

". . of Ed Coogan, former star salesman, now a lowly night watchman, and a loyal T.I.C. employee for more than forty years!" How's that?

JOHN

That's hot stuff, baby, hot stuff.

ED

Gee, imagine me, Ed Coogan, a national symbol!

JOHN

How about this: on the cover of the magazine, a picture of Ed here, seated in his night watchman's uniform. Behind him an American flag on one side and the T.I.C. emblem on the other!

AL

Terrific! You're cookin' with gas. Hey look, why not try out a couple shots right now with the Polaroid, just to see how they look?

JOHN

Hey, good idea. Here, Ed, have a drink. (*Hands him bottle. Ed drinks.*)

AL

(*getting equipment ready*) Get him on a chair there . . Hey, no, I got a better idea — get him on a chair on top of the table — I can get some angle shots.

JOHN

Great, that's the idea.

ED

(*as John gets chair on table and helps Ed up*) Jeez! Who'd of thought, a funny lookin' old geek like me, on the cover of the company magazine!

AL

Just the beginning, Ed, just the beginning.

ED

Hey, maybe I could get a couple prints made and show 'em to my wife . . She was startin' to think I was never gonna amount to anything.

JOHN

She has no faith.

AL

(*getting set*) Okay, now cross your legs and put your hands . . excuse me — hand in your lap. Hey, get that bottle out of there.

ED

Oh. (*chuckles*) That would never do, would it. (*John removes the bottle and takes a drink. He sighs from a combination of exhaustion, relief, and apprehension over what he has started.*)

AL

(*focusing*) Okay, we ready? . . Now, hold your chin up . . turn your head a little . . more towards John . . That's it . . Hold it . . now say cheese.

ED

(*nervously*) Cheese.

BLACKOUT

Scene 2

About 7:45 A.M. — sunlight streaming in the windows. Al and John are asleep, face down, at their desks. Ed is stretched out on one of the tables asleep, as before, with a flower held in his hand. The whiskey bottle, now empty, sits on one of the tables nearby. A few moments, then the phone on Al's desk begins to ring. Slowly he stirs and picks up the receiver.

AL

'Lo . . Oh hi, honey . . (*suddenly realizes where he is and quickly becomes awake*) Oh my God, what time is it? (*looks at his watch*) Ten to eight! My God, everybody'll be at work in a couple minutes! What? . . I know I didn't come home last night; whatta ya think, I don't even know when I don't come home? . . Honey, don't cry, for crying out loud . . I couldn't help it . . I got locked in the office all night . . Honest to God . . I'll explain when I get home . . You did what? . . Well, call 'em back and tell 'em I'm all right . . Yeah, I'm just fine . . a little tired is all . . No, I don't have time to come home. (*condescendingly patient*) Well, that's the job, baby . . No, I'll brush 'em twice when I get home . . Look, honey, I just woke up, I gotta get ready for work . . (*sighs*) I know it was your birthday, but it wasn't my fault . . I'll explain everything when I get home . . All right, baby, goodbye . . Yes . . goodbye. (*hangs up*) Christ! (*He begins moving quickly about the room, cleaning things up and pulling himself together as he does so. He picks up the whiskey bottle, sees that it is empty, mutters "Oh, my head!" and puts the bottle in a wastebasket. Then he thinks better of this, removes it, and puts it in his desk drawer. He snatches the flower from Ed's hand and throws it in the wastebasket, then moves to John and begins to shake him.*) Hey, John . . wake up . . C'mon . .

JOHN

(*suddenly looking straight at him*) What?

AL

(*emphatically*) It's almost eight o'clock.

JOHN

What?

AL

All the early birds start arriving in a couple minutes.

JOHN

(*looking around him, dazed; makes a face*) My mouth tastes like the Russian cavalry slept in it.

AL

We got to hitting it pretty hard.

JOHN

We must've fallen asleep. What time did we go to sleep?

AL

(*shrugs*) I don't know. (*They look at each other a little sheepishly.*) Anyway, Ketchum's liable to come barging in any minute now wanting to see some of those Polaroids from the party. And I don't think he'll be too impressed with the sight of old Ed stretched out on our table there.

JOHN

(*takes a deep breath and lets it out*) No, I guess not. (*Unlike Al, he doesn't seem to find anything urgent in the situation. Looks down at his drawing board.*) Christ, what a mess.

AL

What?

JOHN

This layout for the bride's page.

AL

(*pause as he looks at it*) Yeah. (*pause*) Oh well, you can do it over again. It won't take long . . (*can't resist*) if you just get down to business.

JOHN

Yeah.

AL

C'mon, we gotta do something with old Ed. (*John rises slowly and they go to the table where Ed is stretched out. They stand over him for a moment, silently. John picks up a few snapshots from the table beside Ed.*)

JOHN

(*laughs softly*) Christ, we sure took a lot of pictures of Ed last night.

AL

(*picking up some more pictures*) Took some pretty good ones of ourselves too. We shot up six rolls of film. Here's a charming one of you with the wastepaper basket over your head. (*offers it to John but John waves it away without looking*) Well . . (*referring to Ed and the task at hand*)

JOHN

(*gently*) Ed . . Ed . . wake up, boy, it's mornin' . .

ED

Huh?

JOHN

Up an' at 'em, big fella — people are startin' to come to work.

ED

(*raises up slightly*) Jeez . . turn off the lights . .

JOHN

That's sunshine, Ed — vitamin D.

ED

(*half-sitting*) Whatever it is, I don't need it.

AL

(*nervously*) C'mon.

JOHN

Look, people are gonna be comin' in to start work any minute . . and a . . it doesn't look good — you know . .

ED

(*groggy but agreeable*) Sure, sure, I know — I'll get outta here right away. I don't want to get you boys in any trouble. (*sits up painfully; holds his head in his hand*) Uhhh. I don't know about you fellas, but I really hung one on last night. (*Al begins putting the room back in order.*)

JOHN

Yeah, we all did.

AL

You said it. (*looks at John anxiously*) C'mon . .

ED

Yeah, my old head's ready to explode. Jeez, I need some orange juice or somethin' . . or maybe a hair of the dog.

JOHN

(*gently trying to get rid of him*) Well, you can probably pick up a little something on the way home, then get some sleep.

ED

Good idea. Say, why don't you guys come with me? I know a little place we can get a bite to eat — maybe an eye-opener.

AL

Ugh!

JOHN

Naw, thanks anyway, but we got work to do.

ED

Jeez, ain't ya gonna go home now?

JOHN

We can't, we gotta get this magazine out.

ED

Oh yeah, the magazine. Jeez, you young fellas. (*shakes his head*) I can't do it anymore. Used to be a time I could go on for days but not anymore. I need my sleep. (*Gets off the table, knocking several Polaroid pictures to the floor as he does. He bends, picks them up, looks at them.*) We really had a good time last night, didn't we? (*John and Al grunt assent.*) I sure had a good time. We had a regular party.

ED

(*looking at his watch*) John, I'm not kiddin' . .

JOHN

Yeah, I know. (*to Ed*) Listen, old buddy . .

ED

Jeez, lookit all these pictures of old Ed. Some of 'em aren't too bad, eh?

JOHN

(*looking at pictures*) You're a regular Cary Grant, Ed.

ED

I never had so many pictures taken of me before. Hey, ya really gonna do that story about me? (*John and Al exchange glances.*)

AL

Ahhh, I don't know.

JOHN

We were . . uh . . talkin' it over a little bit before you woke up and . . uh . . we're gonna do it — we definitely decided we're gonna do it . . but we gotta be careful. Something like this, it's dynamite, ya know.

ED

Oh sure, I see.

JOHN

But we're definitely gonna do it. It's just gonna take some more careful thinking and planning. Ya can't go off on somethin' like this half-cocked, ya know. Ya gotta find just the right angle.

ED

Oh that's right. Somethin' like this, one wrong move and powee! — the whole thin's shot right in the ass.

JOHN

Very well put, Ed, that's it, exactly. So ya see, we gotta put some more thought into this. We'll get in touch with ya when we're ready to let fly with this thing.

ED

Well I just want ya to know you can expect full cooperation from me when the time comes. This is the sort of thing that needs to be brought to light. Hell, I'd be tickled pink.

JOHN

Well thanks, Ed — it's good to know we can count on ya. Oh and Ed, mum's the word on this. If this should ever leak out . .

ED

Oh sure, I getcha. (*puts a finger to his lips*) Shhh.

AL

Jesus, would you wrap it up! Any second now . . (*At this moment, Ketchum comes briskly into the room. He is robust, energetic, and confident. He enjoys exercising his power and likes to think of himself as the sort of man that his employees would all like to be some day. Strangely enough, many of them would.*)

KETCHUM

Good morning, good morning. At it bright and early this morning I see.

AL AND JOHN

(*nervously*) Good morning . . yessir. (*Ed withdraws slightly into the background. Ketchum doesn't seem to notice him.*)

KETCHUM

Ah, I like to see that. A lot of people, the day after the Christmas party, call in sick. Hah! Sick, my foot. We know what they're all sick from.

AL

Yes, sir, I can imagine.

KETCHUM

Imagine what?

AL

Well . . that they're . . I mean, what they're all . .

KETCHUM

Well . . (*continuing*) it only comes once a year . . thank God! (*chuckles*)

AL

Yes, sir, thank God for that.

KETCHUM

Say, I thought I'd like to get a look at some of those Polaroid shots you took at the party last night. Some of them ought to be pretty good.

AL

Oh yes, sir, they're right here. (*begins going through his photographic equipment, but can't locate the pictures immediately*) Now, where the hell . .

KETCHUM

(*to John*) Say, I hope you didn't mind me cutting in on you last night.

97

JOHN
Oh no, perfectly all right. Don't think a thing about it.
KETCHUM
Well, I wasn't trying to take her away from you or anything, I just wanted to dance with her a couple times. New girl like that, comes to a big company like this, doesn't know anybody, helps her to feel at home if an executive pays a little attention to her.
JOHN
Sure.
KETCHUM
Makes them realize we look at them as individuals, not just another cog in the old machine. Gives the kid a lift.
JOHN
Sure, that was all right. I mean, I know what you were doing. I wasn't *with* her or anything, we were just dancing. I mean, what the heck, Mr. Ketchum, I'm a married man.
KETCHUM
Sure, sure, so are we all. Well, I looked around for you to return her to you, but you'd already gone.
JOHN
Well, I had some work to do so I . . ah, did anyone else . . get acquainted with her?
KETCHUM
Well, she's such a shy little thing . . I saw to it . . she got home all right. (*Wanting to change the subject, he picks up some of the pictures on the table.*) Ah, are these the pictures?
AL
Oh, no . . those are . . uh . .
KETCHUM
What the hell! Who's this with the wastepaper basket over his head?
JOHN
Oh . . well, that's . . uh . . me . . ya see . .
KETCHUM
(*picking up more*) What are all these, anyway? Who the hell is this?
AL
Oh, that's uh . . Ed . . (*gestures to Ed who stands uncomfortably*)
KETCHUM
(*glances at Ed*) Ed who?
ED
(*weakly*) Ed . . Coogan.

JOHN

He's the night watchman.

KETCHUM

Well, what are all these pictures for?

AL

We were sort of killing time.

KETCHUM

Killing time? With company film? There must be four or five rolls shot up here. What do you mean, "Killing time"? Don't you have enough to do around here?

AL

Well, yes, sure, plenty . . but see, this was about three or four this morning . .

KETCHUM

Three or four in the morning? What the hell were you doing here at three or four in the morning?

AL

Well, see, we got locked in last night.

KETCHUM

Locked in? You mean you were here all night?

AL

Yes, sir, that's right — we were here all night. See, we came back here from the party because we had some work to finish up. But the time lock went on before we could leave and we couldn't get out.

KETCHUM

So you were here all night?

AL

Yes, sir.

KETCHUM

(*laughs*) I'll be goddamned, if that doesn't beat all! (*John and Al laugh with him. Suddenly Ketchum stops laughing.*) What the hell, why couldn't *he* let you out? (*pointing to Ed*) The night watchman's got a key for the time lock, why couldn't *he* let you out?

ED

Well . . uh . . ya see, sir . . uh . . (*He stops, not knowing what to say. There is a pause.*)

AL

He couldn't let us out because he lost the key to the time lock.

99

KETCHUM

You lost the key to the time lock? (*crosses to Ed, being as intimidating as he can*) How the hell did you do that?

ED

I don't know, sir . . I . .

KETCHUM

How long ago did you lose it?

ED

I don't know, sir, how long ago . . about a month ago . .

KETCHUM

A month ago! Why didn't you report it lost? Do you realize what could happen if the wrong people got their hands on that key?

ED

Well . . I thought I'd find it . .

KETCHUM

How long were you going to wait, a year? Five years?

ED

No, sir . . just a little while longer . .

KETCHUM

Have you been drinking?

ED

Drinking? Me? No, sir . . no, sir . . I . . Well, yes, as a matter of fact, I had a little during the night . . it helps me . .

KETCHUM

(*looks at his watch*) I'll meet you at the personnel office in five minutes. I think we better talk this over with Mr. Winkle. (*turns to go out*)

ED

Yessir, five minutes — personnel office — I'll be there.

KETCHUM

(*stops at door — to Al and John*) How's the Christmas issue coming along?

AL

Comin' right along, sir; should have it out by the second week in January.

KETCHUM

Fine, keep up the good work. (*smiles*) And get cleaned up; the two of you look like you've been up all night. (*goes out*)

AL

(*beaming*) Yessir, we'll do that sir! (*sinks back into his chair*) Whew! I thought we'd had it. (*pause*)

ED

Well, maybe *you* haven't, but . .

AL

Listen, Ed, I was sorry we had to bring you into this but . .

JOHN

We? Where do ya get "we"? You were the one that did it.

AL

Well, it was your neck too, ya know! I didn't hear you comin' up with anything.

JOHN

Well ya didn't have t' . .

ED

Forget it, boys, forget it. It isn't worth fightin' over. It wasn't anybody's fault, anyway.

AL

Besides, all those things were true. It isn't as if it were unfair or something.

JOHN

Why you sanctimonious . . !

ED

Forget it, forget it, I said! He's right, it's my own fault. Hell, they ain't gonna do anything to me. I been with this company too long — they remember things like that. Probably just give me a good chewin' out is all. Jeez, I oughta be able to stand that after all these years.

AL

Sure, that's all they'll do. They won't can him.

JOHN

Yeah? Well listen, Ed, if they give ya any heat, tell 'em all to go to hell. I mean, if the writing on the wall becomes clear, don't let 'em walk all over ya just for exercise. Go out with a bang, not a whimper.

ED

Oh hell, you know me. They won't push old Ed around. I'll say, "Look here, I been with this company for . ." (*stops, sighs*) Yeah, well . . (*uncomfortable pause*)

AL

Listen, I'll put in a word to Ketchum for ya.

JOHN

(*contemptuously*) You . . !

ED

Yeah, thanks . . (*picks up some of the pictures*) Say, you won't be usin'

101

all of these — would ya mind if I took a couple of 'em along? I'd like to show 'em to my wife the next time I see her. She's never seen me in my uniform before.

AL

Help yourself.

JOHN

(*going to table and gathering them up*) Listen, Ed, take 'em all. I mean they were just practice shots anyway. When the time comes, we'll take some new ones — you know, complete with everything. (*gives pictures to Ed*)

ED

Hey, no kiddin'. Gee, thanks a lot. I never had very many pictures of myself before.

AL

Sure, you're welcome to 'em.

ED

Well, I better get down to personnel. No sense keepin' those people waitin'.

JOHN

Let us know how things turn out.

ED

Oh, you bet. You'll be hearin' from me.

AL

Take it easy.

ED

Hell, I'll take it any way I can get it. (*laughs*) So long, boys, and thanks a lot for everything. Oh, and hey — Merry Christmas to you fellas.

AL AND JOHN

Same to you, Ed. (*Ed goes out quickly. Long pause.*)

AL

(*finally*) Think he'll get the sack?

JOHN

You know goddamn well he will! Why the hell did ya hafta blow the whistle on him?

AL

It was him or us — what could I do? Besides, I only told the truth; if he gets canned for that then he deserves it.

JOHN

You make me sick!

AL

You don't do much for me either, sweetheart! And if I make you so damn sick, why don't you quit!

JOHN

Are we gonna sing that song again? Look, if you're gonna hold your breath waitin' for me to . .

AL

All right then, listen: if you're gonna stick around here you're gonna toe the mark and play the game according to the rules! And if ya don't, you'll be out of here so fast you won't know what hit ya! And you know I got just the bit of insurance I need to make that happen too.

JOHN

If I ever get hold of that picture I'm gonna rip it up and shove it down your throat!

AL

Don't worry — you're never gonna get that chance.

JOHN

You're . . immoral! That's the only word I can think of.

AL

You call *me* immoral! Don't make me laugh.

JOHN

You are. You're the most immoral person I've ever met.

AL

Well, you can call it anything you want, but you and people like you are a threat to things that I know are right and decent and I'll use any means I have to keep you in your proper place. If that's immoral than I plead guilty! Now get that goddam layout finished! (*He turns to his typewriter, inserts a sheet of paper, and begins to type. Pause.*)

JOHN

(*stands looking out of window — hands in his pockets*) Poor Ed, I wonder what he'll do now. (*no response*) It's starting to snow.

AL

(*continues typing*) Oh well, stop the presses. Snow in December in New York — that's really news. (*silence*)

JOHN

(*softly, mockingly descriptive*) . . And as Christmas shoppers scurried about Manhattan, completing their last-minute buying, a gentle snow began to fall, covering the city . .

AL

(*busy*) C'mon, c'mon.

103

JOHN

And as our thoughts travel westward . . (*stops*)

AL

(*pause*) Well, it's too bad about people like that; I really pity them. But that's the way the world is: it's dog eat dog. (*continues working for a moment, then stops and says*) Arf, arf, arf. (*goes back to work but after a moment stops again and repeats*) I said, it's dog eat dog. Arf, arf, arf. (*No response — John continues to look out of the window. Al turns to him — speaks firmly.*) C'mon. (*pause*)

JOHN

(*sighs*) All right, for chrissakes, arf, arf, arf. (*He turns to his drawing board and begins to work. Al returns to his typewriter and the two of them continue working as the curtain falls.*)

THE END

Visions of Sugar Plums by Barry Pritchard was presented March 31–April 17, 1966, at Theatre St. Paul, St. Paul. It was directed by Rex Henriot.

Cast of Characters

AL HUBBARD	Gerald Hjert
JOHN SCHULTE	Bernie McInerney
ED COOGAN	Gary Gage
PEACHES	Zoaunne Henriot
KETCHUM	Tom Roland

ARNOLD POWELL

The Strangler

A NEW CHOKE ON AN OLD GAG

Cast of Characters

ANDREW VURGLAR, an old man
VIRGINIA VURGLAR, an old woman, his wife
ANNIE VURGLAR, their older daughter
ISABEL VURGLAR, their younger daughter
PAUL VURGLAR and EDDY VURGLAR, their twin sons
UNCLE BUD, Virginia's brother
MARY, the maid
STAGEHANDS

Scenes

Act One. A bare stage, the present. Act Two. The same, a moment later.

THE STRANGLER

ACT ONE

At rise: Nothing. Pause. Andrew, a very old man with great dignity, long white hair, mustache, beard, and a slight limp, enters left and crosses down center leaning on a cane. He is wearing felt bedroom slippers, formal trousers, and a smoking jacket. A stagehand, carrying a chair, follows him on and stands waiting while Andrew fusses about trying to find the exact center of the stage. Finally Andrew, with the cane as pointer, indicates the spot on the floor and turns full front, posed authoritatively until the stagehand places the chair behind him.

STAGEHAND

(Placing the chair and stepping back.)
That okay?
(Andrew tightens his pose, shuts his eyes, and nods. Stagehand crosses left.)
Well, if you need anything else just whistle.
(Andrew, doggedly holding onto his pose, eyes clamped tightly, dismisses him with a wave of the cane.)
See you around.
(Stagehand exits. Andrew slams the floor with his cane.)

ANDREW

Every night.
Every night I give them explicit instructions:
You have only to place the chair

© Copyright 1962 as an unpublished work, 1967 by Arnold Francis Powell. Address inquiries concerning performance or translation rights to Ernest Dobbs, Creative Management Associates, Ltd., 555 Madison Avenue, New York City.

107

Quietly
Efficiently
On the spot indicated
And unobtrusively Un-Ob-Tru-Sively
Exit.
No fuss
No talk
ESPECIALLY NO TALK!
No speech is necessary.
And yet
Every night EVERY NIGHT
They break the mood
Shatter the pose with their backstage prose.
(*Imitating stagehand.*)
If you need anything just . .
(*Violently whistling out the words.*)
Why I've ceased whistling since adolescence!
(*Struggles to control himself. Fails.*)
The world has gone to hell!
(*Pause. Another struggle. A little better.*)
No sense of . .
No feeling for . .
No appreciation of . .
(*Pause. This time he succeeds in relaxing. He looks about him at the bare stage.*)
Well, what can you expect
In this modern-day so-called playhouse
With its no-stage staging?
Not
(*Palms together, oriental bow.*)
Noh stage but
(*Violent gesture of discard.*)
No stage!
Anti-theatrical theatre.
Undramatic drama.
Why should the theatre of all places be anti-theatrical?
Tell me that.
What sense does it make
For something to . . to . .
For something to deny its very essence?

Its . .
Its character?
What it is?
I tell you what:
When a thing turns against itself
You've got nothing left
But chaos.
If the road crosses itself
How can you find the way?
We're lost that's what we are
Lost.
(*Stands gloomily thinking for a moment.*)
But never mind.
We really should be getting
As we say in the theatre
On with the show.
(*Sighs. Becomes nostalgic.*)
I remember when a theatre was a theatre.
Not
(*Gesture of dismissal.*)
A-theatre but
(*Emphatically positive gesture.*)
A THEATRE!
And proud of it.
(*Strikes a pose with chin lifted proudly. Pause. Relaxes.*)
However . .
(*He starts to sit, glances behind him, bangs his cane onto the floor, turns full up to face the chair. With a display of patience and artistic precision, he moves the chair two inches to the left, steps back to inspect, cocks his head, turns the chair a half inch to the right, inspects again, and, satisfied, turns to the audience.*)
In the old days there would have been a mark
And the stagehands would have placed the chair on the mark
Not before the audience
But before the audience
Arrived.
And behind closed curtains.
The actor would have come out
Beforehand
Behind closed curtains

109

And inspected it
Sat in it
Tested it
Before and behind
Before
(*Slows tempo.*)
Sitting in it
(*He sits.*)
Assuming his pose
(*Assumes patriarchal pose. Adjusts.*)
Nodding graciously to the stage manager in the wings
(*Nods graciously to the left.*)
Like a soloist to the conductor of a great symphony orchestra
Cuing him that he was ready
That he had made the transition from the world of reality to the world of
    illusion
And was ready.
And then
(*Another gracious nod to the left.*)
R-r-ring up the curtain.
Tableau!
(*He restrikes his pose as a dramatic change of lights leaves him isolated
in surprise pink. He holds the pose for some moments, quivering with ex-
citement. Finally he speaks in exalted, deliberate tones.*)
I am the father.
(*Pause. Not quite so exalted.*)
Do you know what a father is?
What a . .
(*Pause. Angrily shouts.*)
Line!

STAGE MANAGER
(*Off.*)
What a father does!

ANDREW
What a father does?
What a —
(*Leaps up.*)
There you see
Even if we had decent stages
What do they give us to stage?

110

What can you do
What can an actor do
With lines like that?
With plays that aren't plays?
Bastard plays written for bastard stages
By . .
(*Pause. Calmer.*)
A true soliloquy was one thing:
Full front and spout it out.
Hit the audience full in the face with it.
But from a distance.
It kept its distance.
And if any playwright in my day had been clumsy enough with his ex-
    position to have a character turn to the audience and explain who he
    was he would have been hooted from the stage.
Oh no
We knew how to do it better in my day
Smoother
More subtly:
The butler and the maid discussed it.
Or a long-lost son returned home after a prolonged absence
And asked questions.
A stranger appeared.
And the audience wasn't even aware that it was being informed
Along with the stranger
Or the long-lost son
Or the maid.
(*Reviews the situation.*)
Or the butler.
And illusion!
(*Exalted.*)
Illusion of reality!
(*Deflates.*)
What kind of illusion of reality can you sustain
When a character
Steps out of character
And addresses the audience
As actor
Like this
To criticize the play?

(*Shakes his head sadly.*)

Oh well

Let's try to make the most of what we've got left.

Let's try again.

(*Sits again and assumes patriarchal pose. Holds it for a moment, then speaks slowly.*)

I . . am . . the

(*Breaks from pose genially.*)

The show must

To paraphrase an old theatrical expression

Go on.

(*Resumes pose, slow pace, exalted tone.*)

I . . am . . the . . father

(*Slight pause.*)

Do you know what a father is?

(*An almost imperceptible wince, but he goes on.*)

What a father does?

(*He is warming up now.*)

What a father thinks of?

Broods on?

Dreams up?

Stands for?

(*He stands. A spot of cold white light comes up down right on Virginia, called Gin, Andrew's wife of indeterminate age: she has mixed black and gray hair but an ageless face. She might be either a young woman with prematurely gray hair or an old woman who is exceptionally well preserved, though the small, old-fashioned, steel-rimmed spectacles that she is wearing emphasize her age. She is holding in her hand an opened package of raw meat.*)

GIN

He stands for me

The mother

That's what a father stands for

Respectfully.

ANDREW

(*Posing.*)

The patriarch.

The protector of his little brood

From killers and

Stranglers.

112

The bulwark against evil
And sudden terror.
The earplug against night screams
The nose-stopper against . .
Against . .
The trouble is: one earplug or one nose-stopper isn't enough when every-
    body has two ears and two nostrils just waiting to suck in the slightest
    wheeze or whiff of all that luscious contamination which . .
(*Pause.*)
Which I know
Which I alone know
Saturates the very atmosphere that shrouds
Yes I said SHROUDS this home
And I choose the term deliberately
Because —
But that's my secret
And I wear it in the depths of my bowels like a night-blooming carcinoma.
(*Announces grandly.*)
Bear in mind
It was I who strangled the strangler.
      GIN
He thinks I stand for him
In a metaphysical kind of way . .
      ANDREW
The word, my dear, is "metaphorical."
      GIN
Now isn't he the superior one?
(*Stares straight out.*)
Of course I could handle a little verbal jab like that if I wanted to:
A series of left and right hooks, an uppercut or so, and the old one-two
    would put him out like a light.
Verbally, that is.
Metaphys — ah
Metaphorically
Like a light.
(*Smiles.*)
But that would hardly be a suitable way for a
Mother
To comport herself
Would it?

No

Oh no

That's not the way a mother goes about it.

Here's the way a mother goes about it.

Watch.

(*As the general lights come up onstage, Gin crosses to Andrew and holds out the meat to him.*)

Andrew.

ANDREW

Yes, my dear.

GIN

Will you smell this meat?

ANDREW

I will not.

GIN

I only wanted to see if you thought we should eat it.

If you thought it was good.

ANDREW

Or bad.

GIN

Or bad.

I've only had it a few days but I kept it in the meat saver right under the freezing unit and I don't see how it could possibly have —

ANDREW

Throw it out.

GIN

What? Why —

ANDREW

Throw it out!

GIN

But I can't do that.

It may be perfectly good.

ANDREW

Not any more.

You've planted the seeds of doubt.

You've ruined it.

Throw it out.

GIN

Oh, Andrew.

ANDREW

How many times must I repeat
Don't ask me to smell the meat.

GIN

But somebody has to . .

ANDREW

That's your job.
Women's work.
Women have stronger stomachs.

GIN

(*Studying the meat.*)
I don't really think anything's wrong with it.

ANDREW

Then why did you ask me to smell it?
Why did you spoil it for me?

GIN

I only wanted to be sure.
I noticed this smell and —

ANDREW

If there's a smell
Throw it out.

GIN

But I'm not sure it's the meat that I smell.
(*She sniffs the air, holds the meat to her nose, and sniffs it, mentally weighs the evidence.*)
I'm not sure that's the smell I smell.
(*She turns and looks at him. He quails.*)

ANDREW

Well it certainly isn't me.
(*Trying to recover, weakly.*)
Throw it out . .
(*He attempts several more dauntless poses but can't seem to get comfortable. Finally he hangs halfway between two poses as if balancing on one foot.*)

GIN

(*Observes him smugly for a while, then calls.*)
Annie!
(*Annie, a large unformed girl of fourteen with an intense air of pious dedication, runs in.*)

ANNIE
Yes, Mother?

GIN
(*Hands her the package of raw meat.*)
Take this meat and wrap it better and . .

ANDREW
(*Muttering.*)
Throw it out throw it out . .

GIN
Return it to the butcher.

ANNIE
(*Horrified.*)
Oh no!
Please!

GIN
And demand a refund.

ANNIE
Please don't make me do it.

GIN
Tell him it's spoilt.

ANNIE
No . . no . .

GIN
Tell him it smells bad.

ANNIE
I can't I can't . .
(*She bursts into tears.*)

ANDREW
(*To Gin.*)
Have you no sensibility, woman?

GIN
Have I no what?

ANDREW
Sensibility sensibility
In the older and truer sense of the word sensibility.
Have you no delicacy of feeling
Or no feeling for delicacy of feeling?

GIN
I don't stand for any nonsense.

116

ANDREW
Sending a tender young girl
A callow spring shoot of a green thing
Into the blood-bedewed
The crimson charnel house
Of beasts.
GIN
The butcher shop?
ANDREW
Ah
Look at her flinch
Blench
And fetch her breath in short little startled gasps
At the very thought.
Poor tender young . .
GIN
Look
This tender young hulk of a girl
Could drink your blood and eat your guts
Without missing a single respiratory stroke.
ANDREW
I forbid you!
I forbid you to use such expressions
Such images
In the presence of my daughter.
GIN
She's my daughter too, you know.
ANDREW
Perhaps she can overcome that handicap.
ANNIE
Please please please . .
ANDREW
You see how you've upset her
With all this talk of such things as
(*Spelling.*)
B-l-o-o-d and
G-u-
ANNIE
You don't understand, Daddy.

ANDREW

How?

I don't understand?

I, the father?

ANNIE

No, sir.

It's not the blood and guts that would upset me —

ANDREW

Wait!

Pause!

Pause one moment to consider your choice of words.

Is this the language of young girlhood?

Are these the locutions that should properly issue from the mouths of
maidens?

ANNIE

But you see

(*Assumes pious pose.*)

Matters of the flesh don't touch me.

I'm above such things.

My world is of the spirit alone.

ANDREW

Well then

What was it that upset you so?

ANNIE

The butcher looks at you funny when you take meat back.

It's embarrassing.

ANDREW

I must say you disappoint me.

ANNIE

Do you like to return things

That you've already bought and paid for?

And ask for your money back

And have them look at you like you were a freak

Or something?

GIN

(*To Annie.*)

Can these sticks and stones reach the rarefied heights

Where your proud spirit dwells?

ANDREW

Ah well

Let's not dwell upon these morbid things.
We've so much to be thankful for
Reassured by what we know we mean to each other
In our own little family circle.
Let's be a HAPPY family
Affectionate
Relaxed
Yes, even playful . .
(*Relaxing into jovial playfulness, he turns to Annie.*)
Come here, Squirt.

      GIN AND ANNIE

(*Both horrified.*)
No no no no no no no!

      ANNIE

You've got the wrong one, Daddy.

      GIN

This is your older daughter
Not the baby.

      ANDREW

(*Bemused.*)
Not the kid?

      GIN

She's the one you playfully call "Squirt"
The younger one.

      ANNIE

I'm Annie, Daddy.
I'm your "Dear Child."

      GIN

You're confusing her with Isabel.
Isabel's the younger one.
(*Isabel steps in.*)

      ISABEL

I'm Isabel.
Just call me Squirt.
(*Isabel, though played by an actress who is obviously older than the one playing Annie — both adults — is a little girl of nine.*)

      ANDREW

(*Vaguely.*)
Isabel and Annie . . ?

GIN
(*Raising her voice as if speaking to a deaf person.*)
You have two daughters
Remember?
(*Pointing carefully.*)
Annie's the older
Isabel's the younger.

ANNIE
I'm the older daughter.

ISABEL
I'm the younger daughter.

GIN
Two daughters.

ANDREW
(*Suddenly shouting.*)
Daughters! Daughters! Daughters!
I'm surrounded by women!
Are there no sons in this household?
Do I have no sons and heirs?

GIN
Of course you do.
You have two:
Paul and Eddy.
(*Paul and Eddy march on in unison, come to a military halt facing full out, and salute.*)

PAUL AND EDDY
That's us.
(*Though played by adult actors, they are seven-year-old twins, as identical-looking as possible. Both are dressed in play soldier suits but they are not the same: Eddy wears a child's replica of the latest style of uniform worn by the soldiers of the country in which the play is being performed; Paul wears a child's replica of that worn by the country's current enemy.*)

ANDREW
(*Beaming.*)
Which one's the older?
Which is THE son and heir?

PAUL AND EDDY
We're twins.

ANDREW
Yes but —

EDDY
As sons and heirs
PAUL
We go equal shares.
PAUL AND EDDY
We're twins.
ANDREW
This makes for a rather ambivalent relationship
Doesn't it?
Between father and son?
Come come
Twins or no twins
One had to get here first.
Which was it?
ANNIE
They were identical twins, Daddy.
ISABEL
That's right
Identical.
ANDREW
Identical doesn't mean that.
ISABEL
Identical means same.
PAUL
Identical twins.
EDDY
Identical ages.
PAUL
To the very day.
EDDY
The very hour.
PAUL AND EDDY
To the very minute.
ANDREW
But not the very second.
Gin.
GIN
Yes, Andrew?
ANDREW
You're the mother.

You must know.
Tell me
Which one got here first?

GIN

Neither one.
They both arrived at EXACTLY THE SAME TIME.

PAUL

Photo finish!

EDDY

Dead heat!

ANDREW

That's impossible.
Think, woman, think.
Some PART of one of them must have appeared first:
A finger
A toe
An elbow?
Don't you remember?
Didn't you see?
You WERE there, weren't you?

GIN

You expect me to sit up and watch?
At a time like that?
Twins coming neck and neck down the home stre-e-etch . .
Oy.
(*Pause.*)
What difference does it make anyway?

ANDREW

All the difference in the world.
The older one is my heir.
My son and heir.
He inherits everything I have.
All my worldly goods.
(*Pause.*)
And chattel.
(*Eddy eases forward.*)

EDDY

(*Quietly.*)
Uh . .
I've never mentioned this to anyone but

122

Just before we hit the finish
I tilted my head up and
Won by a nose.
(*General consternation.*)
      PAUL
If you tilted
The game doesn't count.
It means you cheated
And you're disqualified.
      EDDY
That's if you tilt a mechanism.
I didn't tilt my mechanism
I tilted my nose.
      PAUL
You're telling a big lie.
You didn't do any such of a thing.
      EDDY
How do you know?
You had your eyes closed.
      PAUL
I didn't!
I was watching you.
I knew you better than to close my eyes at a time like that.
      EDDY
Don't be silly
Everybody knows a baby doesn't open his eyes till several days after he's
   born.
      PAUL
That's cats.
      EDDY
Babies too.
      PAUL
You're a stinker.
      GIN
I knew I smelled something . .
      EDDY
You're just sore because I won.
      PAUL
I'm not.

EDDY

Oh yes you are.

PAUL

Not.

EDDY

Are.

PAUL

Didn't.

EDDY

Did.

PAUL

Tied.

EDDY

Won.

PAUL

Cheater.

EDDY

Clever.

PAUL

Liar.

EDDY

Poet.

(*They wade into each other and fall to the floor in a rough-and-tumble fight, arms and legs flailing. The girls cheer them on, Annie for Paul and Isabel for Eddy.*)

ANDREW

This is disgraceful.

Stop it, sir.

Sirs!

I forbid you to . .

I order you to . .

Quiet, you girls!

Boys! Boys!

Damnit, I'm your father.

Do you hear?

Obey me!

Obey!

(*The boys continue fighting, the girls cheering.*)

GIN

(*Finally.*)

All right that's enough
Stop now.
(*The boys stop fighting and the girls stop cheering.*)
Do what he says.
> PAUL AND EDDY

(*Heaving for breath and staring balefully eye to eye.*)
Why?
> GIN

Because he's your father.
> ANDREW

That's right
I'm your father.
> PAUL AND EDDY

So?
> GIN

So do what he tells you to do.
(*The boys' trembling hands rise toward each other's throat.*)
Do what he tells you when I tell you.
> PAUL AND EDDY

(*Standing at attention.*)
Yes, Mama.
> GIN

You should be ashamed of yourselves
Fighting over an inheritance.
Brothers.
> PAUL AND EDDY

Yes, Mama.
> GIN

You should apologize.
> PAUL AND EDDY

Yes, Mama.
We're sorry, Mama.
> GIN

Say that to him.
> PAUL AND EDDY

(*To Andrew.*)
Yes, Mama.
We're sorry, Mama.
> GIN

Daddy.

ANDREW
(*To Gin.*)
Yes, dear?

GIN
I was speaking to the boys.

ANDREW
(*Puzzled.*)
You called them "Daddy"?

GIN
The boys have something to say to you.

ANDREW
(*Turning to them.*)
Oh?

PAUL AND EDDY
Yes, Daddy.
We're sorry, Daddy.

ANDREW
(*Pleased.*)
There
That's more like it.
(*Strikes pose.*)
I am the daddy . .
(*Deflates.*)
Isn't it about time these great brutes of boys started calling me something
    more dignified than
Daddy?

GIN
They're only seven years old.

EDDY
Seven years AND
(*Points to himself.*)
One second.

ANDREW
But they're so big.

GIN
What would you like them to call you?

ANDREW
Oh I don't know . .
(*He thinks about it.*)

126

EDDY
Pa?
(*Andrew winces, shakes his head.*)
PAUL
Pops?
(*Andrew thinks, shakes his head.*)
ISABEL
Papa?
ANDREW
That's as bad as Daddy.
ANNIE
(*Accenting the last syllable.*)
Papa?
(*This appeals more, but he finally shakes his head. From here on the suggestions come accelerando as Andrew shakes them off more and more rapidly.*)
EDDY
Pappy?
ISABEL
Dad?
PAUL
Old Man?
ANNIE
Sire?
(*Andrew is on the point of accepting this one, but Paul and Eddy hurry on.*)
PAUL AND EDDY
Pater?
ANNIE AND ISABEL
Pater Familias?
ALL FOUR CHILDREN
Guv'ner?
(*Pause.*)
GIN
Mister President?
ANDREW
Father!
Why not?
I am the father.
Why not call me what I am?

127

GIN

That's not very logical
But if it's what you want . .

ANDREW

How?
Not logical to call a man what he is?
You call a spade a spade don't you?

GIN

Not when I can help it.
I'm a housewife
But I don't want anybody calling me housewife
Or even hussy.

ANDREW

That's beside the point.

PAUL

I'm a *homo sapiens*
But I wouldn't want anybody calling me *homo*.

ANDREW

Please . .

EDDY

How about *sap*?

ANDREW

Never mind never mind.

ISABEL

I'm a member of the bright section of the Junior Fifth Grade of Public
School Number One Hundred and Twenty-Eight
But I wouldn't want anybody to call me
Member of the Bright Section of the Junior Fifth Grade of Public School
Number One Hundred and Twenty-Eight.

ANDREW

If everybody has quite had his —

ANNIE

(*To Isabel.*)
You know you'd love it.
(*Scornfully.*)
Bright section.

ANDREW

QUIET!
Your father is speaking
Your father do you hear?

(*Everybody listens with a great show of patience.*)
Furthermore
I've made up my mind
From now on
I want all of you to call me Father.
Is that clear?
    CHILDREN
Yes, Daddy.
    ANDREW
There.
That settles that.
    EDDY
(*Sniffing the air.*)
Pee-you
Something stinks!
    ANDREW
Watch your language, sir!
    PAUL
(*To Eddy.*)
You and your big nose.
    ANDREW
Go to your room
Both of you.
    PAUL AND EDDY
What have we done?
    ANDREW
Your room your room!
    PAUL AND EDDY
I don't see why —
    GIN
(*Softly.*)
Your room.
    PAUL AND EDDY
(*To Gin.*)
Yes, Ma —
(*She points quickly to Andrew and the boys turn their heads toward him.*)
Daddy.
(*As Andrew watches the boys leave, his attitude softens to fondness.*)
    ANDREW
They're good boys but . .

(Gin and the girls turn full front and recite in bored rote with him.)

ALL

Boys will be boys.

ANDREW

(Gratefully surprised.)

Right!

ANNIE

(Wryly.)

Boys!

They're the lucky ones.

ANDREW

How is that, dear child?

ANNIE

Boys have it all their way.

The world is theirs

And all that's in it.

ANDREW

A woman has her own world

Or her own part of it:

Hers is the domain of the mother.

ANNIE

(Scornfully.)

The mother!

A mother's domain is a country

A quaint country

Bounded on the north by the kitchen sink

   Filled with dirty dishes

On the south by the playpen

   Filled with dirty children

On the east by the bridge table

   Filled with dirty gossip

And on the west by the double bed

   Filled with a dirty old man.

(Isabel bursts into tears and runs across the stage. Gin follows to take her in her arms and comfort her.)

GIN

There, there, you'll get used to it.

(To Annie.)

Your portrait of motherhood is a bit overdrawn

But I must admit there's a general likeness.
I'd recognize the subject who sat for it.

ANDREW

Overdrawn!
It's a travesty!
You're disparaging the very things that are
Holy and good
In motherhood.
What more beatific picture can you conjure up than
The industrious housewife in her natural setting
Her habitat:
Her cozy little home
Her love nest
Joyfully scouring, cleansing
Happily setting her house in order
Blissfully tending her tender babes
Her jewels
Singing her blithesome way
Through the day
At the close of which she can look forward to
(And this is really very modern of me)
All the raptures of sexual gratification
And ecstatic fulfillment
In the arms of the man she loves.
(*Pause.*)
Legally.

GIN

Or the man she loathes.
(*Pause.*)
Legally.

ANDREW

Anyway
Motherhood isn't the only profession a girl can choose.

GIN

Nor the oldest.

ANDREW

There's very little nowadays that a boy can do
That a girl can't.
(*Annie groans.*)

131

All right
For example for example?
(*Annie, still holding the bloody package of half-wrapped meat, turns
front and steps forward, where she is picked up by a spot of artificially
pretty blue-green light, which follows her as she acts out her speech. General lights dim.*)

ANNIE

For example . .
(*She thinks wistfully for a moment, then speaks.*)
A boy can do many many things
So many things that a girl can't do . .
(*Her voice throbs into a lyrical chant.*)
A boy can ride out into the great world
Through pagan realms
In quest of high adventure
And wonderly great deeds
A glorious and besainted defender of the true faith:
Astride that winged horse of Medusa's blood
Pursue the dread eclectic beast Chimaera
Smite it even unto death sorely
To soar to
Foot the proud threshold of the gods' high Olympic home . .
Set sail with those of Pelops' line
To burn the topless towers of Ilium . .
Do daughty defiance to the sirens of the beach
With their cruel cupid's bows so Greekly perfect . .
Wind a clear horn on windy plains of Roncesvalles
Turn to
Meet full on the fell and crafty Saracens
Fearlessly to face
A certain death . .
Lips bedewed with dragon's blood
Follow the woodbird to fire-ringèd Brünnehilde . .
Play pick-up golden Styx
For rod divine
That points the way through woods obscure
To hell
Or past nine heavens to the ultimate
The quiet one . .
Cross the wide sea to King Anguish of Ireland

For the lily-white hand of La Beale Isoud
Liever to die with worship than to live with shame
Harnessèd well
In silver shining armor starry clear
Sword and buckler by his side
Gaily bedight
For God and the right!
(*After a pause, the general lights come up.*)

ANDREW
(*Exalted again.*)
Flesh of my flesh
Blood of my blood
My own
My spirit reincarnate.

ANNIE
That's what a boy can do.
A girl can only change smelly babies and
(*Regards the package in her hand.*)
Return smelly meat to the butcher shop.

ANDREW
(*Still exalted nonetheless.*)
Come here my dear child
Dear child of mine.
(*As Annie turns to go to him, Gin takes the package of meat from her hands.*)

GIN
Here let me take this meat.
It's not a suitable prop
For the tender little scene
Your father's setting up here.
(*Hands the meat to Isabel.*)
You take it back to the butcher
Before we have to bury it.

ISABEL
I don't see why I have to take the old smelly stuff
Just because she . .

GIN
Take it.
And do as I say.

(*Isabel takes the package, sniffs distastefully at it, raises her head, and smells more deeply.*)

ISABEL

It's not the meat.
That's not what smells so bad.
(*Sniffs in the direction of Andrew.*)
It's something else.
Puwee!
(*She goes out right.*)

ANDREW

(*To Annie, who is now standing beside his chair.*)
Sit here, my child.
(*He pats his knee.*)
And let's have a good
Heart-to-heart
Father-daughter talk . . ah
Chat.

ANNIE

Oh now, Daddy . .

GIN

Go ahead
Humor the old man.
It can't last long
What with your heft
And his weak knees.

(*Annie drops onto Andrew's knee. He gasps and braces. The leg sways and wobbles a little as Annie twists and squirms during his speech, but Andrew resolutely supports her, thrusting an arm about her waist to try to ease and disguise the strain, which nevertheless is betrayed by his tight, choked-up voice and his heavy breathing.*)

ANDREW

Now then . . ah . .
Ah . . ah . . ah-h-h-h . .
(*Firms up. Assumes an air of spirited brightness.*)
If . .
(*Decides this is too bright; lowers the pitch.*)
If you had your choice . . ah . .
Of anything . . ah . .
Hmmm
Of anything in the whole world . . ah . .

Of all the professions
That boys can . .
Ah . . Any exciting and . . ah . .
Adventurous profession in the world . . ah . .
What would you choose?
(*He fixes a bright smile in front of the pain on his face.*)

ANNIE

(*Swinging around on his knee with her full weight.*)
Anything at all?

ANDREW

Ah . . anything at all.

ANNIE

(*Shifting heavily again.*)
Anything probable or improbable?

ANDREW

Ah . . anything.

ANNIE

(*Bounces with mounting excitement.*)
Anything possible or impossible?

ANDREW

Anything . . ah . . anything!

ANNIE

(*Another bounce.*)
No matter how incredible?

ANDREW

(*Crying out in pain.*)
Yes yes yes yes yes . . ah . . anything don't you see . . ah . .
Anything!

ANNIE

(*Slow grind.*)
If I could have my choice
Of anything in the whole world
Of all the professions that boys can choose
(*A climax of girlish bouncing.*)
Any EXCITING and ADVENTUROUS and ROMANTIC profession in the
    world . .

ANDREW

(*Writhing in pain.*)
Yes yes!

ANNIE
(*A dramatic pause, then rapturously.*)
I'd be a mortician.

ANDREW
(*Forgets his pain.*)
A what?

ANNIE
A mortician.

ANDREW
Surely you mean
MUSician
Or PHYSician.

ANNIE
(*Shaking her head.*)
MORTician.

ANDREW
(*Carefully matching her rhyme.*)
SPORTician?
(*She shakes her head.*)
PianoFORTician?
(*She shakes her head.*)
AstroNAUtician?
(*She shakes her head.*)
Not BEAUTician?
(*She shakes her head as he lists the following in crescendo.*)
Scientician? . . athletician? . . diplomatician? . . heretician? . . pietician? . . chivalrician, benedician? . . transfician, bishoprician, fiddlestician, ich liebe dician?

ANNIE
(*Doggedly.*)
Mortician.

GIN
It should be clear to you by now, Andrew,
That she wants to be a mortician.

ANDREW
(*To Gin.*)
You don't seem surprised by this at all.

GIN
Why should I be surprised?
It's exactly what I expected.

136

ANDREW
You've seen it coming?
And you did nothing to put a stop to it?
GIN
Why should I put a stop to it?
It's better than hanging around the drugstore
And smoking cigarettes
And reading comic books.
ANDREW
Well yes but . .
(*He groans.*)
ANNIE
What's the matter, Daddy?
ANDREW
It's . . ah . . it's
My leg . .
My leg's gone dead on me.
ANNIE
Dead? O-o-o-o-o-oh!
(*She jumps off his knee, kneels behind it, and cradles his leg in her arms tenderly.*)
Can I take care of it
Can I?
ANDREW
Certainly not.
I don't want it buried
I want it revived.
ANNIE
(*Jumping in his lap again.*)
Please!
ANDREW
No! No!
GIN
Well
I think you're being very inconsiderate not to let
Your own daughter
At a very small cost to you
Get a little practice at the profession
That she's chosen as her life's calling.

ANNIE
I only wanted to help.

ANDREW
(*Writhing.*)
You can help by getting off my leg!
(*She stands, offended. Andrew kneads his leg to bring the life back.*)

ANNIE
(*Gazing piously into the distance.*)
I suppose I should have known
You wouldn't understand.

GIN
Don't let him upset your stomach, my darling.
(*To Andrew.*)
Why shouldn't she be a mortician
If she wants to?

ANDREW
Because it's morbid
That's what it is
Morbid.
(*Andrew rises and paces painfully, limping on both legs and shaking out the right one every step or so.*)

ANDREW
To want to spend the rest of your life
Sorting out the dead relics of the past.
Preserving them in artificial cenotaphs engraved
With inscriptions in a language dead itself long ago:
In memoriam, hic jacet, requiescat in pace.
Why look backward all your life?

GIN
(*Meaningfully.*)
That's a good question.

ANNIE
But it's not looking backwards.
Forward
It's looking forward.
The farthest forward we can go in this life
Is death.
Our ultimate goal
The grave.

GIN
(*To the audience.*)
Now he wouldn't understand that
Because he's going in the opposite direction.
(*Andrew stops pacing.*)

ANDREW
Just what do you mean by that?

GIN
(*To the audience.*)
Oh oh.
He's all ears that one.
(*To Andrew.*)
If your nose were as sharp as your ears
You wouldn't have to ask that question.

ANDREW
I'm sure I don't know what you're —

ANNIE
It's the smell, Daddy.
She means the smell.

ANDREW
Smell? Smell?
What smell?

ANNIE
You don't smell THAT?
(*Inhales deeply.*)
As a matter of fact
I rather like it.
(*She starts following the smell with her nose, crossing down left.*)

ANDREW
I don't smell anything.
Why does everybody around here keep talking about smelling something?
I think we'd best forget about this
Alleged smell.

ANNIE
(*Stops.*)
How?
How do you make a nose forget
The scent it's stuffed with?
Shall we give our noses shock treatments
To jar these fulsome fumes

139

From their thirls of consciousness?
Shall we perform frontal nasotomies?

ANDREW
(*Uncomfortably.*)
I just don't think . . we . . should . .

ANNIE
How can you forget a smell
When the air is thuriferous with it?
(*She turns again to the scent as if resuming an interrupted ritual and proceeds blissfully offstage. Andrew sniffs the air.*)

ANDREW
(*Muttering as he sniffs.*)
Thur . . thurif . . thurifer . .
Maybe it's the dinner
Have you put on the meat to broil?

GIN
What meat?

ANDREW
Why the dinner meat, of course.

GIN
But you said to throw it out.

ANDREW
Surely we have other succulent substitutes
In our richly stocked larder:
A roast, capons, a side of venison,
A brace of pheasants.

GIN
Stew.

ANDREW
Whatever
Don't you think it's about time you got it ready for the table?
Woman.

GIN
(*Sarcastically.*)
Yes, your lordship.

ANDREW
(*Modestly.*)
Oh now
I only want to be what I am.

GIN

Good
How would you like to be a brother-in-law
For dinner tonight?

ANDREW

Not again.

(*Gin beckons to stagehands off right, and they start bringing in a table, chairs, dishes, and placing them up center in the shadows.*)

Don't tell me you've invited him to dinner again.

GIN

It's been a whole week since we had him.

ANDREW

Some people don't have their brothers-in-law to dinner
For years.

GIN

That's brothers-in-law.
Bud's not my brother-in-law
He's my own true brother.

ANDREW

But not mine
But not mine.

GIN

Nobody said he was.
Now you be nice to him.
It won't hurt you a bit.

(*She checks on how the stagehands are setting up the dining room and goes out right. Andrew motions for one of the stagehands to remove the chair, which he does. Then Andrew turns to the audience and advances a step or two.*)

ANDREW

(*To the audience.*)

And so ends
What might loosely be called
The exposition of
What might loosely be called
The play.
Now I'm to do a monologue
In one
A kind of choric commentary
To cover the change of scene

Such as it is.
I really don't know why they bother
To have a covering monologue
In one
When they do the whole damn thing right before your eyes anyway.
What am I supposed to be covering?
In a real production
In a real theatre
They'd have the courtesy to drop a curtain
Between me and this distracting activity
This racket
That drowns out my every word
And line.
And where the hell is
In one
When there's no front curtain to define it?
Ah well
On with the choric comment:
I don't suppose there's any doubt
In anybody's mind by now
That I AM THE FATHER.
Or
For that matter
That Bud
Who will appear in the next scene
Is Gin's brother.
And I'm sure the other family relationships must be clear by now.
Family relationships are important
In this play
As is sex antagonism
Which I'm sure you've noticed
If you've been here more than two minutes.
And that business about
Forward and backward
That's meant to be important too.
Very important.
(*Thinks.*)
What else?
Well I don't think you could miss the fact that
We're on the scent of something.

142

That ubiquitous smell is a patent contrivance to create a sense
Not only of smell but also of
Suspense.
(*Melodramatically.*)
What could it be?
What could their noses be leading them to?
Whatever?
(*Pause.*)
Maybe you think you've already figured it out
But would you be quite so sure of your detective work
If you knew that the stage direction
On Annie's exit
Reads:
Quote paren she turns again to the scent as if resuming an interrupted
    ritual and proceeds blissfully offstage paren end quote?
I might say here that not all the stage directions of this play
Are in such high-flown rhetoric
But then
Not all the stage directions
Were written to be spoken aloud
Like this.
(*Thinks a moment.*)
For the rest
There are some pretty heavy-handed hints
And I won't insult your intelligence
By pointing them out.
(*Suddenly bursts out angrily.*)
It's not WHAT the play has to say
That I find so offensive
It's HOW it says it.
The way the scene
As the French say
Marches!
The way . .
Oh I'll admit there's an occasional
Jocular moment
That may be amusing . .
(*Thinks, smiles.*)
At times actually rather humorous . .
(*Laughs quietly.*)

143

Yes even highly comic . .
(*Laughs with spirit. Stops to recite.*)
"Shrouds"!
(*Bubbles into laughter.*)
"Atmosphere that SHROUDS this home"!
(*He breaks up in a spasm of laughter that finally shatters him in a fit of coughing. When he gains control, he breathes hard for a moment, then wheezes.*)
No
It's not that —
(*Coughs, controls it.*)
Not the content
The subject matter.
It's the total effect:
It leaves you somehow . .
Well you'll see.
Somehow
Dissatisfied.
The amalgam never seems quite to become
(*Pause.*)
Amalgamated.
The point is hardly made
Before it's blunted.
The laughter soured.
The smile frozen.
(*Mary, the maid, enters in the shadows above and rings a small crystal bell.*)

      ANDREW
But enough for now
The scene is set.
Excuse me
I must wash up for dinner.
(*He exits down left. The lights change to low-key general illumination. Gin hurries in quietly from right to watch Andrew as he goes out. She stops center, but continues to follow Andrew with her eyes. When he is off, she motions to the right, and Bud crosses uncertainly to her, feeling his way cautiously in the semi-darkness. Bud is a gaunt, balding, upper-middle-aged man, alternately unctuous and pompous in bearing, consistently mellifluous in tone. He wears extremely thick-lensed glasses through which*)

he peers myopically. Gin has removed her old-fashioned glasses and looks
somewhat less aged and more alert. There is less gray in her hair.)

GIN

(*Sotto voce to Bud.*)
There
Did you see?
Did you hear?

BUD

I couldn't quite make out what he was —

GIN

It doesn't matter WHAT
He was saying it's
HOW he was saying it:
Muttering and jabbering to himself.
You heard him.
And the fact that he was saying anything at all
With no one to listen but himself.

BUD

Well of course
An old man . .

GIN

A SENILE old man
A daft old man.
(*Pause. Slowly.*)
A dangerous old man.

BUD

Simply because he talks to himself?
I fail to see —

GIN

Oh
That's only a symptom.
An effect of the defect.
That's not the main thing.

BUD

Then there IS something else?

GIN

So much else.
Some of the things he does
You wouldn't believe it.

145

BUD
(*Curiously.*)
Well
Try me.

GIN
Horrible horrible.

BUD
Don't you think you'd better tell me?

GIN
Never.
I can't do this to him.
After all
He's my own dear husband.
It wouldn't be right for me to tell you
What a son of a bitch he is.

BUD
But if you don't tell me everything
How can I . . ?

GIN
Never never . .

BUD
Now, Virginia,
You mustn't forget
I'm not only your brother
I'm your physician as well.
Your family doctor.

GIN
True. True.
I must tell you everything.

BUD
All right then.
(*He takes out a little black notebook and pencil.*)
Let's have it.

GIN
(*Hesitates.*)
There's so much
I hardly know where to begin . .

BUD
Just say the first thing that pops into your mind.
First impressions are always more accurate, you know.

GIN

Pineapple chunks.

BUD

How's that?

GIN

(*Savoring the words.*)

Juicy, mouth-filling pineapple chunks.

(*Bud swallows and wipes his mouth.*)

BUD

What has he been doing with

Pineapple chunks?

GIN

Nothing.

BUD

Nothing?

GIN

Why no.

What would he be doing with

Toothsome, luscious, syrup-drenched, tart-sweet, mouth-filling, juicy

Pineapple chunks?

BUD

But you . .

(*Swallows.*)

You just . .

(*Swallows.*)

Said . .

(*Slurps, swallows, and wipes his mouth.*)

Then why did you bring it up in the first place?

GIN

You told me to say the first thing that came into my mind and since it's
    dinner time and I'm hungry I guess the first thing that popped into my
    mind was

Savory, delicious, toothsome —

BUD

Never mind.

Spare me please.

What I meant was

With regard to Andrew's . . ah

Transformation

His distemper
His antic disposition.

GIN

Why didn't you say so in the first place?

BUD

You mustn't quibble with me, Virginia.
After all, I'm not only your brother
I'm your minister as well
Your father confessor.

GIN

True. True.
I must tell you everything.

BUD

(*Pencil poised.*)
So?

GIN

Wel-l-l-l . .
For one thing there's his talking to himself.

BUD

Yes yes
We've observed that.
What else?

GIN

An-n-n-nd . .
His temper . .

BUD

(*Writing.*)
Temper . .

GIN

He has terrible temper tantrums.

BUD

Yes yes go on.

GIN

An-n-n-nd . .
When I ask him to smell the dinner meat
He has LIVID spells.

BUD

(*Writing.*)
Livid spells . .
Tch tch tch . .

GIN

An-n-n-nd . .
He has this phobia about
Blood
And death
And such things.

BUD

Good heavens.
What occasions have there been to evoke this
Phobia?
Has Andrew been having daily encounters
Lately
With blood and death and such things?

GIN

Oh yes.
Occasions of his own making I might add.

BUD

Such as?

GIN

Oh
Just today there was that business of the charnel house
And the blood and guts
And the dead leg
And the mortician
And the cenotaph and the dead language and the grave.

BUD

Gracious
That sounds terrible.

GIN

Not only that but
(*She looks about to be sure no one is listening, bends close to Bud and lowers her voice.*)
Listen to this:
He gets the children all mixed up.

BUD

Mixes them up?
(*Gin nods.*)
What does he . .
(*Pantomimes stirring.*)
Mix them in?

149

GIN
In confusion generally
Though sometimes in anger.

BUD
(*Writing.*)
I see . .
(*Studies his notes.*)
But there still doesn't seem enough to warrant —

GIN
But I haven't told you the worst.

BUD
My dear sister
I have a feeling that you're skirting the main issue.

GIN
No I swear I give you my word there's nothing more to tell I've told you
    everything on my solemn oath please don't press me to tell you
THAT!

BUD
You must remember
I am not only your brother
But your lawyer as well.
Your legal counsel.
If I'm to help you
You must tell me everything.

GIN
All right I will.
But you must promise that you'll help me.

BUD
Yes yes.

GIN
That you'll back me up in everything
No matter what happens.

BUD
You can depend on me.

GIN
Well then
Here it is . .
Oh I hate to do this to him.

BUD
Yes I know.

GIN

But it's for his own good
Isn't it?

BUD

His own good yes.

GIN

It's —
This is in absolute confidence.

BUD

A professional secret.

GIN

Well then it's . .

BUD

Yes?

GIN

It's the SMELL!
There I've said it and I'm glad.

BUD

Did you say SMELL?

GIN

Yes
Hadn't you noticed it?

BUD

Why yes
As a matter of fact I had.
(*Sniffs.*)
That's Andrew?

GIN

Oh no
I mean not necessarily.
I certainly wouldn't think it strange
That Andrew smells BAD.
It's that he smells BADLY.

BUD

What on earth do you mean?

GIN

You smelled the smell
I smelled the smell
Everybody smells the smell
But not Andrew.

He says he can't smell anything.

BUD

Hmmmm.

Perhaps this accounts for his going on so

When you ask him to smell the dinner meat

GIN

But why should that make him angry?

BUD

Well

It's like saying "listen"

To a deaf man or

"See here" to a blind man or

"Speak up" to a dumb man.

A man is sensitive about his little

Foibles and flaws.

GIN

But it's not that he CAN'T smell the smell

In my opinion.

BUD

You mean . . ?

GIN

That he WON'T

Smell the smell.

BUD

That he . . ?

GIN

Deliberately REFUSES

To smell the smell.

BUD

Then you think that . . ?

GIN

He may well be RESPONSIBLE for the smell.

BUD

And . . ?

GIN

Guiltily refuse to face the facts.

BUD

Aha!

Then you think that he smells

Not only badly
But also bad!

GIN

It could be something he's done
Or committed
Rather than himself proper.

BUD

You mean that it might be something improper?
A smell that he has
Caused or
Created?

GIN

Exactly.

BUD

But what on earth could it be?

GIN

That's where I need your help.
Your keen professional mind
Your generous and sensitive nose.

BUD

Mmm yes.

GIN

You will help me won't you?

BUD

Of course of course.
Now then
Let us explore the possibilities
Systematically.
What could be the source of the smell that he has
Caused, created, or committed?
(*Thinks a moment.*)
Has he by any chance been playing with
Finger paints lately?

GIN

Finger paints?

BUD

They have a tendency to decompose you know
And anything decomposing
Usually smells.

153

GIN

Oh.

No, he hasn't played with his finger paints

Lately.

Not since he was four.

(*Thinks.*)

Or was it four and a half?

BUD

(*Writing in his notebook.*)

Gave up finger paints at age four

And a half . .

(*Thinks.*)

Is he addicted to novelties and practical jokes like

Say

Stink bombs?

GIN

Not since he was seven

When one went off in his pocket and he was deathly ill for days

At the smell of himself.

BUD

(*Writing.*)

Does he have a chemistry set?

GIN

Oh I took that away from him when he was eleven

After he threatened to blow up the house.

BUD

(*Writing.*)

What about a memory book?

Does he have a memory book?

GIN

(*Puzzled.*)

A memory book?

Oh

You think it's something in his past?

BUD

No, dear sister.

Not the past

But the paste.

GIN

Oh-h-h

154

Tendency to decompose and . .
>BUD

Exactly.
>GIN

No
He hasn't kept a memory book since he was sixteen.
>BUD

(*Writing.*)
Gave up memory book at age sixteen.
Deuce take it!
(*Thinks.*)
Does he do any fishing?
Could he absently have placed a finny fellow in his pocket
And forgotten him?
>GIN

He hasn't gone fishing since he was a young man.
>BUD

(*Writing.*)
Oh dear!
(*Thinks.*)
How about gardening?
The fertilizer, you know.
>GIN

He gave up gardening when he passed middle age.
>BUD

(*Writing.*)
Well!
Well well well well!
(*He racks his brain impatiently, chews on his pencil.*)
You HAVE given me a puzzler
Haven't you?
(*Paces.*)
What does an old man do?
How does he spend his time?
>GIN

Well
He spends most of his time
Worrying about the state of his
Bowels.
(*Reflects.*)

Of course he also talks a lot about
How much better things were
When he was younger.

BUD

(*Alert.*)
What do you mean younger?
How much younger?

GIN

Oh
To hear him tell it
The farther back the better.

BUD

(*Pressing.*)
You mean all the way back to infancy
When he was a mere babe
In DIAPERS . .
Oh dear
You don't suppose he's . .

(*He sniffs experimentally. Andrew enters from left above the table. He has changed into a dinner jacket which makes him look younger, and he has discarded his cane, though he still walks with a slight limp. In a good-natured, hearty, expansive mood, he hovers over the dinner table, unaware of Gin and Bud.*)

ANDREW

What about some dinner here?
The old man's ravenous.
Flub a dub dub
Bring on the grub!

(*He laughs a good, hearty, Santa Claus laugh. Gin, finger to her lips, motions Bud farther downstage.*)

GIN

Sh!
Observe.

(*They turn up to watch. The light fades out on them so that they are silhouetted between Andrew and the audience.*)

ANDREW

Ah-h-h-h!
I feel as fresh as a Phoenix
And as hungry as a horse!
Mary!

Ring the bell again.
Nobody seems to have heard it the first time.
(*There is a weak tinkle offstage.*)
That's it!
Ring out wild bell
Sound the knell
Put on the scran
And gather the clan.
(*As he laughs another jovial laugh, Annie and Isabel enter down right,
unobserved by him. Gin stops them with a gesture, and they turn up to
watch Andrew.*)
Ah the festive family board
Laden with
Literally groaning with
Goodies
And sugarplums and such
A rasher of bacon and
The goose hangs high on the hog and
A goodly saddle of honest mutton and
The nut-brown ale and
And . .
What could be keeping them?
They should . .
Mary!
Ring it again
Louder!
(*A larger louder bell rings offstage. Paul and Eddy run in down left but
Gin intercepts them and they join the silent silhouetted lineup across the
lower stage, turning to watch Andrew.*)
There!
Those sweet jangled bells should fetch them.
O thrice thrice welc . . ah . . thrice welcome sound
O triple-throated tocsin
Harbinger of hope and joy
Thy heavenly peals
Give promise of fulfillment
Dearest to the hearts of
Kith and kin.
(*Sings.*)
With a hey ho and a nonny nonny no.

(*Speaks.*)
If food be the music of love
Lay on Macduff and
Let the cannikin clink
Clink.
(*Sings.*)
Gaudiamus igitur
Hoc . . ah . .
(*Stops, peers out into the darkness, and calls.*)
Ginny. Annie.
Isabel. Paul. Eddy.
Where could they . . ?
Why . . ?
(*Calls.*)
Ring it again, Mary!
Louder!
(*A very large, very loud bell rings for some seconds while Andrew smiles broadly, if a little forcedly by now, and looks about eagerly.*)
That's it! That's it.
Good girl.
They're bound to hear that
And come a-running
Eagerly to participate in the felicities of
The holy family communion
To partake of the blessings of
(*Begins to taper off.*)
The high point of . .
The climax of
The familial ritual of
Sitting down together
To break together the
Bread of mutual . .
Love . . and . .
Understanding . .
(*Looks about in the darkness and calls.*)
Wife?
Children?
Sons? Daughters?
(*Pause. Lowers.*)
Brother-in-law?

158

(*Pause.*)
I wonder . .
(*Calls.*)
Why don't you answer?
Where are you?
Don't you hear?
(*Desperately.*)
Mary! Again, Mary! A good loud long one this time!
Mary!
(*A tremendous bell rings loud and long as Andrew scurries limping about back and forth above the table, craning into the darkness and calling wildly, though his words are completely drowned out by the bell. During the ringing of the bell Andrew begins weakening and subsiding, so that when the bell finally stops ringing, he is leaning on the table and calling weakly.*)
Dear hearts . . my own . . loved ones . . kindred spirits . . family
    ties . .
Blood of my blood
Stock of my stock
Breed of my very breed . .
Tribal companions . .
Beloved bedfellow . .
(*Pause.*)
Ginny?
(*Pause. He sinks slowly into the center chair at the table, muttering brokenly.*)
Does no one
No one at all
Wish to share this
(*Pause.*)
Quiet time of joy and . .
Solace
(*Pause.*)
Forgetting cares . .
To care for cares . .
Of
Others . . ?
(*He places his chin in his hands, props his elbows on the table, and stares vacantly. Then his head slips slowly down onto the table. Short pause.*)
    GIN
Now.

(*The shadowy tableau breaks up and the children start up to the table as the light comes up generally. Gin turns to Bud.*)

GIN

You see?

Not a word about the smell.

(*Everybody goes quietly to the table and stands behind a chair. Gin, Paul, and Eddy stand lined up at Andrew's right; Bud, Annie, and Isabel at his left. The children engage in subdued giggles and byplay at the joke they've played on Daddy. Gin, indulgently amused, lets the children have their fun. Finally she turns to Andrew.*)

Well, Andrew?

(*Andrew raises his head slowly, looks about at them blankly, then suddenly brightens gratefully.*)

ANDREW

You did come . .

You did hear my . .

(*Shudders back into character, beams.*)

Well!

(*Stands.*)

Well now!

Here we are!

(*Composes himself into patriarchal dignity. Grows two inches in stature.*)

Let us all bow our heads

And close our eyes

In humble thankfulness to the Lord

For his gracious bounty.

(*He raises a hand in an episcopal gesture of blessing. All bow their heads and close their eyes except Gin, who stares at his hand.*)

O Lord we thank thee for —

GIN

Your fingernails are dirty.

(*There is a tense silence. Then everybody looks up and examines Andrew's upraised hand. He keeps his head bowed, his eyes closed, and his hand upraised, quivering for a few moments before he can manage to speak.*)

ANDREW

If you'd had your eyes closed

As is proper

You'd not have noticed.

GIN

Do you think the Lord will have his eyes closed?
Do you think he'll think it
Proper
To address him with dirty fingernails?

ANDREW

It was not with my fingernails
That I intended addressing him.

GIN

Excuse me
The way you were wig-wagging
I thought it might be semaphore that you were —

ANDREW

(*With great patience.*)
Do you mind if we —

GIN

Anyway
Whatever lovely words you might use
You're spoiling the effect
By thrusting those dirty fingernails right up into his face
Like that.

ANDREW

Woman!
Cease thy inane prattle
In the presence of the Lord.

GIN

And speaking of the Lord
Or TO the Lord
Do you think it appropriate for you
A mere layman
To be returning thanks when Bud is at the table with us?
A man of the cloth?
A man of God?
(*Bud lowers his head modestly. Andrew raises his proudly.*)

ANDREW

Is Bud the head of this household?

GIN

Now you know
That we know
Perfectly well

Who's head of THIS household.
(*Andrew flashes her a suspicious look, but she smiles back at him with bland sweetness.*)
It's all right, dear.
You go right ahead.
(*Andrew turns front, closes his eyes again, and raises his hand, this time with a little less authority. Gin interrupts just as he opens his mouth to speak.*)
I'm sure Bud is above indulging in any
Invidious comparisons
Between his own polished professional devotions
And your crude amateur efforts.
(*There is a long pause. Andrew keeps his eyes closed and his hand, which may be trembling a little now, raised.*)
You go right ahead.

    ANNIE
I agree with Mother.
I think Uncle Bud should return thanks.

    ISABEL
That's right
He's the preacher.

    ANDREW
Children at meals
Should be silent as eels.
(*A moment of silence.*)

    PAUL
I vote for Daddy.

    ANDREW
(*Gratefully surprised.*)
My son!

    EDDY
Yeah
Daddy gets through quicker.

    ISABEL
That's because he doesn't know enough to say
That's why.

    EDDY
Uncle Bud goes on and on and on and on and . .

    ANNIE
Brevity is not the soul of blessedness.

EDDY
And on and on and . .

ISABEL
Besides
We can hear Daddy any old time.

EDDY
And on and on and . .

PAUL
But I'm hungry!
I want to eat!

EDDY
And on and on and . .

ANDREW
Children!

EDDY
And on and . .

GIN
That will do.

EDDY
And . .
(*There is silence.*)

GIN
Now do as your father says:
Close your eyes and bow your heads.
(*Pause.*)
And let him have his fun.
(*Another pause filled only by Andrew's quivering. Finally he slams the table angrily.*)

ANDREW
How!
I ask you
How!
Can I possibly
Exercise properly
The rights, privileges, and responsibilities invested
In me
As the father
If you insist on
Pr-r-ricking in public
The bubble of my parental authority?

GIN

You know
That's very well put, Andrew.
I like the implications.

ANDREW

I am not competing with your brother's famous devotional style at the
  moment
I am trying to make a point.
I am trying to tell you —
(*Gin takes his hands tenderly and pulls him to her.*)

GIN

(*Very sweet.*)
Oh, Andrew, don't you see that
Being a father
Is only a by-product
Of your essential role in life?
First of all
YOU ARE MY HUSBAND.

ANDREW

Yes well that's true but —

GIN

(*Slipping her arm around him.*)
First, last, and always:
My husband.
(*She gently strokes his beard.*)
You must play that part too.

ANDREW

Of course you're right
I AM your husband but —

GIN

(*As she speaks with throbbing lyricism, with infinite tenderness and eager
anticipation, she slowly removes his beard as if preparing for an act of
love.*)
I am your wife
O husband mine
Husband mine
Stalwart prop of my life
Sturdy oak to my vine
Husband mine
Husband mine.

THE STRANGLER

ANDREW
(*Left with only a respectable little black mustache, he feels his bare chin experimentally.*)
Ah yes . . yes . .
(*As if trying to remember something.*)
But . .
That doesn't preclude my also being
The father
The head of the house
The —
GIN
Of course not, my dear.
(*Puts beard on the table.*)
You're the children's old man
(*Lovingly removes his white wig, exposing a full head of black hair streaked with gray.*)
And you're my old man too.
(*She kisses him on the forehead.*)
ANDREW
(*Smoothing back his hair.*)
Hmmmm.
Not so old at that . .
GIN
Old enough to be dependable, though.
A good provider.
You've always been a good provider.
(*She puts the wig on the table.*)
ANDREW
But of course
A husband's first duty —
Beyond the obligations of affection naturally —
Is to be a good provider.
I should hope I'm that
Certainly.
GIN
(*Clinging.*)
You'll always take care of me
Won't you, Andrew?
My husband?

ANDREW
(*A pillar of strength.*)
Always.
(*Vaguely.*)
AND the children . .
The children too
As their fa —

GIN
My spouse.
Sharer of my soul and sex.
YOKE mate of mine.
My CONNUBIAL partner!
(*Andrew rises, puts his arm about Gin, and turns to the others.*)

ANDREW
Friends
Won't you join my wife and me
At our humble table?
(*Everyone sits except Andrew. He remains standing, takes up a large bone-handled carving knife, and begins sharpening it with flamboyantly authoritative strokes, enjoying the ceremony immensely.*)

GIN
Of course your fingernails are still dirty.
(*Andrew freezes.*)
Did you wash your hands?
Husband mine?

ANDREW
(*Slowly.*)
Don't you think
That is a question you might ask one of your children
Rather than your husband?

GIN
A wife must look after her husband
As well as her children.

ANDREW
Nonsense.
A husband takes care of his wife.

GIN
And vice versa.
(*Makes a smiling moue at the children.*)

Especially if he doesn't even know to wash his hands before coming to the
  table.
(*The children giggle.*)
    ANDREW
(*Shouting.*)
I washed my hands!
    GIN
Then why are your fingernails so dirty?
(*Andrew looks at his nails but immediately clamps his fists and thrusts
them behind his back.*)
    ANDREW
You might have noticed Annie's fingernails.
They're dirtier than mine.
(*Annie drops her hands into her lap under the table and looks away.*)
Hold them up hold them up.
    GIN
Let me see your hands, Annie.
(*Annie doesn't move.*)
Annie!
(*Slowly Annie brings her hands out and shows them.*)
Why they ARE filthy.
What on earth have you been doing
A girl of your age
To get your fingernails in that condition?
    ANNIE
Why don't you ask your husband
What he's been doing
To get HIS nails so dirty?
    GIN
I will.
(*Turns to Andrew.*)
What on earth have you been doing
To get your nails so dirty?
    ANDREW
I've been gardening.
    BUD
(*Sitting up quickly.*)
What . . ?
    ANDREW
I've been gardening

167

And when you garden
Dirt gets under —
    BUD
(*To Gin.*)
Excuse me
Did he say he'd been GARDENING?
    GIN
That's right.
He loves to garden.
Does it every spare moment he gets.
(*Bud eagerly fumbles out his notebook and checks through it.*)
He's not only my good husband
He's also my good husbandman.
    ANDREW
A good provider.
    BUD
He hasn't given it up?
    ANDREW
I'll always be a good provider.
    BUD
I mean gardening.
    GIN
Oh no
He's got a lot of good gardening years left in him yet.
(*Bud, puzzled, makes a few uncertain notes.*)
    ISABEL
What about Annie?
You haven't made her tell how she got her fingernails so dirty.
    PAUL
That's right.
    EDDY
Make her tell make her tell!
    GIN
(*Turning to Annie.*)
All right, Annie?
    ANNIE
I've been digging too.
    GIN
In the garden
With my husband?

ANNIE
No, ma'am.
GIN
Where then?
ANNIE
In the basement.
GIN
Our basement?
ANNIE
Yes, ma'am.
GIN
And exactly
Why or
What were you digging in our basement?
ANNIE
I was going to tell you when I had a chance —
BUD
(*Sniffing the air.*)
You know
I think that smell is getting stronger.
(*Everybody except Annie sniffs.*)
ISABEL
It sure is.
PAUL AND EDDY
Pee-you!
(*They stand.*)
We're not hungry.
(*They turn to go.*)
GIN
Sit down.
(*They sit.*)
ANDREW
I don't smell anything.
I don't know why everybody's so —
BUD
You don't smell THAT?
(*He holds his mouth and nose as if to keep from being sick.*)
ANDREW
All I smell is the tempting aroma

Of the good rare roasted joint of beef . .
Or stew as the case may be.
    BUD
(*Jotting notes in his book, to Gin.*)
You really ought to do something about that smell.
It's poisoning the atmosphere.
    ISABEL
Nobody can find what it is.
    PAUL AND EDDY
We've looked and looked.
    ANNIE
I've been trying to tell you —
    BUD
You should get an exterminator
To decontaminate the place.
A smell like this
It's unhealthy
Spiritually as well as physically.
And it must be illegal too.
    ANDREW
A good rare joint on the table
And a good rare jointress by my side.
(*He pats Gin's hand affectionately.*)
    GIN
You were trying to say, Annie?
    ANNIE
Can the exterminator
Exterminate
A corpse?
A dead body?
(*Everybody turns to stare.*)
    EDDY
A stiff?
    GIN
Why no.
Why do you ask, dear?
    ANNIE
Because there's one in the basement
And I think that's what everybody's smelling
Except him.

(*Nods toward Andrew.*)

BUD

What?
What did she say?

ISABEL

A dead body.

PAUL AND EDDY

Gaw-w-w!
(*Annie looks modestly down at her fingernails and picks at them.*)

GIN

Are you trying to say
That you dug it up with your fingers
And that's the reason your fingernails are dirty?

ANNIE

Yes, ma'am.

GIN

Well in that case I think we might excuse you for having dirty nails
This time.
But in the future
Try to get your digging done far enough ahead of dinner
To allow time for a good wash.

ISABEL

A dead body in the basement!

PAUL AND EDDY

W-w-w-wow!

BUD

But
Whoever could it be?

GIN

Did you recognize it, dear?

ANNIE

No, ma'am.
There wasn't much left to recognize.

GIN

You think it's been
A long time dead?

ANNIE

(*Tenderly.*)
A long time.

ANDREW
(*Angrily.*)
Nonsense!
 GIN
(*To Andrew.*)
You think it's a newly dead body?
 ANDREW
I don't think it's ANY kind of body.
 GIN
But a body must have some sort of character.
 ANDREW
I don't believe there's any body at all.
(*There is a hushed pause and a chilling fade of lights as everybody turns to stare uneasily at Andrew.*)
 GIN
Nobody at all?
 ANDREW
No body at all.
(*Another pause. Heads turn indefinitely. Gazes glance.*)
 BUD
How perfectly devastating . .
 ISABEL
Ma-ma . .
(*The boys whimper.*)
 GIN
(*To Andrew tensely.*)
In the name of humanity
How can you make such a statement?
 BUD
Yes who do you think you are to make such a —
 ANDREW
I'll tell you who I am:
I am the one who
Strangled the strangler.
(*All gasp in horror.*)
 ALL
The strangler!
(*All except Gin scramble wildly to their feet and cringe away into the shadows. Gin lowers her head into her hands in theatrical pain, as there follows without pause a rapid-fire series of fast-dying echoes.*)

172

GIN
(*Sorrowful.*)
The strangler . .
BUD
(*Indignant.*)
The strangler . .
ANNIE
(*Beatific.*)
The strangler . .
PAUL AND EDDY
(*Thrilled.*)
The strangler . .
ISABEL
(*Terrified.*)
The strangler . .
(*Pause.*)
ANDREW
There now
You finally forced me to admit it.
GIN
Forced you . .
Why you've been admitting it three times a day at meals and as needed
    ever since —
ANDREW
I had hoped to spare you.
GIN
Spare ME?
ANDREW
And the children.
ISABEL
Spare us what?
PAUL AND EDDY
Spare us what?
ANDREW
The pain
The shock
Of evil in retrospect
Of horror remembered.
(*Pause.*)
You see

I've known all along
That there is a body in the basement.
>BUD

You knew it was there?
You knew it all along?
>ANDREW

Certainly.
(*General exclamation.*)
>CHILDREN

(*At random.*)
He knew! He knew it all along!
>BUD

You sly dog!
>ANDREW

Not only that!
But also
I know who it is.
I know!
>GIN

You know?
>BUD

He knows!
>PAUL AND EDDY

I know you know he knows
We know you know they know!
>GIN

Well then
Don't you think it's about time you told us?
>BUD

Yes
Who is it?
>PAUL AND EDDY

Tell us!
>ISABEL

Who is it?
>PAUL AND EDDY

Tell us!
>ANNIE

Who is it?

174

PAUL AND EDDY
Tell us!
(*Andrew holds his hand up for quiet.*)
ANDREW
All right
I'll tell you!
(*All gasp and freeze in attitudes of eager attentiveness. Tableau. There is an extended trumpet fanfare.*)
But not in this act.
(*As the others hold the tableau, he walks around the table and, crossing down center, addresses the audience.*)
The first act ends here
And you'll have to wait until the second act
For what has been set up so obviously here as
The GREAT REVELATION.
(*A single spot of light comes up on him, other lights fade.*)
Now is that piling it on thick
Or isn't it?
I ask you?
Obviously
Oh so obviously
You're supposed to be curious enough now about my impending announcement
To come back for the last act.
To . .
(*The others are noisily and obviously trying to get quietly and unobtrusively offstage in the upstage area of shadows. Andrew glances at them and turns again to the audience.*)
And you're not supposed to notice them
Skulking off back there in the shadows.
Since we don't even have a front curtain
I'm supposed to get up here
And keep you from noticing
Hold your attention
By pointing out to you
What a state of suspense you're in.
Remind you
CLOBBER you
With the SUBTLE hints

That may have escaped you.
IF you're blind.
And deaf and dumb as well.
(*Assumes a mock-suspenseful attitude and tone.*)
Whose is the body in the basement?
(*Pause.*)
And what about the strangler?
  Now how could you miss
  The importance of this?
How could you possibly . .
The TITLE of the play
Is suddenly repeated SEVEN times
Seven times in a row
In varying tones
And overtones
Even in unison
And yet I have to get up here and ask you if it's occurred to you
   that
Perhaps
Just possibly
Something is meant by it.
Well
I have several more superfluous questions that I COULD ask
And I daresay you might have one or two you'd like to ask yourself.
Well
Ask yourself if you like
But don't ask me.
I'm only an actor
And all my lines are memorized.
Even that one.
(*Slowly.*)
E-ven . . this . . one.
(*Considers it.*)
Hardly seems memorable
Does it?
(*Glances around and sees that all the actors are off.*)
But I see they've all gotten off
Thank heaven
So we'll just

To use an old theatrical expression
Take ten.
(*He turns and walks off the stage. The house lights come up.*)

END OF ACT ONE

ACT TWO

At rise: The stage is empty. As soon as the stage lights are up, Andrew hurries in from down left furtively. He looks carefully back over his shoulder, then turns to the audience, finger to lips.

ANDREW

Sh!
(*Gin, Bud, Annie, Isabel, Paul, and Eddy enter upstage and make a great show of getting back to their places in the tableau at table. Andrew watches them until they are all in place and immobile, then speaks to the audience in a stage whisper.*)
They've been up to something
During the intermission
Plotting.
I don't mean the kind of plotting that this play could stand more of.
But scheming
Conniving
Conspiring.
It's not really fair, you know.
Not playing the game.
Because in this play the action is supposed to take up right where it left off.
Nothing is supposed to have happened.
Nothing.
You'll see:
I start right in with the announcement I was about to make
At the end of the first act.
So there's not supposed to have been TIME
For plotting and scheming and conniving and . .
If only you could depend upon people a little
At least to observe the amenities . .
(*Shakes his head sadly, then jerks his chin up to show determination.*)
Well
They won't take me in.
I'm alerted to them.

177

Excuse me.
(*Andrew walks to his place at center above the table and joins the tableau.
A moment of silent, eagerly anticipatory tableau; then Andrew speaks
portentously.*)
It is the body of . .

ALL

Yes?

ANDREW

The STRANGLER!
(*He beams about at them but the general reaction is highly unsatisfactory.
No one seems to take him seriously. They look at each other and shake
their heads or turn and look vaguely away as if embarrassed. An indefinite
little tune seems to hover somewhere in the air at a great distance. An-
drew regards them suspiciously.*)
So
You've decided among yourselves
Not to believe me.
Is that it?

GIN

Why, Andrew,
Don't be silly.
When could we have decided anything among ourselves
When we've been sitting
And standing
Right here all along?
Nobody's left the room. You've heard everything.

ANDREW

There's been an intermission, you know.

GIN

Oh but that's out of bounds.

ANDREW

To persons of honor and integrity
Actors who not only play the part
But also play the game.

PAUL

The game.

EDDY

The game!

PAUL AND EDDY

Let's play the game!

GIN

Not yet, boys
Not yet.
(*To Andrew.*)
So it's the body of . .
(*She simpers at the children, they snicker back.*)
The strangler?

ANDREW

(*As if making the announcement for the first time.*)
The STRANGLER!
(*This makes everybody uncomfortable all over again.*)

ANNIE

But how could it be the strangler?

ANDREW

Why not?

ANNIE

This one doesn't look like a strangler.

ANDREW

And what does a strangler have to look like?

ANNIE

Well
I don't know but . .
What DID he look like?

ANDREW

The strangler?
Oh . .
(*Preening.*)
He was BIG!
STRONG!
MEAN!
Why it was all I could do to —

ANNIE

Was he an old man
With white hair
And a white beard?

ANDREW

(*Laughing her to scorn.*)
Certainly not.

ANNIE

That's what this one is.

ANDREW
Old? White hair?
And beard?
ANNIE
(*Nodding.*)
Mm-hm.
BUD
Besides, Andrew,
That was so long ago
Years!
The body could not be just now decomposing and
Smelling.
ANDREW
Why not?
Who are you to tell a body just when it can decompose
And smell?
BUD
Why I'm sure I don't —
ANDREW
The cool dry air in our basement
Could act as a preservative.
GIN
Dry?
Our basement?
ANDREW
And as for the beard and the hair and all
It's a well-known fact
To most people
(*Cuts his eyes to Bud.*)
And practically all doctors
That the hair continues to grow after death.
ANNIE
And turn white?
ANDREW
Why not?
If it turns white on live people
As the years pass
Why not on the dead?
Alive or dead
It's all the same.

BUD

I like to think there's SOME difference.

ANNIE

But you said he was big.
And strong.
This one's not much bigger than you
If any.

ANDREW

Well I'm not exactly a midget
You know.

GIN

Why don't you admit it, Andrew?
(*Pause. Everybody concentrates on Andrew curiously.*)
Why don't you stop trying to fabricate
A world that doesn't exist?

ANDREW

I'm sure I don't know what you —

GIN

Why don't you face the facts?
That's not the strangler
Buried down there in the basement.

ANDREW

Well I'd like to know who it is then
If it's not the strangler.
I ought to know.
I killed him with these hands
And buried him there myself . .
(*Everybody is turning away, bored.*)
Nobody seems impressed by that
At all.

GIN

Boys
Be impressed.

PAUL AND EDDY

Gee!

GIN

Girls.

ANNIE AND ISABEL

Ah-h-h!

ANNIE

He killed the strangler!

ANDREW

(*Proudly.*)

Strangled him.

ISABEL

Strangled him!

PAUL AND EDDY

Gee!

BUD

And buried him?

In your own basement?

ANDREW

(*Still proud.*)

That's right.

BUD

But why?

Why didn't you call the police and let them —

ANDREW

(*Suddenly frightened.*)

What right have you got to cross-examine me like this?

I demand a lawyer before I —

GIN

He IS your lawyer, Andrew.

ANDREW

If he's my lawyer

Why is he trying to —

GIN

He's only trying to help you, dear.

ANDREW

By advising me to call the police

When I've killed a man?

What kind of help is that?

You don't need to be a lawyer to know that

You have to keep such things *sub rosa.*

Or in this case

Sub terra.

BUD

But if he was a killer

A strangler

And you killed him in self-defense
There surely was no need to hide anything.
To bury it.
To keep it a secret.
(*Andrew is nonplussed. There is a long pause.*)
>BUD

IF it was self-defense.
(*Another long uncomfortable pause.*)
>GIN

(*Finally.*)
The truth is
It was not done in self-defense.
>ANDREW

No . . that's true . .
(*Lunging brightly.*)
It was a selfless and
Disinterested and
Generous act.
I was defending another:
My father.
>GIN

Your father?
>ISABEL

The father!
>GIN

You weren't defending HIM.
Or if you were
You didn't do it very well because
The strangler strangled him.
>ISABEL

The strangler killed the father?
>GIN

Killed him.
>PAUL AND EDDY

Killed him dead killed him dead!
>GIN

And what's more
That's not the strangler buried down there
Or un-buried now
It's the father.

PAUL AND EDDY
The father! The father!

ISABEL
(*Sadly.*)
The father.

ANNIE
I THOUGHT he looked familiar.

BUD
(*To Andrew.*)
Aha!
So that's why you tried to ignore the fact
The smell.
That's why you felt guilty.
You knew it was the father all along
Not the strangler at all.

ANDREW
(*Uncertainly.*)
But . . it wasn't the father . .
All along . .

ISABEL
Anyway
Wasn't the strangler a woman?
Or at least partly so?

ANDREW
Don't be absurd!

ISABEL
Are you sure?

ANDREW
I hope these hands would know the difference
Between a man's throat and a woman's
Even partly so.

GIN
(*Interposing quickly.*)
You're on the wrong track, Isabel.
Don't get in over your head.
(*To Annie.*)
Annie
You'd better keep an eye on her.

ANNIE
Yes, Mother.

184

GIN

(*Turning to Andrew.*)
Now let's see what we've got here.
You insist, Andrew,
That the body down there is the strangler's?

ANDREW

With these very hands
I killed him.
I buried him there.

ISABEL

Killed him.

PAUL AND EDDY

Killed him.

ISABEL

Buried him there.

PAUL AND EDDY

Buried him there.

GIN

Just to clear things up
Why don't you go take a look?

ANDREW

I don't see why I should —

BUD

Oh come now, Andrew
What harm could there be in —

ANDREW

And I'll thank you to stop meddling in my affairs!

BUD

A minister of God is not meddling, Andrew
When he is looking after the affairs
Of your soul.

GIN

(*Coaxing.*)
Why don't you just go and look?
There's a dear.

ANNIE

Go and look
Please?

ISABEL

Please go and look.

EDDY
Go and look.
PAUL
Go and look.
PAUL AND EDDY
Pretty please?
ANDREW
All right all right I'll go.
Just to settle the matter
Once and for all.
(*He walks away from the table to down right where he stops, still on the stage, and stands facing out.*)
GIN
Now
In the meantime
We might as well sit down at the table.
(*They sit.*)
I'm afraid that
What started out to be a good hot family dinner
Is in danger of ending up as
Cold cuts among strangers
What with a fifteen-minute intermission
And now all this do about a body.
ISABEL
(*Stands. Smugly, the clever child showing off.*)
I just thought of something.
GIN
Yes, dear?
ISABEL
A strangler is only a stranger
With a little 'ell added.
PAUL AND EDDY
(*Sarcastically.*)
Ha ha.
GIN
Why that's very good, dear.
BUD
Charming charming.
ISABEL
I'm not through.

GIN

Oh? What else?

PAUL AND EDDY

We can't wait.

ISABEL

And yet you can make an angel
Out of a strangler
But not out of a stranger.
There's only anger there.
(*Bud laughs a startled simpering laugh. The boys imitate him in unison, mockingly.*)

ANNIE

(*Quietly.*)
You can make a saint out of either one.

ISABEL

(*Piqued.*)
Only an abbreviated one. I'm through now let's eat.
(*Sits.*)

PAUL

Stranger spelled backwards is regnarts.

EDDY

Strangler spelled backwards is relgnarts.

ISABEL

(*Imitating Bud.*)
Charming charming.

PAUL

(*To Eddy.*)
Copy cat.

EDDY

Ah shut up.

PAUL

Shut up yourself
Nosey.

EDDY

Junior!
(*They fight.*)

GIN

And they were doing so nicely for a while.
(*To the boys.*)
That will be enough of that.

(*The boys stop fighting.*)
Anybody would think you were
Men already
With your independence and self-assertion.
(*Ominously.*)
I wouldn't rush into growing up
If I were you.
(*Pause.*)
And perhaps you'd better come over here and sit by me, Eddy.

EDDY

(*Rising.*)
As the older
The son and heir
I accept the honor.
(*He goes to Andrew's vacant chair and sits in it. Paul grips the edge of the table and tensely rises.*)

GIN

Sit down, Paul.
(*Paul sinks back down into his chair.*)

ANDREW

(*Sadly.*)
A subtle maneuver
Oh so fiendishly subtle.
Mither mither . .

GIN

Is that you, Andrew?
Are you back already?

ANDREW

Yes.

GIN

What did you find?

ANDREW

I found the body.

GIN

And whose body was it?

ANDREW

It was the father's.
You were right.
The father is dead.

GIN

I could have saved you the trouble of that trip.
I told you it was the father all along.
I told you so.

BUD

Dear dear
This has very serious implications.
(*Rises like a prosecuting attorney to cross-examine the witness.*)
You say that
YOU
Buried the body in the basement?

ANDREW

Yes.

BUD

The body of the person whom
YOU'D strangled?

ANDREW

Yes.
(*Bud paces in deep concentration.*)

BUD

Now I must ask you to be very careful in your answer to this next
Question.
(*He stops, takes a drink of water, and puts the glass down.*)
Think it out.
Take your time:
Is there more than ONE body buried in the basement?

ANDREW

No. Only one.

BUD

And THAT
Is the body of the father?

ANDREW

(*Wearily.*)
That's right.

BUD

(*Turning triumphantly to the others.*)
Then I submit
The conclusion is inescapable:
ANDREW strangled the FATHER.

189

ALL
(*Softly.*)
Ah-h-h-h . .
(*They applaud and laugh.*)
GIN
Well now
That settles that
And we can eat in peace at last
(*Bud sits smugly at his place.*)
Come sit down, Andrew, and eat your dinner.
You'll feel much better with something in your stomach.
ANDREW
(*Remains where he is, facing front.*)
No . . no . .
I'm not the strangler . .
I know things look bad for me
But
I didn't kill him.
Why should I kill him?
I'm . . the husband . .
Not . . the strangler . .
GIN
(*Impatiently.*)
Do sit down, Andrew.
(*Pause.*)
ANDREW
(*Not moving.*)
Someone is sitting in my chair.
ISABEL
(*In a high squeaky voice.*)
Someone's been eating my porridge.
PAUL AND EDDY
(*Imitating her.*)
And ate it all-l-l-l up!
ISABEL
(*Deep gruff voice.*)
Someone's been sleeping in my bed.
PAUL AND EDDY
Cuckoo! Cuckoo!
(*The children laugh happily.*)

190

GIN

Quiet, children.

(*Rises and goes to Andrew.*)

Never mind, Andrew,

You can sit in Eddy's chair there.

ANDREW

And shall I sit in a child's chair?

GIN

The chairs are all the same size, Andrew.

ANDREW

But not in the same position

At table.

GIN

Why they're all faced squarely up to the . .

ANDREW

Relative position.

Relative.

GIN

You know I sometimes think, Andrew, that you place far too much emphasis on relatives and family and such.

ANDREW

I'm speaking about protocol!

What about protocol?

GIN

What ABOUT protocol?

ANDREW

I am the husband.

The husband should sit at the head of the table.

GIN

No, that's the father, dear.

The father sits at the head of the table.

ANDREW

Well I'm also the . .

A husband can be a father too

Can't he?

GIN

Not when the father's dead.

ANDREW

If the father's dead

All the more reason for the husband

To sit at the head of the table!
>GIN
(*Patiently.*)
I'll tell you what
(*She smiles about at the others.*)
Suppose we simply
Rename the parts of the table.
We'll call THAT the head of the table
And you can sit there.
>ANDREW
But it's NOT the head of the table!
You can't change a thing into something it's not
Simply by naming it something it's not.
>GIN
Don't be so literal-minded, Andrew.
Do you expect to find hair growing on the head of the table?
Don't be such a big baby.
(*Pause.*)
>ANDREW
(*Slowly, softly.*)
What
Are you trying to do
To me?
>GIN
I am simply trying to keep peace in the family
By separating the boys.
Do you want to eat your dinner to the tune of their wrangling?
>EDDY
A strangler can be a wrangler.
>PAUL
A stranger can be a ranger.
>GIN
You see?
It's bad enough with them separated like this.
>ANDREW
(*Shouting.*)
I will not surrender my rightful place at the head of the table to Eddy!
>GIN
(*After a moment of speechless shock.*)
Don't tell me that you're . .

(*To Eddy.*)
Stand up, Eddy.
(*He does.*)
Come to mother.
(*He does. She puts an arm about him and faces Andrew.*)
Don't tell me that you're JEALOUS
Of a seven-year-old boy!
(*Andrew turns to look at them. He doesn't seem at all reassured by the sight of the full-grown actor playing the role of Eddy who smiles mockingly at him. Gin turns to look at Eddy, then Paul.*)
They ARE growing up
Aren't they?
Much too fast.

    ANDREW
(*Doggedly.*)
I only want my rightful place at table.
(*There is a long moment of impasse.*)

    BUD
If I may make a suggestion . .

    ANDREW
(*Under his breath.*)
Oh God.

    GIN
Certainly, Bud dear.

    BUD
Why don't we let a higher power than ours
Decide how we should settle this issue
Of who sits where?

    ANDREW
Now don't go ringing God in on your side.
I'm outnumbered already.

    BUD
What an idea.

    ISABEL
(*Jumping up.*)
I know!
I know how we can settle it.

    GIN
How, dear?

ISABEL

He wanted us to play a game.
Let's play a game:
Musical chairs!

GIN

Why that's a splendid idea.
(*Gin and the children push the chairs back from the table.*)

ANNIE

I adore music.
It's the quintessence of the spirit.

PAUL AND EDDY

We like games.
They're fun.

BUD

(*Hesitating.*)
But
To leave the choice entirely up to
Chance . .

GIN

(*Pushing back Bud's chair and then Andrew's.*)
Think of it this way, dear padre,
Dear Father Bud:
We won't be TAKING a chance
But rather GIVING a chance
To the higher powers to decide the issue
Without any meddling on our part.

BUD

True . .

ANDREW

But it's not an issue to BE decided.
It's already —

GIN

All together now:
(*Sings.*)
Oh-h-h-h
(*She cues them and they sing and dance very gaily about the table, trapping Andrew in the procession and pushing and buffeting him around the table with them.*)

ALL

(*Singing, except Andrew.*)

194

Love somebody, yes I do
Love somebody, yes I do
Love somebody, yes I do
Love somebody, but I won't tell who.
Love somebody, yes I do
Love somebody, yes I do
Love somebody, yes I do
And I hope somebody loves me too.
(*During the dance, as they shove Andrew about, they swap places care-*
fully so as to end up — a little hurriedly to make it come out that way —
with the two girls at the left of the table, the two boys at the right, Gin at
the father's place up center, with Bud on her right and Andrew on her
left. Everybody except Andrew drops into his chair on the last word of
the song and has a good long laugh. Andrew stubbornly refuses to sit.)

GIN

Well!
Look who's the daddy.

ANDREW

It's not fair, I wasn't ready and besides you're not supposed to swap about
    that way.
It's not right.

BUD

Don't be a bad loser, Andrew.

ANDREW

I'm not a loser bad or good.
I wasn't even playing the game.
I didn't have a chance.

GIN

You want another chance?

ANDREW

Certainly I want another chance.

GIN

All right
UP again and take your places, everybody.
(*Everybody stands.*)
Ready?
(*She raises her hand to give the cue.*)

ANDREW

Wait a minute.

195

I want a better place in line.
Where you can't block me.
    BUD
Quibbles quibbles
Picayune quibbles.
    GIN
It's all right, Bud dear.
Let him have every advantage.
Then he can have no complaint.
(*To Andrew.*)
Go ahead
Choose your place.
(*Andrew looks the situation over uneasily, does some quick calculating under his breath and on his fingers, then crosses around Gin and Bud to be at their right or in front of them in the line of dance.*)
    GIN
Are you ready now?
(*Andrew, holding himself tautly poised like a sprinter on his mark, nods.*)
    GIN
Well then
Here we go.
(*She raises her hand to cue them.*)
    ANDREW
And no swapping about this time.
    GIN
(*Sings.*)
Oh-h-h-h
(*She cues them and they start dancing around the table as they sing.*)
    ALL
(*Singing.*)
Love somebody, yes I do
Love somebody, yes I do
Love somebody, yes I do
Love somebody, but I won't tell who.
Love somebody, yes I do
Love somebody, yes I do
Love somebody, yes I do
Love somebody and it may be-e-e-e-e-e-e
(*Andrew having ended up at the father's chair up center, they prolong*

the next-to-last word until they have shoved him past it, then finish the song.)
You.
(*Thus they end up with Bud in the father's chair, Andrew shoved into the chair on his right and Gin into the chair on his left, the children being where they were to begin. They laugh gaily.*)

GIN
Oh dear
I lost my place.
But I'll accept the toss of the coin
The bounce of the ball
The crumble of the cookie
Cheerfully
And in good part.
(*Turns and leans across to Andrew.*)
Now are you satisfied?
(*Andrew stares grimly out front.*)

GIN
I said
Are you satisfied?

ANDREW
Let's make it two out of three.

BUD
Oh now really.

GIN
(*To Bud.*)
No no
Let him call the tune
If he's to pay the piper.
(*Brightly to the rest of the table.*)
UP again, everybody.
(*Everybody stands.*)

ANDREW
And this time I WILL call the tune.

GIN
All right
If you think you can.

ANDREW
And the tempo.

GIN

As you wish.

Anything else?

ANDREW

Yes

I want a completely new line of march.

BUD

Now I think that's going too far.

GIN

Let him alone.

BUD

I don't HAVE to play, you know.

GIN

Humor him.

(*To Andrew.*)

Go ahead

Line us up.

Where do you want us?

(*Andrew studies the situation very carefully. He goes to the father's place and pushes the others aside.*)

ANDREW

(*To Gin.*)

You come over here.

(*Motions her to his right. She goes there. Speaks to Bud.*)

And you go over there.

(*Points to the downstage chair at left of table. Bud goes there.*)

The rest of you fill in between.

(*They do, complaining and grumbling. Andrew surveys the situation. Speaks under his breath.*)

There

That will take care of that little collusion.

(*Aloud.*)

Now remember

I'll set the tempo

No deviations.

Is everybody ready?

ALL

Ready.

ANDREW

(*Raises his hand.*)

All right.
(*Sings.*)
Oh-h-h-h-h
(*He cues them and leads them in a staccato rapid-time song and dance around the table, constantly eyeing and measuring his chances for the father's place.*)

ALL
(*Singing and dancing.*)
Love somebody, yes I do
Love somebody, yes I do
Love somebody, yes I do
Love somebody, but I won't tell who.
Love somebody, yes I do
Love somebody, yes I do
Love somebody, yes I do
(*At this point it is likely that Andrew will end up at the father's chair, so everybody reverses the line of dance, pushing Andrew back down left of the table as they sing the last line.*)
Love somebody just like you.
(*On the last word, Gin gives Andrew, who is already off balance, a push, and he reels across below the table to drop into the downstage chair at the left of the table. Bud is in the father's chair again.*)

ANDREW
You cheated you cheated!
(*He throws himself onto the table, sobbing and beating the table top with his fists. Everybody watches for a moment. Then Gin rises, removes her gray wig, revealing coal-black hair done in a more youthful style, takes out her compact and with a few deft strokes plasters on an oversimplified and rather artificial-looking youthful face. She then comes across to Andrew, raises him to a sitting position, and lowers herself into his lap, her arms about his neck.*)

GIN
Now you mustn't go on so.

ANDREW
(*Through his tears.*)
I've gambled away my heritage
My rightful place
My position
As husband.

GIN

Well now
Is that so very important?
(*She caresses him.*)
Would you rather have the position of a husband
Or that of a lover?

ANDREW

(*Raises his head.*)
They use different positions?

GIN

Of course.
Just think of the implications of the two phrases:
The formal awkwardness of the one
The lithe grace and warmth of the other
Which would you rather be?

ANDREW

But I don't see why I can't be both a —

GIN

You are my lover.
And I am your beloved.
(*She kisses him passionately. He responds with increasing eagerness and prolongs the kiss until she pulls back and holds him off.*)
Wait.
(*As he, breathing hard and trying to fondle her, murmurs over and over again,* "True love . . true love . ." *she parries his advances, removes the rest of the gray from his hair, takes off his mustache, and using her compact again, touches up his face to make it more youthful. Finally she speaks.*)
There.
Now you are my own true love.
(*She submits to his fumbling passion. He seizes her in a wild embrace, kissing her hungrily. The vigor of the embrace mounts until they writhe onto the top of the table, scattering dishes heedlessly.*)

BUD

(*Rapping on the table.*)
Gin
Ginny
Young man.
Is this the proper deportment
At table?

(*Andrew, still embracing Gin on the table, raises his head and turns to the audience.*)

ANDREW

In the old theatre
The classical theatre
This kind of thing would never have been permitted
ON stage.
They've forgotten the meaning of dramatic decorum nowadays.
(*He returns to the embrace with vigor.*)

BUD

(*Again rapping the table.*)
Please!
Please!
If nothing else will appeal
Think of the china.
Our best china.
Our COMPANY china!
(*Gin and Andrew break apart and sit up.*)

GIN

Company?

ANDREW

Company?
(*They climb down off the table and stand apart, awkwardly embarrassed.*)

BUD

I see now, dear girl,
That I hardly understood what you meant
When you asked if you might
HAVE your young man for dinner.
(*Gin and Andrew hang their heads, see the scattered china, quickly occupy themselves with picking it up and setting the table straight again.*)
I thought you wanted the family to meet him
Your young man
For him to meet the family
To get acquainted
With the family.
Yet the two of you seem interested solely in establishing a
Closer acquaintanceship with one another.

GIN

I'm sorry, Father dear.

ANDREW

Sorry, sir.

(*He bows stiffly.*)

BUD

Well then

Well then all right.

Suppose we take our places again

Our SEPARATE places

At table

And continue with dinner

In a civilized manner.

GIN

Yes, sir.

ANDREW

Thank you, sir.

(*Gin goes back to her place at the left of the table. Andrew goes to his place at the right of the table. Both sit stiffly in place. Everybody sits self-consciously, Andrew glancing furtively at the others from time to time and the children frankly staring at him, whispering and giggling.*)

BUD

Mary!

(*Mary, the maid, brings in a large salad bowl and starts passing it. Just as Andrew is trying to help himself, the boys begin to chant.*)

PAUL AND EDDY

Ginny's got a feller

Ginny's got a feller

Ginny's got —

(*Andrew, startled, gives the serving implements a jerk that scatters lettuce leaves about on the floor.*)

BUD

(*To the boys.*)

That will do!

Let them alone.

They are behaving themselves now.

(*Looks suspiciously at Andrew who is now bending beneath the table to retrieve the lettuce leaves.*)

Or are they?

(*Shouts at Andrew.*)

Keep your hands above the table, young man!

(*Andrew's hands fly up into the air and flutter there a moment as he tries*

*to indicate the great distance — the length of the table — between him and
Gin.*)
And no playing footsie, either
Keep your feet to yourself also.
(*Andrew stretches out a leg to prove that he couldn't reach her with his
foot either.*)
Speaking of feet
We seem to have gotten off on the wrong one.
I think we'd better start all over again.
First impressions are so important, you know.

    ANDREW

Where shall we start from?

    GIN

The beginning of course.

    BUD

Let's start . . ah
With the introductions.

    GIN

All right.
(*She and Andrew stand.*)
Father
I want you to meet Andy.
Andy
This is Father.

    BUD

(*Keeping his seat.*)
How do you do, young man?

    ANDREW

(*Starts to hold out his hand, withdraws it.*)
Very well, sir.
(*The hand hovers out again, and back.*)
I am delighted to make your acquaintance.

    BUD

(*Smiles knowingly.*)
For a very good reason, I'm sure.

    GIN

And this is Annie and Isabel and Paul and Eddy.

    ANDREW

(*A polite little bow to each.*)
Annie, Isabel, Paul, Eddy.

(*The children stare at him hostilely or giggle.*)

BUD

Shall we go in to dinner?

GIN

Yes, Father.

ANDREW

Thank you, sir.

(*He and Gin sit down.*)

BUD

Now then —

ANNIE

I smell something.

(*Everybody tries to ignore her. They laugh politely at each other.*)

I said

I smell something.

(*This freezes them. They await further developments.*)

May I be excused?

BUD

Certainly not.

Eat your dinner.

(*Annie rises and crosses off down right.*)

BUD

(*To Gin.*)

How can I be the father

If nobody pays any attention to what I say?

GIN

WE'RE paying attention

Aren't we?

BUD

Well yes . .

GIN

You're doing fine.

Keep it up.

BUD

I'll try once more.

(*Brightly, authoritatively, to Andrew.*)

Young man . . ah

Andy I believe they call you?

ANDREW

Yes, sir.

BUD

What is your way of life?

ANDREW

(*Without hesitation.*)

Fishing, sir.

BUD

Fishing?

ANDREW

Yes, sir.

I love fishing.

I fish every day that I possibly can.

(*Bud turns to Gin.*)

BUD

Excuse me

You told me he hadn't fished since he was a young man.

GIN

But he IS a young man.

BUD

Ah yes . .

(*To Andrew.*)

But . . ah

FISHING as a way of life?

ANDREW

Yes, sir.

Fishing is my all in all.

GIN

(*Hurt.*)

Your all in all?

ANDREW

I could not love thee dear so much

Loved I not fishing more.

GIN

You're my lover boy

That's what you are.

(*Blows him a kiss.*)

Loverkins.

ISABEL

(*Giggles.*)

Look! Look!

PAUL AND EDDY
They're doing it again!
They're doing it again!
BUD
Never mind.
It's all right if it's only verbal.
And you're not supposed to notice.
We'll never get them together if you keep staring at them like that
And hanging onto every word they say to each other.
(*Annie darts into the room down right.*)
ANNIE
I found what it was.
(*Everybody turns to pay polite attention to the child.*)
BUD
(*Genially.*)
What what was, my child?
ANNIE
The smell.
(*Bud rises hastily and hurries her aside.*)
BUD
(*Sotto voce.*)
Please!
We have company!
We know what the smell is.
Must you drag our family skeleton out of the closet?
With company present?
ANNIE
But it's not a skeleton
It's a body
And it's not in a closet
It's in the cellar
And it's not it
It's THEY.
BUD
It's what?
ANNIE
It's they.
There are two of them now.
BUD
Two bodies?

But whose is the second one?
> ANNIE

Mine.
> BUD

It's YOUR body?
> ANNIE

They're both mine.
I found them
And finders keepers.
> BUD

No no no
I mean . . ah
Who . . ah
That is
Of whom is the second body . .
That is
Who
Inhabited it in . .
Or . .
> ANNIE

You're not very good with words are you?
> BUD

Oh now . .
> GIN

(*Full out.*)
You needn't try to hide it.
There's nothing to be ashamed of.
It's the body of the husband
Isn't it?
> ANNIE

Why yes it is.
How did you know?
> GIN

The husband is dead.
(*Gazes triumphantly at Andrew.*)
Long live the lover.
(*Andrew looks about behind him uncomfortably. Gin stands, loosens her bodice, and lets one strap fall off her shoulder. Andrew, staring in fascination, grips the edge of the table. Gin sits on the table, crosses her knees, draws her skirt up, and swings her leg provocatively. Andrew slowly pulls*

*himself up onto the table and starts creeping toward her on his hands and
knees. The children, also staring in fascination, rise to get a better view.
Bud leaps to his feet.)*

BUD

IF

The ladies and children will retire
The gentlemen will remain for brandy and cigars.
(Andrew hurriedly slips back into his chair.)

CHILDREN

Aw-w-w-w.

*(Gin rises and beckons to the children who also rise. Gin and the girls
cross toward down right, but the boys stand at their places at table. Gin
and the girls stop to look back at them.)*

PAUL AND EDDY

We're staying.

PAUL

We're tired of being treated as children.

EDDY

We're tired of always having to go with the ladies.

PAUL AND EDDY

And girls.

PAUL

We want to be men.

EDDY

(Sitting, propping his feet on the table.)
Bring on the brandy and cigars.
(Paul sits too. Long pause.)

GIN

I thought they'd been showing too much curiosity lately
In the ladies' rest rooms.
(Sighs.)
Oh well
I suppose
In the course of time
Such things have to happen.
(To the boys.)
I'm sure you'd both much rather
Play a nice game
Now wouldn't you?

PAUL AND EDDY
(*Interested.*)
Game?

GIN
Yes.
(*To Annie.*)
Why don't you teach them
The game?

ANNIE
(*Eagerly.*)
THE game?

GIN
Yes that's the one.
(*To the boys.*)
You boys go with Annie.
She'll show you how to play.
(*The boys hesitate.*)

ANNIE
(*Undulating over to them.*)
Come on.
(*Runs her fingers through their hair and gently tugs at them.*)
It's fun.
(*She grinds across right and off, with the boys drooling after her.*)

GIN
(*To Bud and Andrew.*)
It's all yours,
Gentlemen.
(*She goes out with Isabel.*)

BUD
Sit down, young man.

ANDREW
Thank you, sir.
(*Andrew goes to a chair, but hovers.*)

BUD
Sit down, sit down.

ANDREW
Thank you, sir.
(*He sits. Pause.*)
Thank you, sir.

BUD
(*Expands.*)
Well!
(*Rings bell and calls.*)
Mary!
(*Mary enters left above the table.*)
    MARY
Yes, sir?
(*Looks about.*)
But where's everybody going?
    BUD
It's time for brandy and cigars.
    MARY
Already?
How could you possibly have . . ?
    BUD
Just bring the brandy and cigars
If you please.
    MARY
Yes, sir.
(*To the audience as she crosses out.*)
I keep forgetting it's not realism.
(*She goes out and returns immediately with decanter, glasses, and cigars on a tray. She pours the brandy, passes the cigars to both men and goes out. Bud goes through all the proper motions with the brandy, passing the snifter under his nose to inhale the bouquet, touching his lips to it tentatively, rolling a little of it around on his tongue, etc. Andrew watches closely and imitates him assiduously. Then, Andrew still observing and imitating, Bud slips the ring off the cigar, passes the cigar under his nose, holds it to his ear and rolls it between forefinger and thumb, bites off the end and spits it out, then places the cigar in his mouth. Mary enters on cue with a lighter with which she lights the cigars of the men, and goes out again. Bud leans back with the cigar in one hand and the brandy snifter in the other.*)
    BUD
Now then, young man,
I believe you had something to say to me.
    ANDREW
(*Uncomfortably.*)
Yes, sir.

BUD
Concerning perhaps
My daughter?

ANDREW
(*As if happily surprised.*)
Yes, sir.
As a matter of fact
It is about your daughter.
(*Gin steps back onto stage.*)

GIN
No no.
You've got it all wrong.
You're headed the wrong way.

BUD
Headed the wrong way?

GIN
Going in the wrong direction.

BUD
Oh-h-h . .

GIN
(*To Andrew.*)
Try it the other way round
Loverkins.
(*Andrew turns to smile foolishly at her. She thrusts out her lips and makes kisses at him. Andrew glances nervously toward Bud, then makes kisses back at her.*)
Wuv oo.

ANDREW
Wuv oo too.
(*She starts backing out, giving him a little wave close to her chest.*)

GIN
Remember
Uvver way wound.
(*She wrinkles her nose at him and exits. Both men resume the positions they were in when Gin entered.*)

ANDREW
Daughter your about is it.
Fact of matter a as
Sir, yes.

BUD
Daughter my?
Perhaps concerning?

ANDREW
Sir, yes.

BUD
Me to say to something had you believe I
Man young, then now.

(*Mary backs in with the lighter, lights their cigars in reverse and backs out. As the men continue to do the brandy and cigar pantomime in reverse, the lights dim down on them and a single cold spot of light dims up down center. Eddy and Paul hurry quietly into the light carrying a love seat, which they place in the center of the light facing out.*)

PAUL
Now this time
I get to be the strangler.

EDDY
No no
I'm the strangler.

PAUL
You're always the strangler.
I never get to be the strangler.
I'm not going to play.

EDDY
You were the strangler last time.

PAUL
I've never been the strangler.

EDDY
Sure you were.
Don't you remember?

PAUL
You've always been the strangler.

EDDY
Oh for Christ sake
It's just a game.
You act like it was a matter of life or . .

(*He stares at Paul. Paul stares back. There is a long pause.*)

PAUL
Life or
What?

THE STRANGLER

(*Annie steps into the light above the love seat.*)

ANNIE

I tell you what.

PAUL

What?

ANNIE

You can both be the strangler.

EDDY

But there's only one strangler
There can't be two.

ANNIE

How do you know?
Do you know who the strangler is?
Or who the stranglers are?

PAUL

Why it's the husband.
Didn't you hear Uncle Bud prove that it was?

ANNIE

You didn't BELIEVE that
Did you?

EDDY

Well
He made it sound logical enough.

ANNIE

Since when did logic have anything to do with it?
Besides the husband's been strangled too.
How could he have strangled himself?

PAUL

But if we're both the strangler
Who'll be the victim?

ANNIE

You can both be that too.

EDDY

How?

ANNIE

I'll show you.
(*Points to the left of the love seat. To Eddy.*)
You get down and hide over there
On that side of the love seat . .

PAUL

I wonder why they call it a love seat . .

ANNIE

Never mind

It's just a name.

(*To Paul.*)

And you hide on the other side.

Then you can both sneak up on the victim

In the middle of the love seat

And by the time each of you gets there

The other will be there to be the victim.

See?

PAUL AND EDDY

Oh-h-h-h . .

ANNIE

Now

Take your places

And when I count three

You both start.

(*Paul crouches at the left of the love seat, Eddy at the right. Both laugh and giggle in happy childish excitement.*)

Ready?

PAUL AND EDDY

(*A tense whisper.*)

Ready.

(*They break into excited snickers and guffaws.*)

ANNIE

One . . two . . three . .

Go.

(*Paul and Eddy, alternately ferocious and laughing eagerly, stalk each other around the love seat ending up on opposite sides. After much dramatic skulking and peeping, they both crawl stealthily over the arms of the love seat, and come face to face in the middle. After a brief confrontation, in dreamlike slow motion they bring their hands up to grasp each other's throat. Annie stands watching them with prurient satisfaction, as their happy, rocking, laughing game of strangling slowly becomes tauter, more realistic and grim. Each one, without in the least slacking his hold on the other's throat, quite realistically strangles, gasping, gurgling, coughing, retching, first in crescendo, then in diminuendo, until both topple*) *over onto the floor in front of the love seat and lie motionless. Annie speaks in an ecstatic whisper.*)

Dead heat right down to the wire.

(*She hurries around to bend over them, feel their pulses, listen to their hearts, etc. Then she stands, looks left and right, takes hold of one leg of each and starts pulling toward right. Suddenly Isabel appears at left.*)

ISABEL

Aha!

(*Annie stops and stares resentfully at her, still holding onto the legs.*)

So you're the one.

You're the strangler.

ANNIE

Don't be silly.

Whose side are you on anyway?

Come help me.

ISABEL

Help you?

Oh no

No you don't.

(*Shouts.*)

Daddy! Daddy!

ANNIE

(*Running to her and clapping a hand over her mouth.*)

Shut up, you little fool.

(*Drags her around to the feet of the twins and tries to make her take hold of their legs.*)

Here

Come help me.

Help me help me!

ISABEL

(*Breaking into great baby tears.*)

Daddy Daddy Daddy . .

Help help help . .

(*Bud and Andrew hurry down to stand behind the love seat and stare aghast at the dead boys.*)

BUD

Dear dear

What's going on here?

ANDREW

What have you done?

ARNOLD POWELL

ISABEL
She killed them.
Look.
She strangled them both
And now she's trying to drag them off before —
ANDREW
Oh this is terrible.
The boys murdered.
Murdered!
And Annie
My child
What have you done?
ANNIE
Look
Will you try to get it through your thick head that —
ANDREW
You can't talk to me that way.
ANNIE
Why not?
ANDREW
Because I'm . .
You're . .
We're . .
(*Helpless pause.*)
ANNIE
When you get it figured out
Let me know.
(*She starts dragging the bodies off.*)
ISABEL
Isn't anybody going to do anything?
ANNIE
That's right.
Somebody give me a hand here.
ISABEL
She's the strangler.
She strangled them.
ANNIE
(*Stopping again.*)
Oh stop being hysterical.
You don't know what you're talking about.

THEY were the stranglers.
This proves it.
They strangled each other
I saw them.
>ISABEL

They did not.
You did it.
>ANNIE

They did it I tell you.
You little fool.
>GIN

(*Entering with a large book under her arm.*)
Never mind never mind.
(*The girls become quiet. Isabel lowers her eyes fearfully. Annie stares at Isabel with cold fury.*)
It's an academic question at best.
No matter who killed them
The fact remains
They're dead
And need burying
AND
Since Annie needs the practice
If she's ever to learn
I think it's an excellent idea
For her to undertake it.
(*Beams at Annie.*)
She's my enterprising girl.
(*To Isabel.*)
Help her, Isabel.
And you too, Bud.
>ISABEL

I don't see why I should have to help
With her bodies.
>GIN

They're your bodies too,
Squirt.
Or should be.
(*Looks at her narrowly.*)
Mummy doesn't like to hear that kind of talk,
My darling.

217

(*Isabel quails under the combined steely gazes of Gin and Annie and reluctantly picks up an ankle. Gin looks at Bud and nods toward the bodies.*)

Bud.

(*Bud hesitates, then gingerly picks up the last remaining leg by the ankle.*)

BUD

I loathe this sort of thing.

GIN

Don't be silly
It can't hurt you.
Whoever heard of anybody being bitten by an ankle?

BUD

I'm not at all sure about this.
Isn't this going a little too far?
I mean
I'm willing to cooperate
Up to a point
A point still within the limits of
Human decency
But —

GIN

I'm disappointed in you, Bud.
(*Shakes her head sadly.*)
But of course I knew it would come to this
Eventually.
After all
You're only a man.

BUD

I'm only human.

GIN

Well do this one last thing for me
And we'll try to spare your delicate masculine feelings
Any further strain
Won't we, Annie?

ANNIE

Yes, ma'am.

BUD

I still don't like it . .
At all . .

GIN

Come come
Get a hold of yourself.
And of this leg.
(*She presses his hand about the ankle.*)
Now
All together
Heave.
(*They tug at the bodies. Andrew starts to cross to them.*)

ANDREW

Maybe I'd better help.

GIN

No.
You stay here.
They can manage.
(*To the others.*)
Now give it a good try.
(*They tug again and start dragging the bodies off, as Gin calls encouragement to them.*)
That's it
Keep pulling
You can do it.
Put a little body into it.
That's right
I knew you could
That's fine
Fine . .
(*They drag the bodies off down right. Gin turns to Andrew.*)
Alone at last.
Come sit down.
(*She crosses to the front of the love seat and sits.*)

ANDREW

Oh. So that's why you . .
Oh boy.
(*He crosses to front of the love seat, sits, and plunges into clumsy love-making with Gin, but almost immediately freezes, with Gin in his awkward embrace, and turns his head to the audience.*)
I have an idea that
This is where the peripeteia would come
In a really well-made play.

219

But they don't even know what the word means
Nowadays.
Oh well . .
(*He resumes his clumsy love-making.*)
GIN
(*Submitting mechanically, murmurs.*)
That's my big boy.
ANDREW
I'm your lover.
GIN
And my big boy.
ANDREW
Mainly lover, though.
I'll bet you never had another lover like me
Did you?
GIN
Why, Andy,
What an idea.
ANDREW
No really
Tell me
Aren't I the best lover you've ever had?
GIN
Of course you are.
ANDREW
Better than the husband?
GIN
Certainly.
ANDREW
Or the father?
GIN
By far.
ANDREW
(*Happily.*)
I am the lover.
GIN
You're my big boy.
ANDREW
(*Suddenly cooling and backing away.*)
Why do you keep saying that?

220

GIN

Because it's true.

ANDREW

In a ha ha metaphysical kind of way?

GIN

In a ha ha literal kind of way.

ANDREW

What do you mean?

GIN

(*Slowly.*)

Has the time come at last?

Are you really ready to know now?

ANDREW

To know what?

Tell me.

GIN

Yes.

Both the time and you

Are ripe.

(*She unpins two golden brooches from her dress, calls.*)

Annie!

(*Annie enters down right, dusting off her hands and forearms which are grimy with mud and dirt up to the elbow.*)

ANNIE

Yes, Mama?

GIN

(*Handing her the brooches.*)

Take these golden brooches

And hide them.

I have an announcement to make to Andrew.

ANNIE

(*Taking the brooches.*)

Yes, Mama.

(*She goes out.*)

ANDREW

An announcement?

You sound as if you were going to address

A whole group of people

A multitude

Instead of simply
Your lone lover.
>GIN

You ARE my multitude.
>ANDREW

Oh now that's very flattering but —
>GIN

Do you want to know the truth?
>ANDREW

Well naturally.
>GIN

No matter how much of a shock it may be to you?
>ANDREW

(*Timorously*.)
The truth
Is shocking?
(*Gin hands him a large book*.)
>GIN

Here
You'd better take this while I tell you.
It will give you something to hold onto.
>ANDREW

(*Taking the book*.)
Why
It's my memory book.
My old memory book.
>GIN

Yes.
Open it.
(*Andrew opens it*.)
Now leaf through it
While I talk.
(*Andrew starts leafing through the book and immediately becomes absorbed in its pages*.)
>ANDREW

Look at that.
(*Laughs*.)
The senior class picnic.
Look at old Molly . .
(*Chuckles*.)

222

GIN
Now listen carefully to what I have to say.
ANDREW
(*Preoccupied with the book.*)
Yeah sure go ahead . .
Golly Moses look at all the hair on Joe . .
GIN
Do you remember
The FATHER
That you killed?
ANDREW
(*Preoccupied.*)
Yeah yeah I remember . .
GIN
It was
YOUR father.
ANDREW
(*Preoccupied. Turns page.*)
That's right . .
My father . .
GIN
He was also
The HUSBAND.
ANDREW
(*Preoccupied.*)
Mm-hm.
(*Points to page and snickers.*)
GIN
MY husband.
ANDREW
(*Preoccupied, snorts.*)
I bet old Suzy wishes she was as skinny as that now.
(*Chuckles.*)
GIN
So you see
If he was YOUR father
AND
MY HUSBAND . .
(*Pause.*)
What does that make you?

And me?

(*Andrew freezes, raises his eyes to stare full out, then slowly closes the book. Slowly he turns to stare at Gin, and they gaze into each other's eyes for a long time. Then Gin takes him into her arms and cradles his head on her bosom. She chants.*)

My boy
My big boy.
My son.

ANDREW

Mother . .
Mother . .
I've missed you so.

GIN

There there
It's all right now.
Everything's going to be all right.
From now on.

(*Andrew begins whistling a low undistinguishable tune, which he continues under the following dialogue. Annie darts in down right.*)

ANNIE

Mama.

GIN

Yes, dear?

ANNIE

There's another body.

GIN

Yes
I know, dear.

ANNIE

You know?

GIN

It's the lover
Isn't it?

ANNIE

Yes it is . .

GIN

The lover is dead.

(*Assumes madonna and child pose.*)

A son is born.

(*She holds Andrew away from her and looks him over.*)

Why you poor boy.
Shrouded in all those heavy hot
Men's clothes.
(*To Annie.*)
Annie
Look in the second drawer of my chifferobe
And bring your brother something cooler to put on.
    ANNIE
Yes, ma'am.
(*She runs out down right.*)
    GIN
(*To Andrew.*)
Now
Let's get you out of that heavy old thing.
(*As she helps him take off the coat, the memory book falls to the floor.*)
    ANDREW
Oh
My memory book . .
(*He starts to pick it up, but Gin stops him.*)
    GIN
Never mind about that
You won't be needing it anymore.
(*She gets the coat off and lays it on the back of the love seat. Andrew is wearing a short-sleeved white shirt.*)
This stuffy old tie!
(*She takes the tie off and opens the collar.*)
How can a boy romp and play
When he's being literally strangled?
There now.
Mother's made it better
Hasn't she?
(*Andrew stands, faces full out, and recites in childlike rote.*)
    ANDREW
I don't know what I'd do without you.
You're the sweetest, grandest mother in all the world.
You do everything for me.
I don't know how I can ever repay you.
I realize only too well that you gave yourself
Your very self
In order to give me

225

Being
That you risked your life
Your very life
In order to bring me into the world
That you sacrificed your whole existence
Your very whole existence
In order to assure for me
Comfort and joy
And security
And blessedness . .
Uh . .

GIN

(*Prompting him.*)
At your knee . .

ANDREW

At your knee
I have received those high moral truths
And virtuous precepts
That will make me a better boy.
Your guiding hand has set my feet
Upon paths of righteousness.
(*Steps forward and places his hand on his heart.*)
M is for mother
O is for other
T is for t'other
H-E-R- that's her
My mother.
(*Suppresses a sob and hangs his head shyly.*)

GIN

(*Proudly.*)
My boy.

ANDREW

I hope you'll always be proud of me.

GIN

I know you will always give me reason
To be proud.
(*She starts loosening his belt and unbuttoning his trousers.*)

ANDREW

I think I'd like to play with my chemistry set now.
I feel like blowing something up.

GIN

Oh no no no no
Little Andy isn't old enough for that yet.

ANDREW

(*Sulkily.*)
I'd like to know why not.

GIN

(*Pulling two small round objects from his pocket.*)
Here's one good reason.
Or rather two.
You're still playing with stink bombs.
You're just a little boy.

ANDREW

(*Sinks to his knees and clutches at her skirt, frightened.*)
I'm . .
I'm just a little boy.
Don't leave me.

GIN

Leave my little fellow?
You know Mummy would never do that.
(*Annie runs in down right, carrying a large box.*)

ANNIE

Guess what.

GIN

(*Nodding wisely.*)
More bodies?

ANNIE

I've got enough to go into business.
Set up shop.
Nine bodies.

GIN

Nine?

ANNIE

You guessed it.

GIN

But I don't think I can account for

NINE

(*She is trying to get Andrew's trousers off.*)
Here.
Come help me.

(*Annie puts the large box on the floor to one side and helps Gin pull off Andrew's trousers and his shoes and socks. She speaks as they work.*)
There's the father
And the husband
And the lover
(*Annie nods.*)
And the twins make five.

ANNIE

That's right.

GIN

And the sixteen-year-old boy.

ANNIE

That's six.

GIN

And the eleven-year-old boy.

ANNIE

Seven.
(*Gin thinks.*)

GIN

Well that's all I can . .
The seven-year-old boy hadn't already . . ?

ANNIE

No.
Guess again.

GIN

I give up.

ANNIE

Why Isabel and Uncle Bud of course.

GIN

(*The light dawning.*)
Of course of course I should have known.

ANNIE

And that makes nine.
(*Tears of happiness well up into Gin's eyes as she embraces Annie.*)

GIN

My own true daughter.
Mother's little helper.
(*Reverts to business.*)
Well.
(*Hands Annie the coat, trousers, shoes, and socks that she has taken off*

Andrew, who is now dressed like a little boy in short pants and short-sleeved shirt.)

Take these and dispose of them.

(Annie takes them.)

And hand me those others that you've brought.

(Annie pulls the large box over beside the love seat and takes out a smaller box which she places on the floor in front of the love seat.)

ANNIE

And I thought he might like to play with this.

(She skips out down right.)

ANDREW

What that she bwing Andy?

(He slips down off the love seat onto all fours and crawls to the box.)

O-o-o-o-o-o-o-o!

My widder finger paints.

Andy wuvs finger paints.

Ah-h-h . .

(Andrew smears red finger paint blissfully about, first on the box and floor, then all over himself. When he sees what a mess he has made of himself he begins to fret and cry, then wipes both eyes with his paint-smeared fingers. He throws back his head and screams with pain. Gin goes to him and pulls him to the love seat.)

GIN

Here here here here . .

What a mess you've made.

(She gets a cloth from the large box and wipes his face and hands clean.)

My my

I guess he'll have to wait several more years before he's ready for finger
    paints.

Aw-w-w

Did um get um pigment in um's little eyes?

Here Mama'll get it out

Don't you worry . .

There

Now let's get some nice clean clothes on

My little fellow.

(She takes from the box a long white baby dress and slips it on Andrew over his clothes.)

ANDREW

Nite nite.

(*Gin takes an embroidered baby cap from the box and ties it on Andrew's head.*)

GIN

Now he's Mama's little
Spick and span babykins.
Come to Mama.

(*She pulls him over into her lap, cradles him in her arms, and rocks him gently back and forth. She calls.*)

Annie!

(*Annie brings her a baby bottle. Gin takes it and holds it for Andrew, who eagerly starts sucking on it. He stops sucking and turns to the audience.*)

ANDREW

In reality
I was breast-fed
But there are certain things you simply can't do
Even on the modern stage.

(*He goes back to nursing the bottle happily.*)

GIN

(*To Annie.*)
Have you got his bed ready?

ANNIE

I'm digging it now.

GIN

Good.
Only a little one will do.
A little little one.
For he's my tiny little babykins.

(*Andrew pulls away from the bottle and looks lovingly up into Gin's eyes.*)

ANDREW

Ma-ma.

GIN

Isn't that sweet?
His last word was
"Mama."

(*Gin hands the bottle to Annie, who exits with it. She sings.*)

Lullay lullay lullay lullay
Lullay lullay lullay
Lullay lullay lullay lullay
Lullay.

(As she sings, Andrew slowly curls up into the fetal position and the lights begin fading. When he is finally tightly folded into a little ball, Gin suddenly interrupts her lullaby with a groan that is as lascivious as it is agonized, and her legs stretch out and apart. She calls.)
All right, Annie,
You can call the midwife now!
(Another groan with even more sensuous fulfillment.)
My time has come!
(As her legs slowly spread more and she rolls over toward Andrew, Andrew sneezes and the lights go to black.)

END OF PLAY

The Strangler by Arnold Powell was presented August 11–13, 18–20, 1966, at Scott Hall Auditorium, University of Minnesota, Minneapolis. It was directed by Lee Adey.

Cast of Characters

ANDREW VURGLAR	Richard Ramos
VIRGINIA	Lorraine Steiner
ANNIE	Candace Birk
ISABEL	Judy Weiss
EDDY	Larry Stout
PAUL	Thomas Drake
UNCLE BUD	Warren Kliewer
MARY, the maid	Valerie Vaux
STAGEHANDS	Donald Seay, Russell Ratsch

KEVIN O'MORRISON

The Long War

Cast of Characters in the Order of Their Speaking

CHARM VENDOR
LEOGORAS, father of Andocides, an aristocrat
ALCIBIADES, Commander in Chief, Expeditionary Forces
POLYDOR, Leogoras' slave
DIAGORAS, a poet-philosopher
CHARICLES, a fat merchant
MENIPPUS, chairman of the Naval Committee
CRITIAS, chairman of the Military Committee
ANDROCLES, a leading demagogue
METON, a soothsayer
CHARMIDES, Leogoras' young nephew
PISANDER, a young general, friend of Charmides
ANDOCIDES, son of Leogoras
OLD WOMAN, Andocides' great-grandmother
ADAMANTEA, a young slave in Leogoras' house
POLYSTRATUS, President of the Assembly and a general
EUPHILETUS, a young officer, friend of Andocides
PULYTION, Captain of the Home Guard
DIOCLIDES, a public informer
MELETUS, a young officer, friend of Andocides

Characters with No Lines

LYSIPPUS, Androcles' slave   HOPLITE GUARD
RECORDING CLERK   CITIZENS

The Setting

THE TIME: The seventeenth year of the Peloponnesian War. Late spring.
THE PLACE: Athens.
THE SET: Three platforms of varying height. On one side, a platform faced with three or four steps to accommodate the Sitting Assembly curves from down right, or left, to center. On the other side, there is a similar platform of perhaps one or two steps on which a longish bench is permanently set. Center, a flight of steps — perhaps six or seven; the Herm is permanently set on its top. A pair of Doric pillars on each side of the stage might be helpful but are not essential. The rest is light and movement.

THE LONG WAR

PROLOGUE

A piping tune is heard — a wistful tune, full of gaiety, courage, and rue. At the rise, the piper is discovered leaning against the Herm. He is Diagoras the Poet. It is just before dawn. In the street below him a charm vendor cries at a drunken passerby.

CHARM VENDOR

(*like "Fish — get your fresh fish!"*) Havoc! Havoc and woe! Buy a charm, sir, a charm against your Fate . . (*pursuing him off*) A charm against headaches — a charm against your wife . .

(*Leogoras and Alcibiades enter from the other side, followed by the slave Polydor. The two men are gently mulled. Party music and a babble of cheery voices accompany them on.*)

LEOGORAS

(*calling*) Farewell, Agathon, farewell —

ALCIBIADES

Farewell, friends —

VOICES

(*off*) Farewell, Leogoras . . The gods be with you, Alcibiades.

LEOGORAS

A lovely party, Alcibiades. I shall carry its benison to bed with me.

ALCIBIADES

I envy you your bed, Leogoras. A long night's map-work lies yet before me.

© Copyright 1966 as an unpublished work, 1967 by Kevin O'Morrison. Address inquiries concerning performance and translation rights to Bertha Case, 42 West 53rd Street, New York City.

LEOGORAS

Even the sun must rest, dear boy.

ALCIBIADES

But not the commander who would be victorious.

CHARM VENDOR

(*coming on*) Buy a charm, Alcibiades — a charm against defeat.

ALCIBIADES

(*amiably*) Don't you fellows ever sleep?

CHARM VENDOR

(*mocking*) With dread Omens all about us? Buy a lucky charm, sir — a charm against Omens.

ALCIBIADES

(*lightly*) Omens are only for the uncertain, my friend.

CHARM VENDOR

Then buy a charm against your Fate.

ALCIBIADES

(*laughing*) And he who would bargain with Fate is a fool.

CHARM VENDOR

(*His eye pierces Alcibiades'.*) Still — one never knows — does one. (*He has shaken the General. He mocks as he goes.*) Charms against Omens. Charms against the night —

LEOGORAS

(*offers his hand*) Good luck and a valiant heart go with you to Syracuse tomorrow. May her walls crumble before your warlike look.

ALCIBIADES

(*lightly, now: confident*) Armed with your good wishes, Leogoras, I shall be — invincible. (*He goes.*)

LEOGORAS

(*calling*) Farewell, dear boy, farewell. (*He suddenly wiggles a finger in one ear.*) Do you hear a piping, Polydor?

POLYDOR

A piping, sir?

LEOGORAS

Never mind, there's the fellow. Say, you, there. Who is that piping to the night?

DIAGORAS

(*Through the scene, his tone is light.*) You mistake the hour. I am piping to the dawn.

LEOGORAS

By your voice — Diagoras the Poet?

DIAGORAS

I would your conscience were as quick as your ear. Athenians call me Diagoras the Blasphemer: Are you Athenian, Leogoras?

LEOGORAS

Oh, my friend, not I.

DIAGORAS

Odd. Until this moment, I had thought you were.

LEOGORAS

Were what?

DIAGORAS

Athenian. Was it a good party that you left?

LEOGORAS

We missed *you* — but you mistook my meaning in the dark. I meant I do not call you Diagoras the Blasphemer, but Diagoras the Wise Man.

DIAGORAS

Then I mistook your meaning in the light.
For I would swear I heard you call me Blasphemer, just yesternoon when I was tried before the commons in the Assembly. Did Socrates say *wondrous* things tonight?

LEOGORAS

Oh, perish Socrates — you never heard me call you so!

DIAGORAS

Oh, never with your tongue.
But yesterday at my trial, the many-tonguèd silence shouted out the name. Androcles read the charge against me, and in the hush that followed, silently — like all the rest — you called me "Blasphemer." So call me, now, before I leave your country, as you have judged me.

LEOGORAS

You do me wrong, I never called you so. I voted on your side.

DIAGORAS

And yet, I did not hear you say in my defense, "It is not so."

LEOGORAS

I could not. All the things Androcles said you said, I heard you say. (*pleading*) My *friend* — we are at *war*. The commons are inflamed at the very hint of treason.

DIAGORAS

I was not charged with treason, but with blasphemy.

LEOGORAS

One charge serves as well as another, in times like these. Call it blasphemy, then — the line between blasphemy and curiosity is a thin one.

DIAGORAS

(*mock alarm*) And I think you overstep it. Be careful, Leogoras — for I think that you are telling me that I was condemned, not for *my* doubts, but for *theirs*.

LEOGORAS

No, no! I meant, your thoughts were too complex for simple telling. The commons would not understand such complex matters in so short a time as trial permits.

DIAGORAS

And yet you understood them, once — in a time that took no longer. Are you wise, Leogoras?

LEOGORAS

Not wise, but understanding.

DIAGORAS

You are fortunate: Are they large or small, these things you understand?

LEOGORAS

I understand that you are bitter, now.

DIAGORAS

Then it is little that you understand. I am not bitter. This is not my home. I am an alien who long ago came to Athens mistakenly. Alien still, I shall go the way I came.

LEOGORAS

How do you mean?

DIAGORAS

I came here because I learned to read Athenian faultily. I must now leave because I speak in the same blunt error of my learning.

LEOGORAS

I do not follow you.

DIAGORAS

And yet you may.

As to my meaning: On the small island of Melos, where I was born, we built an altar and dedicated it to Zeus. On it we inscribed in gold those precious words you Athenians carved on your own altar — to celebrate your victory over the Persian King:

(*He makes Leogoras "see" the altar.*)

> "The Greeks,
> When by their zeal for Truth and Right
> Repelled the Persians and their Might,
> This altar raised in commonality
> To Zeus —

238

(*Leogoras repeats the last, dear, familiar words with him.*)
Who guards the Brave and Free."

I believed those words upon the altar where I worshipped, on the small island of Melos. And I was proud to share a world with men who thought so nobly. (*He chuckles.*) I was not then educated in the subtleties and nuances of Athenian speech. The idiom is difficult — it has taken me a lifetime in your midst to learn it: for one word may have a thousand shades of difference and meaning. Truth, for instance, hereabouts means Dogma. Right means Might. Brave means Circumspect. And Free means To Conform. I had to go to trial to learn that. But the dullest mind learns fast in the hot sun of trial before the commons.

LEOGORAS
Oh, my friend, my gentle friend — how we have wounded you.

DIAGORAS
(*shrugging off his hand*) A flesh wound, only. But the sword with which you cut *me* has two edges. It cuts up as well as down. Go armed, Leogoras. He who would live in Athens must go armed.

LEOGORAS
It will soon be light — shall I see you to your ship?

DIAGORAS
Go home, sad man. Look to your house.
I have a song to pipe.
(*As he goes, piping, dim to blackout. His piping is swallowed up in a low rumble of timpani: a sound of threat.*)

ACT ONE

Scene 1

Androcles' house, a little later. Lights dim up, stage right, on Charicles and Menippus.

CHARICLES
Well, I don't mind telling you, Menippus — I had half a mind to tell Androcles' slave I wouldn't come.

MENIPPUS
That would indicate half a mind.
(*Leogoras enters. Charicles sidles over to him.*)

239

CHARICLES

Well, Leogoras. I see that Androcles has got you out of bed, too. What do you suppose he wants of us?

LEOGORAS

(*with a look of distaste*) Our reputations, most likely, Charicles.

(*Critias enters. Charicles goes round Leogoras to welcome him.*)

CRITIAS

(*as though Charicles didn't exist*) Greetings, Leogoras. (*He now stares full at Charicles.*) We're an ill-assorted little group, aren't we.

(*Charicles rejoins Menippus.*)

LEOGORAS

Have you any idea why Androcles has called us at such an hour?

CRITIAS

No — (*eyes the other two*) but he seems to be summoning one of every political faction in the city.

LEOGORAS

Tch — Why do we permit ourselves to be ordered about by such a creature —

CRITIAS

(*icily*) For the same reason we yield him the powers of our offices: to refuse him is to invite an attack upon our characters before that mindless rabble in the Assembly.

(*Androcles enters bearing a roll of maps as though it might be a scepter.*)

ANDROCLES

Gentlemen. My apologies for disturbing your sleep, but it was urgent that I call you all together. Less than an hour ago I learned that Alcibiades is planning something larger than our campaign against Syracuse.

LEOGORAS

(*stiffly*) I was not aware that you were in his confidence.

ANDROCLES

(*blandly*) I'm not. But I am in the confidence of his mapmaker. (*He opens maps.*) And these leave little doubt that our "Supreme Commander" intends to use Syracuse as a base from which to extend the war — attacking, first Carthage, then all the cities of Italy.

CHARICLES

Well — why not. We have the fleet for it. We have the allies.

ANDROCLES

Not since the Slaughter of Melos, we haven't. That blunder —

CHARICLES

(*angry*) What do you mean, blunder! The Slaughter —

ANDROCLES

Spare us what we've had to tell the public, Charicles. The Slaughter was stupid. A show of naked force against a weaker state. Which has made many of the "allies" you speak of, reluctant allies. At the slightest diplomatic or military reversal, they would fall away from us.

CRITIAS

They wouldn't dare. Our sea power is absolute.

ANDROCLES

Really. Then you will be interested to learn that one day last fall our "sea power" was stretched so thin we lost control of one little part of the sea — the part our wheat comes from. There was only two weeks' supply of grain in the city, at the time. (*He regards the stunned men with satisfaction.*) Only by scavenging a ship, here, a battered hulk, there, were Menippus and I able to scrape together a squadron and dispatch it in time to save the city. (*They all stare in anger at Menippus.*)

LEOGORAS

Menippus and *you*! (*to Menippus*) Since when is Androcles on the Naval Committee!

MENIPPUS

Well . . the . . uh . . the Naval Committee had no funds, so I . .

CRITIAS

So you acted privately in a public matter! (*to Androcles*) Why weren't we told of this!

ANDROCLES

Where would you have told it, Critias — in the Assembly? The issue would have been decided in the field while we all wrangled in partisan disarray over whose fault it was.

CHARICLES

Well, whose fault was it!

ANDROCLES

(*full in his face*) How many of you gentlemen voted against the Fleet Maintenance Tax last summer — friends, seventeen years of war has emptied your purses.

CHARICLES

Well, then, Syracuse will fill them up again.

ANDROCLES

No, Charicles, it won't. We have already spent more gold to outfit the invasion fleet than there is in all of Sicily.

CHARICLES

(*not believing his ears*) But — *you* led the cry in the Assembly. When Alcibiades asked for one ship, you screamed at us to give him two.

ANDROCLES

(*again, full in his face*) Yes, Charicles! And I got them! From the same greedy men who refused me the monies to keep the fleet we *had* at minimum strength.

CHARICLES

You! What statute gives you the right to tamper with my purse — you hold no public office!

ANDROCLES

And therefore can never fail that office. Meanwhile, as a citizen, I can point out their mistakes to those who *do* hold public office — either privately, or when necessary, before the Assembly.

LEOGORAS

By all that's holy, you take too much upon yourself!

ANDROCLES

Only because others do not. You, yourself, have the same freedom as I to watch over the public business.

LEOGORAS

Well, I do not like your methods!

OTHERS

Nor I!

ANDROCLES

In my place, where would any of you have done differently? (*They stare stubbornly at him.*) Gentlemen, I am a democrat, and passionately so. But I know the limits of democracy.

MENIPPUS

What do you propose, then?

ANDROCLES

(*briskly, now: like equations*) The public purse cannot afford extension of our military effort. Alcibiades is determined to extend that effort. I propose a league to stop him. By overthrowing him, if possible — but in any case, by undermining his credit with the people.

MENIPPUS

I should not like to challenge Alcibiades — and fail. He holds the Army securely in his hands.

ANDROCLES

He has rivals in the Army.

MENIPPUS

None who will dare let that rivalry show before the commons. Even you can't stand against him with the commons.

ANDROCLES

Don't worry about the commons. While he is in the field, we shall parade his every mistake before their eyes in the Assembly. Step by measured step we shall lead them, and they shall not know how they have arrived at their destination — But our ends must be accomplished before Syracuse falls. After the victory, Alcibiades would sweep everything before him.

CRITIAS

And the Army?

ANDROCLES

The important thing is for you and your Military Committee to secure the Home Guard to us. I think I know just the man for the job.

CRITIAS

My committee would never permit the removal of so good a man as Captain Pulytion.

ANDROCLES

The man I have in mind outranks Pulytion. By merely assigning him to the Guard, he would succeed to the command.

CRITIAS

Who is he?

ANDROCLES

An ambitious young commoner: General Pisander.

CHARICLES

The one who led the charge at Melos? (*Androcles nods.*) He's a good man . . but he'll be sailing with the fleet.

ANDROCLES

We-ell, perhaps we can do something about that. *You've* been supplying our Allied Generals, have you not?

CHARICLES

(*puzzled*) Yes —

(*As the men gather around Androcles, cross fade on them and up on Meton the Soothsayer, in limbo: his face shadowed by a cowl, Meton points an indicative hand.*)

METON

> Hear me, O Athens
> The gods are moving amongst us
> They are turning our swords inwards
> Didymus is dead

243

(*Fade down on Meton as Pisander enters, carrying the limp, drunk Charmides over his shoulder.*)

CHARMIDES

(*singing*)

> My mother was a Theban, My father came from Troy.
> His wife, *she* came from Argos, and I'm their
> little boy.

(*He pulls Pisander's sword from its scabbard and whacks happily away at Pisander's rump.*)

TOGETHER

> Oh, I'm a jolly bastard, I fight for whom I
> please.
> And so far I've pleased no one yet, but
> Al-ci-bi-a-dees.

(*They are off.*)

METON

> The gods are turning our swords inward
> In our bellies they turn them
> Mighty Didymus is dead

Scene 2

Leogoras' house, a few minutes later. Leogoras enters, accompanied by Polydor.

LEOGORAS

Just listen to that idiot! (*calls*) Close your windows and go to sleep, Meton! There's the mark of our uncertain times, Polydor: When every misfortune is taken for an Omen, soothsayers grow rich enough to buy houses in our street. (*Pisander, with Charmides still slung from his shoulder, enters and collides with Leogoras.*)

PISANDER

Make way there, old man.

LEOGORAS

Make way — this is my house!
I don't believe I know you, sir!

CHARMIDES

(*Raising his head, he points a finger.*) Oh, you should, Uncle dear — you *should*.

244

LEOGORAS

Charmides — you're drunk. (*Charmides wriggles off Pisander's shoulder.*)

CHARMIDES

(*mocking*) In-*dooby-tabby-tib*ally.

Uncle, may I present . . General Pisander. (*prompting, as his uncle stares*) Come, now, Uncle. Surely you recall — Pisander. Of Melos.

LEOGORAS

Oh. Certainly. I — I should have made your acquaintance earlier, young man, but for the affairs of a busy life. Perhaps you will now accept the intention for the deed, and forgive me.

CHARMIDES

Yes, Pisander, *do* forgive my uncle. The poor man has had so much on his mind of late — the bloodlines of his prize pheasants, for instance. Terribly complicated business, pheasants. Then there are his epigrams to keep polished — they tarnish so quickly in our climate. With such grave distractions from the common need, you can see why it might take him eight months to thank you for saving the life of his only son.

LEOGORAS

I hope you will forgive my nephew, as well, General. In my day, young men had respect for their elders. I would that day might return.

CHARMIDES

Oh, please let's not return to your day, Uncle. For then I should have to live *my* day all over again. And I've loathed every minute of it. (*The swing of his arm — a travesty of gaiety — spins him in easy collapse into Leogoras' arms.*)

LEOGORAS

(*with as much aplomb as he can muster*) You must call on us another time, Pisander. If you will excuse me, now.

PISANDER

Good night, sir. (*He goes. Charmides — on the threshhold of consciousness — wriggles in his uncle's arms.*)

(*Fade up on Meton the Soothsayer, in limbo.*)

METON

> Didymus the Archer is dead
> On the Altar of the Twelve Gods he killed
>   himself
> As he plunged his sword into his belly
> Mighty Didymus cried, "As to Melos, so
>   now to Athens!"

(*Fade out Meton.*)

245

CHARMIDES

(*an energetic chant*) Oh, Pamphylia, Pamphylia, the virgin pros-ti-toot! (*He skews his head around.*) I wan' go back 'n' see Pammmphyl-i-yah! (*His eye focuses on his uncle.*) J'you know Pamphylia 'sa princess? (*enthusiastically*) Breasts big as mushmelons — 'n' soft 's down cushions. (*makes fluffing gesture*) Wan' go back 'n' fluff 'em up a li'l' — (*He collapses.*)

LEOGORAS

Tch — what are our young men coming to — (*He waves Polydor to take Charmides off, then sags to a seat.*) Oh, god — it hurts even to breathe —

ANDOCIDES

(*from the shadows*) Be glad. For then you know you are alive.

LEOGORAS

Who said that! (*turns*) Polydor, do you presume —

ANDOCIDES

No, Father. It is I who "presume." (*He moves into the half-light. Wine and grief have taken him beyond drunkenness.*)

LEOGORAS

Oh, son. You startled me. What are you doing here alone?

ANDOCIDES

I am not alone, Father.

LEOGORAS

I see no one with you.

ANDOCIDES

And yet they crowd about us.

LEOGORAS

Who?

ANDOCIDES

The unnumbered and unregarded dead.

LEOGORAS

Andocides — have you been drinking?

ANDOCIDES

Yes, Father. But not enough. Not enough. (*As he steps into the light, fresh blood on his tunic glistens.*)

LEOGORAS

Son — you've been hurt.

ANDOCIDES

Don't be alarmed, Father. This is not my blood — Didymus just died in my arms.

246

LEOGORAS

Oh — yes — tch. Such a — (*fumbles for a word*) violent thing to do.

ANDOCIDES

(*flatly*) Violence is the portion our fathers have bequeathed us.

LEOGORAS

(*stunned*) What — ?

ANDOCIDES

You have willed us a never-ending struggle with Sparta: and that we endure because it seems we must. But what of Syracuse — must we endure that, too?

LEOGORAS

Syracuse — what have I to do —

ANDOCIDES

Father, under this roof I have heard you agree with Socrates that our whole campaign against Syracuse "is an ugly essay in greed." Could you not say that in the Assembly?

LEOGORAS

No. There are too many powerful men committed to that greed. If I made such a charge they would not hesitate to strip me even of my honor.

ANDOCIDES

Is honor a bauble that you wear about your neck, that other men may take it from you? I had thought it something else — a state arrived at in the privacy of conscience.

LEOGORAS

I chose my words badly. I meant, the demagogues would not permit me to discuss the charge.

ANDOCIDES

Then could you not persuade Socrates to speak?

LEOGORAS

He would fare no better than I. They would drown his voice in a clap of thundering irrelevance.

ANDOCIDES

And does Socrates, too, withhold his lightning for fear of the thunder that follows? Then carve upon the tombs of us who soon must fall at Syracuse: "Now we are as silent as great Socrates."

LEOGORAS

Andocides!

ANDOCIDES

Forgive me, Father. That was too blunt. Too lacking in wit for an Athenian gentleman's taste. I shall improvise it in a verse for you:

247

The lightning spoke not, nor now do we.
The lightning spoke not, for fear of thunder.
Now Socrates is silent above the ground,
And we — under!

LEOGORAS

That's unfair!

ANDOCIDES

Father, I admire the soaring flight of the eagled mind.
I am fascinated by the stinging flash of the viper'd tongue.
But the clipped wing, and the hobbled tongue hold no charm for me: I take no pleasure from the performance of talented cripples!

LEOGORAS

Oh, son, son, it is bitter to think that you despise me so.

ANDOCIDES

I DON'T DESPISE YOU, FATHER — I LOVE YOU!

LEOGORAS

If you did, you would respect my age!

ANDOCIDES

I *have* respected your age, Father. For part of it was my age, too. But one day last fall, I stood upon the after-threshold of that age. At Melos. The victory was ours, at Melos. Not a proud victory, but perhaps better than defeat. We disarmed the men of Melos and sent word of our victory to the Assembly. For three days — while the men of Melos huddled in their conquered houses — we watched the sea for word of their disposition. The word came. (*His face is terrible as he remembers.*) The word came — on a fateful ship, freighted with doubt — a fatal word: Death. To the disarmed. To the faltering old. To the newborn. "Death to the Males of Melos."

LEOGORAS

Andocides, please —

ANDOCIDES

You are not to speak yet!
"By decree of Alcibiades, Endorsed by the Assembly," the ship captain said. And honoring our oaths of service, we did the bloody dishonor.
That night, the women of Melos buried their dead.
That night, with the blood of babes upon *us*, we buried our age of innocence. Never again may I respect your age, Father, except to pay respects of grief and mourning.

LEOGORAS

What's done is gone, it cannot be recalled.

ANDOCIDES

Recalled! It comes unbidden!

In the dark infinity of my mind, there is no "now" or "then" — but only a shadowed, trackless wilderness, peopled with the sackclothed shapes of mourning women. A voice-filled Void whose lipless mouths cry from five thousand guiltless graves, "Guilty!" "Guilty!"

LEOGORAS

Son, son, you are not alone in your concern —

ANDOCIDES

Concern — what of guilt! *The ballot is as bloody as the sword that it invokes!*

LEOGORAS

Guilt, too. You don't know how I grieve for that ill-considered action.

ANDOCIDES

THEN CRY OUT YOUR GRIEF IN THE ASSEMBLY — to tell it only in secluded walls leaves the living grief entombed!

ALCIBIADES

Forgive me for intruding, cousins. (*Resplendent in armor and purple cloak, he surveys the two startled men. He is all charm.*) One farewell was not enough, Leogoras. I have come for another.

LEOGORAS

(*to cover embarrassment*) Well — I — I had better have Polydor fetch you some wine.

ALCIBIADES

(*staying him*) I took the liberty of sending Polydor to his quarters.

LEOGORAS

Then — I had better see to your escort's needs.

ALCIBIADES

I brought no escort. Pulytion will call for me later.

LEOGORAS

(*genuinely surprised*) You are alone?

ALCIBIADES

(*his opening gambit*) To be Alcibiades is to *be* alone, Leogoras.

ANDOCIDES

Only because he will not look down. If he would bend his neck a little, he should find the rest of us about his knees.

ALCIBIADES

Your flattery is like a spring breeze, cousin — it chaps and reddens the cheek it kisses.

249

ANDOCIDES

Only if the cheek be unused to exposure. If you will excuse me, I'll fetch you some wine. (*He goes.*)

ALCIBIADES

(*eying the uneasy Leogoras*) What is troubling you, old friend?

LEOGORAS

(*pause: blurts it out*) I have seen your war maps.

ALCIBIADES

Good! Then Androcles has already sought you out.

LEOGORAS

You knew — ?

ALCIBIADES

(*amused*) That he had tracings taken from my maps? Before I had worked five minutes I saw the marks of the stylus.

LEOGORAS

Then I must tell you that I am unalterably opposed to your ambitions.

ALCIBIADES

Not my ambitions, cousin, but our necessities. Androcles and I see the world from different vantage points. (*He leads him, as to a dock.*) He stands down upon the merchants' docks, amid the masts and spars of commerce. The world he sees from here is huge — at his back, Sparta presses from the land. To seaward, forbidding distances conceal from him unknown dangers — lurking accidents of Fate. He husbands his strength against these accidents — which we call war — and strives to keep on a firm, fiscal footing.

LEOGORAS

Well, I'd say that was an uncommonly sound view.

ALCIBIADES

(*leading him up a step or two*) Would you? Then come with me and let me fit the whole, vast world into your Olympian eye. From here, the great swelling ocean looks like a small puddle. And on it, nations send out fleets of tiny boats — like nutshell navies launched by little boys after a quick rain — to sail in ever-widening courses until they collide with one another. From here, the world has shrunk to the hailing distance between two hostile war-galleys. There are no "accidents of Fate": conflict is inevitable, and peace an illusion — unless we dare to claim the sea as ours, and rule it as we would the land. (*His face is frank and resolute, now.*) I intend to smash Carthage, then one by one, the cities of Italy. They are ascendant: we are already near our zenith.

LEOGORAS

I . . I don't like your view from Olympus. It has no mercy in it. (*Andocides — in a fresh tunic — enters with Polydor, who bears a wine tray. They are arrested by the intent manner of the two men.*)

ALCIBIADES

There is no room for mercy in this narrow world!
Is it merciful to send boys like Andocides out to drown in the wreckage of a policy to drift? Do you want this war to drag on for *another* seventeen years — Sparta shows no sign of weakening. She devours the land. But if we can take the sea as our domain, Sparta can have the land — and choke on it.

LEOGORAS

I — I suppose you're right. What do you want me to do?

ALCIBIADES

Keep me informed on — (*grins*) your conspiracy against me.

LEOGORAS

I'm unpracticed in the role of dissembler, but —

ALCIBIADES

What is it?

LEOGORAS

(*pointing off*) An Omen — the city has disappeared — the winds have wrapped it in a misty winding-sheet . .

ALCIBIADES

(*exuberantly*) Nonsense, old friend. That is the gossamer gown, through which the Lady Earth — with wanton modesty — will now tempt the ardor of the rising sun. (*A knock on the door, off. Polydor goes.*) That will be Pulytion. (*He takes Leogoras' arm in the soldiers' handshake.*) Send him any word that you want to reach me. (*He exits briskly.*)

LEOGORAS

(*to himself*) I shall do what I can — (*He sees Andocides and goes to him as in a dream.*) One day you will have a son — and when you do — you will find that he is more precious to you — than even — (*touches his face*) your honor . . (*He drifts off.*)

ANDOCIDES

(*a sigh from his bowels*) Oh, Father — some perverted power has made you deaf to all but words — (*sinks wearily on the steps*) that same power which lashes *me* — from victory to victory — down all the bloody alleys of necessity . . while all my life slips by without my having used it . . (*He hears the echo of his own words and considers their implication.*) But — who am I — to use my life or call it mine. Didymus, dead, is forever The

251

Archer. How must *I* be called in days to come, if my unowned life is taken from me at Syracuse . . (*He is looking at himself dispassionately.*) I was born: Andocides, son of Leogoras, grandson of Andocides the Peacemaker. Heir to the House of Odysseus, grandson of Hermes . . What a charge to greatness. I do not recognize myself in it. No. I am—what I have done. And what I have done since I can remember, is kill, and prepare to kill. For a hundred justified reasons and a hundred necessities of State, I have been the articulate, deadly answer to every question put my race and country . . Were there no alternatives . . Are there none now—in the name of honor . . in the name of pride . . in the name of a country . . or in the name of . . self? Self! What is there to me—I have lusted, with never time for love. Friendships—all shaped on the battlefield. Skills—what else besides destruction am I skilled in. Ambitions? What yet, but to do more efficiently what I have done. This, then, is how I must call myself, to recognize myself, if I should die some soon tomorrow: Andocides the Butcher!

OLD WOMAN

(*off*) Who is there? (*Andocides turns to see a young slave girl enter. She is Adamantea, servant to his great-grandmother.*)

ADAMANTEA

You have disturbed my mistress, Master Andocides.

OLD WOMAN

Who is there—I heard someone— (*She is on. Adamantea turns to support her. She is very old and nearly blind, but quite straight in her bearing: a woman of grace, of great sentiment and feeling, but—like her young companion—devoid of any trace of sentimentality. And, despite her age, she is dryly sophisticated.*)

ANDOCIDES

It is I, Old Woman.

OLD WOMAN

Are you up so early, my son?
This hour is only for the old, who cannot sleep.

ANDOCIDES

It is not only the old who cannot sleep in Athens.
I have not been to bed.

OLD WOMAN

(*smiling*) I see. And which of my sons are you?
I find it hard to tell, these days.

ANDOCIDES

(*gently*) Your sons are all long dead, Old Mother. I am Andocides.

OLD WOMAN

Andocides — Andocides is dead. He was my brave one.

ANDOCIDES

Your *son* is dead. I am his grandson, Old Mother.

OLD WOMAN

Ah! I have you now.

And so you have not been to bed. Were you chasing pleasure through the night, son? (*She smiles.*) Pleasure is a woman's truth, and like a woman, best had by indirection.

ANDOCIDES

(*returning her smile: this is a game they play*) It was not pleasure I pursued. The truths that I was after were men's truths.

OLD WOMAN

(*chuckling*) Then you could not sleep, no matter what your age. And did you manage to evade them?

ANDOCIDES

Evade, Old Woman — why would I evade what I was seeking?

OLD WOMAN

Is that not the way men seek men's truths — as though they were enemies?

ANDOCIDES

(*putting an arm about her*) To hear you talk, a man would think — in spite of all the sons you've borne — you do not like the race.

OLD WOMAN

I've loved men, son — having had small choice else. But I would not be one.

ANDOCIDES

Why not, Old Mother — is it so grand a thing to be a woman? To sit by, while men do all the mighty deeds and wonders?

OLD WOMAN

Not grand, no. But to be a woman is to know who you are — and what is yours. And what man can say that? To be a man is never to see the day one lives. A man worries at the meaning of yesterday and tomorrow — he debates the meaning of infinity — while today's needs hammer at the door for reckoning.

ANDOCIDES

(*smiling*) You disapprove of a man's mind?

OLD WOMAN

No. Only the use he puts it to. For a man seeks Justification, rather than Justice. And to do this, he invented Logic, to defeat the evidence of Sense — using Logic as a club with which to beat the Mind to death.

ANDOCIDES

(*laughing*) If you do not like logic, what would you use in its place?

OLD WOMAN

I cannot say. But it is not a woman's way to call war the Logical Way to Peace. No woman having labored to bring forth life ever glorified death. But a man — not knowing how to live — rushes forth gladly, like a child trying to please its mother, to show that he knows how to die. And only a man — having done so pitifully foolish a thing — would expect the bereaved woman to applaud his wanton childishness.

ANDOCIDES

(*nettled*) Would you have us all be cowards?

OLD WOMAN

(*cutting through the masculine pomposity he is on the verge of assuming*) No. But I would have some of you be braver than you are. What man is brave enough to rise in the Assembly, to tell them that they've spent the treasure of the ages to destroy their enemies — and that their enemies still live. While they and the earth they live upon are the poorer for it. What man will rise to say that as they've spent their wealth and young men, so have their enemies; and that war has failed to solve any problem yet — excepting how to die. What man will dare to say that since war has failed, let us find another way to deal with men: Let us now spend our wealth to restore this earth we've ravaged. Will you rise to say that, son?

ANDOCIDES

(*as to a loved, but un-understanding child*) I cannot, Old Woman. For I think that war is not so simple as you put it.

OLD WOMAN

Then sleep nights, son. Or spend them drinking. Spend them gaily and reverently giving some woman love and pleasure — and perhaps a race of men who one day will grow wise. But do not waste your strength pursuing truth. For Truth sits patiently mendicant on your doorstep, where you shall stumble over it — going and coming — morning and night. I fear we women shall outlive you men of mighty deeds and wonders. And one day we shall inherit the earth.

ANDOCIDES

(*kisses her*) And then you shall laugh at the mistakes of all your simple men-children.

OLD WOMAN

(*returning his kiss*) No. We shall weep. For it will be a barren earth. Come, Adamantea. We shall sit in the sun — and talk women's talk. (*Her irony brings Andocides out of himself. He watches as they go.*)

ANDOCIDES

(*softly*) Well, I shall try what I can with them, Old Mother . . But what *can* I? The Assembly is a beast — its will coiled, poised for conquest. What if I stand against it and — merely anger it — dare I? But dare I not . . I have never once taken my own time into my hands, to use it as I would use it. I have questions I would ask before I'm killed . . or kill another. If I cannot change my Fate, then before I embrace it, I will have it honestly declared for what it is. I will have the Assembly call it — and me with it — by our proper names. (*He turns — with upthrust arms — to the Herm.*)

> Oh, Hermes! Mighty Cousin!
> God of Eloquence and Discourse!
> Let me be your tongue today in the Assembly!
> Help me find the word to bend stiff pride . .

(*The lights are down to silhouette, and his prayer is drowned in a rumble of timpani and roar of voices, as the Assembly members begin to mill about him — baiting him in the dark as they take their places.*)

CHARICLES

SIT DOWN, LITTLE BOY! (*laughter*)

ANDOCIDES

GENTLEMEN, LET ME TALK!

POLYSTRATUS

YOU'VE TALKED ENOUGH! SIT DOWN!

EUPHILETUS

LET HIM SPEAK!

CHARICLES

WE DON'T WANT TO HEAR HIM!

ANDOCIDES

YOU ARE FORCING ME TO SAY WHAT I WOULD NOT SAY!

MENIPPUS

THEN DON'T SAY IT, LITTLE BOY! (*laughter*)

ANDOCIDES

POLYSTRATUS, I HAVE COMPLIED WITH ALL POINTS OF LAW IN PREPARING THIS PRESENTMENT. THE LAW NOW REQUIRES THIS ASSEMBLY TO LET ME READ IT!

POLYSTRATUS

TRUE. BUT THE LAW DOES NOT REQUIRE THIS ASSEMBLY TO LISTEN TO IT. (*laughter*)

ANDOCIDES

THE LAW DOES REQUIRE THEM NOT TO INTERRUPT ME!

Scene 3

The Assembly, later that day. Lights up fast on the Assembly in session: officers to one side, Assembly proper to the other. Alcibiades sits next to the Presiding Officer, Polystratus. Pulyion, as Captain of the Guard, is up center. Andocides, a Presentment in one hand, is facing his tormenters, center.

CHARICLES

(*half-standing in his place*) Gentleman. Observe. Children now instruct their elders in the law. (*The elders laugh patronizingly.*)

ANDOCIDES

When the elders have forgot the law, someone must instruct them, Charicles.

POLYSTRATUS

Young man, we have been very patient with you.

ANDOCIDES

(*turning to his adversary*) Not so patient as I have been with you! And not for a few moments, only — but for a lifetime. I am now past all patience!

VOICES

Oh, sit down! Quiet! Sit down, for the gods' sake!

POLYSTRATUS

Son, I think you had better be seated. You're disrupting —

ANDOCIDES

I demand that you let me finish reading this Presentment!

POLYSTRATUS

Captain Pulyion, if this young man will not be seated —

PULYION

Sir! Andocides and I are comrades in arms.
Would you have me violate both that comradeship *and* the law? (*Meletus, Euphiletus, and Charmides nod vigorous approval from their places on the benches.*)

MENIPPUS

Oh, perish the law — haven't we wasted enough time on this sulky boy? Let us press on to the more urgent business of the fleet.

ANDOCIDES

This is the business of the fleet, Menippus.
What good is the stoutest ship, if the hands upon its oars are enfeebled by doubt? And, gentlemen, there has come among your sons a doubt for

256

which we've found no name — yet we have heard it, plainly, crying in wild lament above the din of battle —

DIOCLIDES

(*calling*) Were you standing still, or running, at the time, Andocides? (*The elders laugh. The young men glare at them.*)

ANDOCIDES

I was pulling my spear from the throat of a youth of Melos, Dioclides. And as his own blood choked him, his eyes caught mine in fatal disbelief. I closed my eyes against his death — for I was weary of that day's killing. And on my wetted lids I saw my home — my city — white and gold in the sun. And a specter in my bowels cried, "What of the cost? What of the cost?"

POLYSTRATUS

You can't see the play without buying your ticket, son.

(*The elders laugh.*)

ANDOCIDES

I have *always* paid the price the gods and this Assembly have asked of me — but not so, you! (*He turns back to the Assembly.*) Gentlemen, I do not complain of the hardships of war. I would merely ask you all this question: If we destroy one people to gain a narrow security for ourselves; if, to fill our purses, we loot another — by what subtle distinction shall our friends recognize us from our enemies? (*applause from the young men*)

CHARICLES

The times offer even our friends hard choices, Andocides. But I would say they will recognize us by our power. (*The elders laugh.*)

ANDOCIDES

Gentlemen! Our forebears once sailed, in pride, from Troy. They, too, scorned the guilt of pride. The gods cast *them* upon alien rocks.

ALCIBIADES

We-ell, the gods are a thousand years older than they were in that far time. They are older, cousin, and wiser, and more prone to see that guilt and pride are only a matter of your point of view. (*The elders laugh.*)

ANDOCIDES

There is no point of view, Commander, which could justify your orders at Melos!

ALCIBIADES

(*urbanely*) Oh, indeed there is. Because we were firm there, those who might otherwise defy us will think long and hard before they dare incur our displeasure — thereby saving Athenian lives. (*He has appealed over Andocides' head to the elders. They respond with a patter of approval.*)

ANDOCIDES

I have fought for seven years without asking such ransom. If my life must now be purchased by the life of a suckling babe, then you may have my life! (*Meletus, Euphiletus, and Charmides nod approval.*)

ALCIBIADES

Not your life, then, but the life of your son. You have fought for only seven years. A suckling babe when *I* began to fight today could kill an Athenian soldier. (*to the Assembly*) I am an Athenian commander! Who loves every valiant Athenian heart committed to my hands! I cannot weep for the death of such an enemy! (*A scattering of fervid applause from the elders. The young men look at them with contempt.*)

ANDOCIDES

Oh, cousin! Say me a better reason for the Slaughter of Melos than that you fear a nursing infant might one day strike down my unborn and un-conceivèd son! Say me a better reason, O Lover of the Valiant. Or you shall have to weep *here*. And *now*. For I shall laugh so bitterly it will split my heart! (*hearty applause from Meletus, Euphiletus, and Charmides*)

ALCIBIADES

All right, cousin! I'll say you a reason! A cold — hard — practical reason: The sea is ours! One way and another it has become ours! From the pillars of Heracles to Judea, from the Propontis to Egypt, it is our sea! And it must remain so! (*solid applause and cheers from the elders*)

MELETUS

Then should we not administer that sea justly?

ALCIBIADES

It was not a question of justice, Meletus. We could not let Melos defy us with a demand for neutrality. Our enemies would have read that as a sign of weakness.

ANDOCIDES

Then let me tell you, Commander, that our *friends* have read the Slaughter as a sign of arrogant desperation! Until the Slaughter, every nation thought us invincible: the serenely strong who could tolerate freedom in others. Our friends now see us as merely stronger than themselves — and dangerously so. They now fear that strength which once they trusted. You have purchased a barren scrap of land at the price of our invincibility! (*The young men respond with vehemence.*)

ALCIBIADES

(*with mock applause*) A talented speech, cousin. It has the same virtue as good poetry — it is idealistic, rather than practical. (*The elders laugh.*) In the workaday world, I'm afraid the weaker *must* yield to the stronger.

ANDOCIDES

(*over the laughter of the elders*) Oh, *you* should have been at Marathon, General. Or Salamis. The Persians — outnumbering us twenty to one — could have sent you to point out that practical fact to our *im*practical grandfathers. Who *im*practically believed free men might break the power of a tyrant. And — believing that — were *im*practical enough to fight, and *win*, a totally *im*practical victory. The gods deliver us from the dead hand of your "practicality"! (*The young men cry*: "Hear! Hear!")

ALCIBIADES

Just a moment, cousin — curb your admirable fervor. We fought Persia only for our independence. We fight now for somewhat larger stakes: we now bestride the world! (*The elders now cry*: "Hear! Hear!")

EUPHILETUS

Give up, Andocides. Poor Athens was just. Rich Athens cannot afford justice.

ALCIBIADES

That puts it rather baldly, Euphiletus, but — (*He shrugs for the crowd. The elders laugh.*)

ANDOCIDES

Well, let us not mince words, gentlemen! If Athens once had a soul which lighted the world, let us say so, and proudly. If she has now pawned that soul, to buy chains with which to secure her possessions, let us say so, too. And if not proudly, at least valiantly. It will not do to "bestride the world" nervously! (*The young men snicker and hoot.*) Gentlemen, the conqueror's mantle does not suit Athenians. Even so arrogant an Athenian as Alcibiades looks, somehow, vaguely comical in purple. (*As he points, a bold snicker from the young men makes Alcibiades flush in anger.*) Citizens, let us shrug off the purple for more humble garb: the rough cloth of penance. Let us say to the world that we have done wrong. And we are sorry. And will atone. (*Meletus and Euphiletus cry*: "Hear! Hear!")

ALCIBIADES

(*in cold fury*) Even our enemies have never suggested that we go into battle on our knees. I find it rather sinister that on the eve of an invasion, you should do so.

ANDOCIDES

Sinister! Oh, cousin — would you play Androcles! Don't challenge my motives. Motives are at issue only at public trial.

ANDROCLES

(*mildly*) In the Assembly, all men are at public trial, Andocides.

ANDOCIDES

Your kind have made it so, Androcles. And our enemies rejoice to see our
honest mistakes equated with high treason. Decent men will now no longer
seek high office. Those men who do are lesser men and timid in their practice. (*The young men cry*: "Hear! Hear!")

DIOCLIDES

By "decent men," I suppose you mean aristocrats?

ANDROCLES

Or oligarchs? (*He smiles.*) You see, I've heard about your little "political"
club.

ANDOCIDES

Only by rumor, I trust. I shouldn't like to think you'd get closer than that.

ANDROCLES

Take care, Andocides. (*Under his geniality, there is a note of threat.*)

ANDOCIDES

(*pause*) Would you threaten me?

CHARMIDES

Yes, cousin, *do* take care. Or he might have one of those "anonymous informers" he keeps on the public payroll — (*points directly at Dioclides*)
lodge a bill of information against you. (*to Dioclides*) By the way, Dioclides, what's the going rate for second-class informers, these days? (*The
Assembly laughs in spite of itself. Dioclides glares in naked hatred.*)

ANDROCLES

When his time comes, Charmides, I'll charge him, myself.

ANDOCIDES

In that charge I'll keep the best company. Promise only that you'll never
praise me. I could never live that down.

ANDROCLES

Much as I've enjoyed this little exchange, I must beg your leave. Affairs
of State. You'll excuse me? (*He makes a little bow and starts off.*)

ANDOCIDES

Only for your absence.

ANDROCLES

(*half-turning*) You're clever, Andocides. Not very, but clever. You'll
bear watching. (*The continuing threat in his manner enrages Andocides.
As he leaves, Andocides retorts.*)

ANDOCIDES

And where shall you watch from — the house you've purchased with the
reputations of better men than yourself! (*He turns now, on Alcibiades.*)
General, I am an Athenian soldier. I sail for Syracuse tomorrow. How do

you charge me with my mission: Do I go to loot its treasury? Then charge me, "Andocides, Brigand of Athens, do thus and so." And I will do it! (*a gasp of shock from the Assembly*) Do I go to extend the war, itself — that in war's confused compulsions, you may call on me to do what I otherwise would not do? (*cries of* "Silence him!" "SILENCE!") Then charge me, "Andocides, Servant of Alcibiades, do thus and so." And I will do it! (*cries of* "Treason!" "Villainy!") DO I GO TO MAKE MY PEOPLE SAFE! (*They are momentarily silent.*) Then charge me, "Andocides, Son of His People —" But when you call me so, explain to me — and all of us here — how I shall make them safe, and from whom. And I will take such a name unto myself and wear it proudly — to victory or my grave. (*again*: "Silence him!" "SILENCE HIM!") How do you charge me, General?

ALCIBIADES

Leogoras, your son is humiliating our tribe.

LEOGORAS

Son, I beg of you, sit down.

ANDOCIDES

Father, will you stand with men who would send me into exile!

LEOGORAS

Exile — what are you talking about?

ANDOCIDES

They would silence me! (*He glares at the Assembly.*) And silence is a kind of exile! (*Leogoras backs into his seat. There are cries of* "SHAME, SHAME!") Yes! It is a shame! Not that I should speak so, but that I should be driven to speak so! This morning, another youth was driven by you even further — (*He holds aloft his tunic of early morning.*) This is all that now remains on earth of gallant Didymus. The rest of him you can see ascending heaven from his funeral pyre — (*He points off.*) Gentlemen, if my words have no power to move your hearts, look now upon his blood! (*He lets the tunic fall open for all to see.*)

ALCIBIADES

(*alert to opportunity*) Andocides! You are standing before a sacred altar. Have you dared to bring a garment defiled by death into these sacred precincts! (*panicky cries from Assembly*: "Unclean!" "UNCLEAN!")

ANDOCIDES

This garment is no more defiled than any of you! (*cries*: "Call the priests!" "UNCLEAN!")

ALCIBIADES

Polystratus, I demand that this Assembly be adjourned until the priests can purify it. (*cries*: "YES!" "WE HAVE BEEN DEFILED!" "UNCLEAN!" *Meletus and Euphiletus try futilely to stem the rout.*)

CHARM VENDOR

ANDOCIDES

Yes! Run! Run! The fierce shadows of warlike babes pursue you! Run! Run!

POLYSTRATUS

Gentlemen, we stand adjourned.

ANDOCIDES

(*as they all bolt*) Run! Run! The breath of a question is at your backs! Oh, Syracuse! These are the mighty men who would storm your walls. (*A rumble of timpani — as of fleeing thousands — drowns his voice. Meletus, Euphiletus, and — to one side — Charmides, watch in concern as darkness swallows them.*)

CHARM VENDOR

(*in the blackout*) Charms — charms against Omens. Charms against Fate. Buy a lucky ch —

CRITIAS

Make way there. Make way for Alcibiades!

CHARM VENDOR

A charm for Alcibiades. Buy a lucky —

CRITIAS

MAKE WAY, YOU BLOODY BASTARD! MAKE WAY, I SAY!

Scene 4

The Market Place, outside the Assembly, a moment later. As the lights come up, Alcibiades and Critias are adjusting their clothing — disarranged by the mob through which they've had to push their way.

CRITIAS

Charms, indeed. (*a malicious smile*) Although, for a while in there, the boy made you look like you needed one.

ALCIBIADES

(*good-humoredly*) You know, Critias, it will be a relief to get back to the simplicities of war. I'm weary of one petty crisis after another.

PISANDER

(*coming on*) Alcibiades! Alcibiades!

ALCIBIADES

(*as he sees the young General*) You see? (*He sighs, then turns — all charm.*)

PISANDER

Alcibiades — a word with you.

ALCIBIADES

Ah, the valiant Pisander. I see that you have your new orders with you.

PISANDER

Yes!

ALCIBIADES

Well, I must ask you not to thank me for them.

PISANDER

(*dumbfounded*) Thank you — for taking away my command?
(*Androcles enters — pausing to watch.*)

ALCIBIADES

Our heroes *deserve* some respite from the risks of war.

PISANDER

Listen — I want my command *back*!

ALCIBIADES

Of course you do. The valiant are always only too eager to offer up their lives to Athens. But Athens must not always take from her brave ones. She must give, too.

PISANDER

No! Listen — !

ALCIBIADES

That is why I said not to thank me. The gift is not really mine. It is Athens who is the giver — my hand, merely the instrument of giving. (*Smiling graciously, he sweeps Critias along with him as he departs.*)

PISANDER

You smiler — you damned, damned smiler! You take, and call it giving. But take care, smiler. For I swear by the almighty gods that if ever your imperial cloak sweeps over my fallen hand, I will grab its folds, and pull you down, and choke you in your own purple!

ANDROCLES

That's a charming thought. But don't you leave too much to chance?

PISANDER

Chance — what chance have I got, but chance? I'm alone! How else could he have stripped me of my little power? And why! Why! He has so much — why should he take away my little?

ANDROCLES

(*offhand*) He had no choice. An embassy from our Allied Generals demanded that the Senate remove you.

PISANDER

(*stunned*) Why — ?

ANDROCLES

They *said* you were the reason they had not been meeting with our General Staff. That they could not — with honor — sit with a man who had slaughtered a beaten people.

PISANDER

But — Alcibiades *ordered* the slaughter. Are they going to sit with him?

ANDROCLES

They are now. (*He chuckles.*) That was the whole point. They had never been asked to sit with the General Staff. Demanding your removal gave them a forceful way to point that out to the Senate. You were merely — a convenience to them.

PISANDER

A convenience — *I* am thrown away for a convenience. Every hand in heaven is turned against me.

ANDROCLES

In heaven, perhaps. But closer to home, there are many who will offer their hands in sympathy.

PISANDER

Sympathy is too soft a word. Give me one that will hold an edge, and I will bury it in his ribs.

ANDROCLES

You might be better advised to join forces with some others, against him.

PISANDER

A conspiracy — ?

ANDROCLES

A *confederacy* — of the more patriotic men of the city.

PISANDER

Well, I'll admit that sounds glossier — it's like you, Androcles, to strike at a man only behind his back.

ANDROCLES

Oh, don't be so virtuous, Pisander. It doesn't suit you.

PISANDER

(*stiffly*) I take it you don't believe in virtue.

ANDROCLES

Only in public, Pisander. *Never* in private.

PISANDER

What good would I be to you? I'm no politician, I'm a soldier — and I haven't even got a command.

ANDROCLES

You *could* have one. An advantageous command.

PISANDER

What.

ANDROCLES

The Home Guard. I have your orders, here.

PISANDER

Aaaah — an office job. I'm no good in an office. I need a battlefield to get ahead on.

ANDROCLES

What is getting ahead? Position — or power? (*The word "power" brings Pisander to attention.*) Power, real power, is here. And this job will keep you close to it . . What's the matter, now?

PISANDER

You smile at me today. But how do I know you won't attack me in the Assembly tomorrow.

ANDROCLES

(*blandly*) You, yourself, can guarantee that.

PISANDER

How?

ANDROCLES

By being above reproach. (*He presses the orders into Pisander's hand.*) Along with your new orders, you'll find a list of likely candidates for your honor guard.

PISANDER

Honor guard — ?

ANDROCLES

For the parade to the embarkation.
Those you choose will be flattered — and obligated to you.
You see? You won't be so alone as you thought.

PISANDER

(*This is moving too fast for him.*) Won't they have picked a guard already — I mean, with the fleet sailing tomorrow —

ANDROCLES

Every commander is entitled to a guard of his own choosing. Besides, I doubt it shall sail tomorrow.

PISANDER

But everything is ready. You proposed the date yourself.

ANDROCLES

Did I? Why bless my soul — how unfortunate that tomorrow begins the Feast of Adonis.

PISANDER

Aah — who cares about a woman's festival —

ANDROCLES

The troops going to the ships will, I can assure you. At every street corner they will meet the city's women — in mourning. Everywhere they turn, women will be singing the Lament for the Dead to the effigies of the dead Adonis. I doubt that the more superstitious of the men will regard it as a good Omen — General Nicias, in particular: *He* examines the bowels of chickens before making a decision to oil his hair. (*He smiles at Pisander's unabashed awe.*) Now, the *next* day — when Adonis rises from the dead — the fleet *may* sail. Amid the women's love, lust in the streets, and rejoicing. Symbolic, don't you think? The delay will be a trivial one. But it will be remembered.

PISANDER

You're clever, Androcles — very clever, indeed.

ANDROCLES

We-ell, thorough, at any rate.

CHARMIDES

(*off — calling*) Andocides — Andocides! (*Andocides runs on from the Assembly, Charmides closely following.*) Andocides — wait! (*Andocides pauses in his flight.*) Where are you going?

ANDOCIDES

(*beside himself*) To Cynosarges. To practice hurdles.

CHARMIDES

Cousin, please — that horse of yours is dangerous enough when you are in command of yourself.

ANDOCIDES

(*icily*) Thank you for your concern, cousin, but I was never more in command of myself. (*He turns and runs off. Charmides shrugs, then turns to see Androcles.*)

ANDROCLES

Well, my boy, should you feel you need me, my house is always open to you. (*Androcles goes. Charmides eyes Pisander as he studies the orders and list for his guard.*)

CHARMIDES

Greetings, Pisander —

266

PISANDER

Hmmm?

CHARMIDES

Are you going to exchange the bronze sword for the verbal dagger?

PISANDER

(*absently*) What — ?

CHARMIDES

I thought you might be contemplating a course in plain and fancy dema-
gogy. (*He gets no response. He shrugs.*) They tell me you hauled me
home last night. I'll do as much for you, sometime. (*He is ready to leave.*)

PISANDER

(*looking up from his orders*) You — you can do something for me now.
You can get me into your club.

CHARMIDES

I don't belong to any club.

PISANDER

Androcles said you did.

CHARMIDES

(*puzzled by his intent manner*) When?

PISANDER

Just now. In the Assembly.

CHARMIDES

(*gets it now*) No, Pisander. He said *Andocides*. Not me.

PISANDER

Well, you're his cousin, for the gods' sake! You could get me into it! With
a political club behind me —

CHARMIDES

"Political" club — there's not one of them old enough to hold office.

PISANDER

But I am! And they have influence — they're from the best families in the
city!

CHARMIDES

Oh, my, yes. Andocides, for instance, is not only descended from the
great Odysseus, but from Hermes, himself. For if tradition is to be believed — as I'm sure you'll agree it must — Odysseus was the great-great-grand-
son of Hermes: the gods took a more personal interest in us — particularly our women — in those days. And, since Andocides and I are from the
same root and branch, you may kneel and kiss my — hand.

PISANDER

(*stiffly*) It's all very well for you to take them lightly, Charmides. You were clothed, from birth, with rank. You don't understand what it's like to be naked before the world.

CHARMIDES

Oh, come, Pisander. You have your own rank — a rank you've earned. To be a general at thirty is no small thing.

PISANDER

(*bitterly*) I thought so, too — until this morning. Now I know that to be *merely* a general, is to be — a convenience. A marker in a game of bones, to be moved about at anyone's whim. That's why I've got to ally myself with the powerful families.

CHARMIDES

Fine. But not with those scatterbrains.

PISANDER

Blast your eyes, I haven't been asked to!

CHARMIDES

Well, I have. And my invitation will reveal to you the level of their profound "political" minds. "Dear Charmides," it said, "I have just received a consignment of uncracked Samian wine and three Ionian slave girls, in the same condition. Would be pleased to have your company for the enjoyment of either, or both." It was signed by that political savant, Master Euphiletus, and I've always treasured it — both for its wit, and its depth of feeling. (*Euphiletus and Meletus, hurrying on, break into elaborate casualness at the sight of Pisander. Pisander looks at them in frustration.*)

PISANDER

Well, then — I'll ask him, myself. He owes me his life. (*He turns abruptly, and goes.*)

EUPHILETUS

(*excited, feverish*) Where did Andocides *go* — we lost him in the crowd.

CHARMIDES

To take his daily fall from that mallet-headed ox he calls a horse.

EUPHILETUS

(*irritated*) At a time like this? (*Behind them, Pulytion enters, crossing toward an exit.*)

CHARMIDES

Oh, he's become fanatically punctual about it. He and the sun disappear over the west wall of the riding academy every afternoon, at precisely the same time. They now change guard by him.

MELETUS

(*intensely*) How was he — feeling?

268

CHARMIDES

How would you feel, Meletus, to be baited like a bull?

PULYTION

(*in passing*) It was quite a speech, though — what he managed to say.

CHARMIDES

(*as if agreeing*) *Unpopular*, but quite a speech.

MELETUS

(*fervent*) Well, I say, more power to him.

CHARMIDES

(*becoming aware of a special urgency in the two boys*) Power, yes. Excess, no.

EUPHILETUS

It's about time we had a little excess on our side. (*He is looking pointedly at Charmides.*)

PULYTION

I'm for excess in moderation — whatever side.

MELETUS

Aaaah — you know what's the matter with you, Pulytion? You have no ambition.

PULYTION

On the contrary. I have a most particular ambition. (*He takes a step or two back toward them.*) Gentlemen, I am twenty-six years old. For seventeen of those twenty-six years, Athens has been at war, or preparing for war. At eighteen, I was blooded in an odd little war that was not quite a war — or so I was told. At twenty, I very nearly was killed, in a peace that almost certainly was not a peace. I was reasonably sanguine about all this — until I took note of a paradox: From victory to victory — in pursuit of Freedom — we had somehow climbed the heights of Conquest. And the view from that high place had made my elders dizzy. Refusing the bright name of conqueror — but refusing to give up the fruits of conquest — yet we conquered. And, gentlemen, I can tell you that victory-in-the-name-of-something-else is bloody expensive. After Melos, I began to have a shrewd suspicion that my elders just might victory me to death. And, so to speak, I went in business for myself — I'm Captain of the Home Guard.

MELETUS

Yes, yes. But what is your ambition.

CHARMIDES

Why, he just told you.

MELETUS

(*exasperated*) What!

PULYTION

To survive.

EUPHILETUS

Is *that* all!

PULYTION

For me (*bows modestly*) it is enough. (*He goes.*)

EUPHILETUS

Survive! Didn't he hear those pigs cheer when Alcibiades called it "our sea"? They're ready to swallow the world, whole. And Alcibiades will drag this war on until we're all old men (*meaningfully stares at Charmides*) unless — somebody — stops — him. (*Meletus glares sharply at Euphiletus.*)

CHARMIDES

What do you have in mind this time, Euphiletus — painting the Athena blue? Peeing on the Prytaneum? You know — the trouble with you two is you have no faith. So I'm going to give you one — something to hang onto when the going is rough: In this best of available worlds, if something can go wrong — it will. (*He surveys them both with level contempt.*) Well, gentlemen, I must be off to pick up my importunate cousin. Judging by the sun, he should be flying over the west wall just about the time I get there. (*He goes.*)

MELETUS

(*furious*) Well, why didn't you just tell him our whole plan!

EUPHILETUS

I would have, if he'd shown the least interest.

MELETUS

What!

EUPHILETUS

He could bring Andocides around, if anyone could.

MELETUS

Now you listen to me — what we've planned is a capital crime —

EUPHILETUS

Not unless we're caught.

MELETUS

Our lives are at stake.

EUPHILETUS

Our lives have been at stake since I can remember — that's what this whole thing is about, isn't it? *Listen*, we'll throw the city into a panic. The troops will think the gods, themselves, are after them!

MELETUS

Yes, but everyone who could even *suspect* us has to be involved!

EUPHILETUS

Suspect *us*? On the night before embarkation — with the city jammed to the rafters with foreign troops? Who would suspect *us* of mutilating the faces of our own patron god?

MELETUS

Well, but, I don't know —

EUPHILETUS

Listen, we'll spread the rumor that the Megarians did it.

MELETUS

Yes, but somebody might see —

EUPHILETUS

Meletus. We'll all be at a *party*. At *your* house. Our slaves will swear to it — if they're ever asked.

MELETUS

Just the same, I think we ought to call it off. The people are too — jumpy.

EUPHILETUS

That's just the point, you idiot! They ran! From just the sight of a little dried blood! Show them a thousand smashed faces of their household god, and we'll scare them to death. They'll be too shaky to *walk* to the ships — much less *sail* them to Syracuse. (*He points, excitedly.*) Just look at those clouds scudding in! By nightfall, you won't be able to see your hand in front of your face — it's going to be perfect!

MELETUS

(*almost convinced*) What about Andocides?

EUPHILETUS

Leave Andocides to me. Just get everyone together at your house.

MELETUS

The boys won't move without Andocides.

EUPHILETUS

I *told* you, I'll take care of him.

MELETUS

(*stubbornly*) How? He as much as called you a traitor.

EUPHILETUS

(*winking*) That was last night. The Assembly has clawed him, since. Just have everyone at your house in two hours. (*Meletus, convinced, starts off, stops.*)

MELETUS

You're sure you can handle him alone?

EUPHILETUS

I can handle him best, alone. (*Meletus grunts, and goes. Euphiletus laughs.*) Tonight, I could move heaven and earth — (*Hurrying clouds darken the air about him. There is a low roll of summer thunder.*) But I will settle for merely — chaos!

CURTAIN

ACT TWO

Scene 1

Androcles' house, before dawn, the next morning. At the rise, a ray of moonlight breaks through scudding clouds and glitters coldly on the face of the Herm, revealing a hideous, jagged disfigurement of its face. There is an urgent tattoo on Androcles' front door. The lights come up on Androcles, in night clothes, working on some papers.

ANDROCLES

(*calling*) Lysippus! Lysippus! What's that confounded racket! LYSIPPUS! What is it! (*The hammering stops.*)

PISANDER

(*off*) It's me — Pisander. (*He comes on in a rush — sword drawn — and runs past Androcles to look at his Herm.*)

ANDROCLES

Oh, god in heaven, man — I was about to go to sleep. Can't it wait until morning — (*He takes in Pisander's sword and armor.*) You're in odd dress for a social call —

PISANDER

This isn't a social call — it's an emergency!

ANDROCLES

Indeed. Well, now that you've disturbed me, I'm all quivering attention. What is it? (*The dryness of his tone unsettles Pisander. He is like a student before a professor held in awe.*)

PISANDER

Someone mutilated the Herms.

ANDROCLES

Have you been drinking?

PISANDER

No! I tell you every Herm in the city has been mutilated. Yours is split off to the ears.

ANDROCLES

I don't believe it. I came in only an hour ago —

PISANDER

Did you *look*? No, of course you didn't. You take it for granted.

ANDROCLES

(*crossing up to him*) Well, how did *you* — (*He now sees his own Herm.*)

PISANDER

A group of us were on our way home from — a brothel. I was on the wall side. Our torches lit up a Herm — right in my eye! Its nose and chin had been split off. Gave me a chill, it was so deliberate-looking. Then I noticed every Herm we were passing was mutilated — I got scared. I pointed them out to my friends — they got as scared as I was. There were four of us. We divided up in two's and combed the neighborhood. There wasn't one image left untouched.

ANDROCLES

Where are your friends, now?

PISANDER

At my house — bound by the most sacred oaths to stay there until I could talk to you. I came here directly on my way to call out the Guard.

ANDROCLES

(*harshly*) The Guard — why!

PISANDER

(*taken aback*) Why — to maintain order —

ANDROCLES

Order! You make a show of force and you'll create a mob — they'll tear you to pieces! The Guardian of their City has been defaced, man!

PISANDER

But I'm the Commander of the Guard —

ANDROCLES

Then let me ask you, "Commander" — have you ever seen an overheated wine jar explode? (*He stares insistently at Pisander.*) Fear is more explosive than wine — if you bottle it up. And every man in those streets out there will be mad with fear that the gods are attacking him — personally! Get in their way and they'll destroy you.

PISANDER

Then we — just let them run wild?

ANDROCLES

By no means. (*He is measuring Pisander. He decides.*) My boy, I am going to teach you how to pick up the weapons of power. Now, listen closely, for we haven't much time: As each citizen discovers the mutilation of his

273

house's Guardian, he will cry out. Hearing his neighbor's cry, there will be an anxious comparing of misfortunes. An angry moiling through the streets. Slowly — almost directionless, at first — they will sweep in a general tide to the Market Place. At that moment — as they enter the Market Place — seeing themselves coming from the four quarters of the city, they will first realize how universal their misfortune is. At that moment — as panic is about to seize them — *you* shall meet them. In full armor. (*Pisander is seeing it all.*) Flanked by a guard of your own choosing. *Not* to head them off. But calmly, with authority and dispatch, to go in pursuit of their desires.

PISANDER

Yes! (*pause: candidly*) How will I know what their desires are?

ANDROCLES

(*smiling at his naiveté*) You will *suggest* them to them. You will call for a Special Committee of Inquiry: demanding that it be given exceptional, emergency powers. You, of course, will be elected to that Committee. But in the general excitement, make certain that someone else is chosen to head it up.

PISANDER

(*indignant*) Why? *I'm* perfectly capable —

ANDROCLES

The criminals will not be found overnight, Pisander. Give someone else the chance to fail — (*lets this sink in*) while *you* are merely zealous in the public interest. After the Committee has been chosen, summon the Senate —

PISANDER

The Senate — I haven't the authority.

ANDROCLES

You will have the authority of the mob in the Market Place. No one will question that authority, and live. Now, as to the Committee itself — the friends who were with you might make a logical choice. Who are they?

PISANDER

Menippus, Polystratus, and Charicles.

ANDROCLES

(*appreciatively*) You keep diverse company, these days. (*He chuckles.*) Fat Charicles in a brothel. Tell me, however does he — (*He breaks off at Pisander's impatient glare.*) Well, never mind. They'll be fine. We'll add — Critias. And — Meletus. That gives us a small, workmanlike Committee, yet represents nearly all political factions — (*grins*) including the youngsters. It's time we began giving them a little responsibility. Now, for the serious work.

PISANDER

There's MORE?

ANDROCLES

My boy, the business of government is work. Mastery of detail. Planning with an end in view. The Assembly will want action. We shall have to give them activity, instead: As first order of business, see that the Committee proposes a large reward for information — say, a thousand drachmae. It shan't produce any spectacular results, but the public is always impressed with large figures, whether they mean anything or not. Then, this evening — when the Assembly and Senate are about to adjourn — you, personally, will decree a reward of ten thousand drachmae.

PISANDER

Ten thousand —

ANDROCLES

It will give the animals something healthy to occupy their minds overnight. And it will make *you* a public hero. (*beginning to steer him to the door*) For a moment, you'll eclipse even our friend, Alcibiades.

PISANDER

(*his face tightening*) I wouldn't be surprised if he were behind this!

ANDROCLES

Oh, come, Pisander. There are limits to which you can indulge an aversion — even to Alcibiades.

PISANDER

(*like a small boy with a "terrible" secret*) I tell you, I know things about him!

ANDROCLES

And I tell *you*, he couldn't possibly have been stupid enough to have done this. He *wants* the invasion of Syracuse, and this catastrophe might just cause that invasion to be called off. Why do you think I'm setting up this Committee for you?

PISANDER

(*still with his "secret"*) Well, all I know is, whoever committed this crime has no reverence for the gods —

ANDROCLES

Have you?

PISANDER

I don't *mock* them! But Alcibiades has not only mocked the gods, he has mocked the Sacred Mysteries of Eleusis!

275

ANDROCLES
What!

PISANDER
At a party. He play-acted the god Dionysius himself. In front of non-initiates. And slaves! At Pulytion's!

ANDROCLES
(*with quiet exultation*) A capital crime — who told you about this party?

PISANDER
Pythonicus.

ANDROCLES
Can Pythonicus prove this?

PISANDER
Yes. His slave's brother was there and saw it. And so did Agariste.

ANDROCLES
A woman, too! Pisander, Alcibiades is a dead man.

PISANDER
(*pulling away*) Well, I don't know about that —

ANDROCLES
(*amused*) Why — I believe you're frightened.

PISANDER
I was thinking of the slave! He'd be afraid of the torture. At the public hearing, he'd deny everything.

ANDROCLES
Then we'll grant him an Immunity from torture.

PISANDER
That's against the law —

ANDROCLES
The people are the law, Pisander. Remember that when your Committee balks — as it will — at something you think best. Hold the people over them like a whip, and you'll soon bring them to heel. (*A woman next door begins the Lament for the Dead.*)

PISANDER
What's that!

ANDROCLES
Just a woman practicing the Lament for the Dead. (*Pisander looks blank. Androcles explains.*) For the festival. Now, go and pick your guard, my boy. (*Pisander starts off, stops, turns, and salutes — sword hilt to heart — then goes. The Lament for the Dead swells up, full voiced, continuing into the next scene.*)

Scene 2

Cross fade to the women's quarters, Andocides' house, a few minutes later. The Old Woman and Adamantea are tending Andocides, who lies unconscious on a low pallet. His head is bandaged and his left arm is strapped to his body with bandages. He is also strapped to his pallet. To one side, weary with sick vigil, Leogoras and Charmides doze. Andocides stirs.

OLD WOMAN

He's becoming conscious. (*The two men go to him, Charmides squatting down to look at him. Andocides opens his eyes.*)

ANDOCIDES

Old — Mother. Hullo — Charmides — (*He tries to sit up. The straps, and Charmides, restrain him.*)

CHARMIDES

(*gently*) Easy. The doctor says you are not to move.

ANDOCIDES

(*struggling, irritated*) Why am I — strapped down!

CHARMIDES

You've had a fall — your collarbone is broken.

LEOGORAS

You — uh — your horse threw you into a wall.

ANDOCIDES

(*straining at his straps*) Undo these straps!

CHARMIDES

(*doubtful, with a look at the others*) All right — but you are not to move. (*He undoes the straps.*) Your head may be broken, too.

ANDOCIDES

What — time is it?

LEOGORAS

Nearly sunrise, I think.

ANDOCIDES

(*sits up — startled*) I've been unconscious all that time?

CHARMIDES

(*concerned, supports him*) In a manner of speaking.

ANDOCIDES

(*pause*) You had all better get some rest. (*to Leogoras' attempt at protest*) I'll be all right.

LEOGORAS

Well, but the doctor —

277

OLD WOMAN

We can manage, the girl and I.

ANDOCIDES

Good night, Father. Good night, cousin. (*as they start off*) Cousin. How did I get here?

CHARMIDES

Euphiletus and I carried you. He thought it was an enormous joke — laughed all the way here. Sleep well, cousin. (*They go.*)

ANDOCIDES

(*after a moment*) Why was I strapped down. *If* I was unconscious? (*The two women look at each other.*)

ADAMANTEA

You had a fever, sir.

ANDOCIDES

And they had to strap me down.

ADAMANTEA

Yes, sir. (*He struggles, shakily, to his feet.*)

OLD WOMAN

You should not be up. You have just ridden your horse into a wall.

ANDOCIDES

(*acidly*) Let us just say that I rode him hard, and neither of us noticed there was a wall. (*He realizes she has trapped him into an admission.*) *I would like to know why I was strapped down like an animal.* (*The girl looks to the Old Woman.*)

ADAMANTEA

Very well, sir . . It was because you said you *were* an animal.

ANDOCIDES

What — ?

ADAMANTEA

A mindless animal. And you cursed *me* for having made you so. (*Incredulous, he looks from her to the Old Woman, and back to her.*) Not really me — you thought I was Athena. You were raging. "Bitch Goddess of the Mind," you called me. "We have built you a temple of bloody splendor. Splendor is what men erect to what they no longer believe in, yet still serve." (*She says the raging words solemnly, in everyday tones, then regards him for a moment.*) You are a strange race. You butcher my people, then mourn — for your own lost nobility.

ANDOCIDES

You are impertinent.

ADAMANTEA

(*meeting his eyes, levelly*) I am the daughter of a king — and my mistress' servant. (*There is a loud hammering on the house door.*)

PISANDER

(*off*) Where is your master?

POLYDOR

(*off*) In the women's quarters, sir, but —

PISANDER

(*off*) Then show me the way. Move! (*Pisander enters, in full armor, with drawn sword — followed by the helpless Polydor.*)

ANDOCIDES

Greetings, Pisander — it's an odd hour, but welcome.

PISANDER

May I see you alone!

ANDOCIDES

Certainly. (*to the Old Woman*) Would you excuse us? (*The Old Woman and two slaves withdraw.*)

PISANDER

(*taking in the bandages — as they go*) What happened to you?

ANDOCIDES

I fell from my horse — nothing serious. (*an awkward pause*) You're in uniform — is this a duty call?

PISANDER

(*seizing the opening*) In a way. We've been attacked!

ANDOCIDES

What?

PISANDER

From inside — every Herm in the city has been desecrated.

ANDOCIDES

Oh, god —

PISANDER

I'm forming a Committee to investigate.

ANDOCIDES

(*as in a nightmare*) And — you want me to serve on the Committee?

PISANDER

No — what I want from you is — get me into your club!

ANDOCIDES

What?

PISANDER

It's the chance of a lifetime! With me running the Committee, and the rich families behind us, we can seize the power — we'll grind the commons under our boots. You and I will rule Athens in a week! (*Self-hypnotized, he doesn't notice that Andocides is staring at him in shock.*) What do you say!

ANDOCIDES

(*softly*) No.

PISANDER

(*not believing his ears*) No, what?

ANDOCIDES

I can't help you.

PISANDER

What do you mean, you can't help me — you've *got* to. You owe me your life!

ANDOCIDES

I owe you gratitude. And gratitude I shall try to repay —

PISANDER

THEN GET ME INTO YOUR CLUB! This is an empire, man — an empire just waiting for us to pick it up.

ANDOCIDES

Then you shall have to try to pick it up alone.

PISANDER

Why? (*His cry is almost that of a small boy. As he searches Andocides' closed face, an angry suspicion mottles his own.*) I'm a commoner — that's why. ISN'T IT! (*He grabs Andocides' free arm and pulls him close, making him gasp with pain.*) I'm not good enough for you! I'm good enough to save your rotten life, but I'm not good enough to sit with you! You'd throw away an empire to keep from rubbing asses with a commoner! (*He shakes Andocides like a rag doll.*) You SNOB! You lousy — snob! You blasted — bloody — aristocrat! (*He slings him in an arc to the floor, still holding him by the good arm. Adamantea enters.*) Andocides, I'm going to climb up over you so high, it will break your stiff neck to look up at me. I am going to step down upon your face and grind it into the dirt. I am going to pull this house down, stone by stone, and sow the ruins with salt. When I get through with you, no one will remember your name, except to curse! (*He hurls Andocides to the floor, stunning him, then looks up to find Adamantea — staring at him in cold hatred — as Leogoras and Charmides run on.*)

LEOGORAS

What is the matter — what's — (*sees Andocides*) happening — ?

PISANDER

Ask the slut. (*He blocks Charmides' attempt to pass him.*) Charmides, you come with me. (*Charmides tries to move by him; he grabs his arm.*) I said, come with me. You're going to be Captain of my Guard.

CHARMIDES

Pulytion is Captain of your Guard. And take your hand off me.

PISANDER

Pulytion will be dead by noon. And you will come with me. (*He releases him. They stare, eye to eye.*) That's an order. (*With a look of contempt at the others, he goes. Charmides, with a stunned look at the others, follows Pisander. Leogoras, in a daze, goes to his son, and Adamantea bends to tend him.*)

(*The lights dim to blackout.*)

VOICES

(*even as the lights fade*) Villains! *Villains!* VILLAINS!

ANDROCLES

COUNTRYMEN! You are sending forth a mighty fleet — upon a perilous expedition! The commander of that fleet — has been holding celebration in *mockery* of the Holy of Holies — the Sacred Mysteries of Eleusis!

(*The lights come up to silhouette the mob in the Market Place and Androcles, in mid-harangue.*)

MOB

Death to Alcibiades! Death to the blasphemers!

ANDROCLES

And there were others with him!

MOB

Death to them! Death!

ANDROCLES

He has done this — in the house of *Pulytion*!

MOB

Death to Pulytion! Death to Pulytion!

ANDROCLES

I can prove this —

MOB

Prove it! Prove it!

ANDROCLES

If you will grant — to *my* witness — an Immunity!

MOB

Grant the Immunity! Grant it! Grant it! DEATH TO PULYTION! KILL HIM!

KILL! Immunity! KILL HIMMMM! (*Timpani thunder up as though they were the mob itself, hit a crescendo; then there is abrupt silence.*)

Scene 3

The Committee Hearing Room, before noon. The lights discover the Committee in a moment of pause: Charicles, up center, presides. Critias, Menippus, and Meletus flank him. Standing, down center, Pisander reads a report. As Captain of the Guard, Charmides is to one side. A recording clerk and a Hoplite guard are in attendance. Among the spectators is Leogoras. Euphiletus — like Pisander, Charmides, and Meletus, in armor — watches nervously, alone and apart.

CRITIAS

Citizen Charicles. While we are waiting for Pulytion to be brought, couldn't we stretch our legs? These benches are hard, and some of us are not so well padded as some others.

CHARICLES

(*with a glare for the allusion to his bulk*) Five minutes' recess. (*Euphiletus signals Meletus to join him.*)

EUPHILETUS

(*low and nervous*) I don't like it. I think Pisander knows something!

MELETUS

He knows what everyone else knows. Get hold of yourself, man!

EUPHILETUS

I c-can't help it — I d-didn't know it would be like this!

MELETUS

(*feeling everyone looking in their direction*) Stop trembling — you're attracting attention!

POLYSTRATUS

Gentlemen. (*Meletus and Euphiletus turn, to see Polystratus just below them. Blood drips from a slight wound on his forehead, and his cloak is torn.*)

CHARICLES

(*shocked*) General Polystratus —

POLYSTRATUS

(*a slight bow*) Citizens.

CHARICLES

You — you're bleeding.

POLYSTRATUS
We were set upon by the mob.

MENIPPUS
What mob?

PISANDER
(*curtly*) Where is the Accused Pulytion?

POLYSTRATUS
The Accused Pulytion is dead.

MENIPPUS
Dead?

POLYSTRATUS
Yes, Menippus. Dead. The mob took him from us and tore him to pieces in the street.

PISANDER
(*sternly*) The Accused was the property of the people.

POLYSTRATUS
The people took him for their property. (*He turns his back on Pisander.*) Citizens, there is one happy exception to this morning's melancholy. On my way to arrest Pulytion, I passed the Great Herm. Of the Aegean Tribe —

ANDROCLES
(*coming on, peremptory*) General Pisander, a word with you.

POLYSTRATUS
(*glaring at Androcles for his rudeness*) As I was saying — I passed the Great Herm of the Acgean Tribe. The one in front of the house of my neighbor, Leogoras. It remains unharmed! (*Meletus grabs the wrist of Euphiletus, and twists it. Pisander — who has had a very interested ear turned toward this news — now joins Androcles.*)

PISANDER
What is it?

ANDROCLES
(*handing him a paper*) Here are the names the slave has denounced, so far.

PISANDER
(*reads*) He — he's denounced two of my Committee!

ANDROCLES
(*nodding*) It will be sticky to handle, but you'll manage.

PISANDER
How? Polystratus, for one, is President of the Assembly. And he's popular with the troops.

283

ANDROCLES

He'll stand Accused — and Pulytion is dead just for being Accused.

PISANDER

He'll fight —

ANDROCLES

If he tries to, just mention that he was a pupil of Anaxagoras.

PISANDER

(*his attention on the Committee*) What Anaxagoras?

ANDROCLES

The Philosopher. He was exiled eighteen years ago, and —

PISANDER

EIGHTEEN YEARS AGO! Eighteen years ago I was a little boy! I don't see —

ANDROCLES

(*between his teeth*) Will you *listen*. I'm spelling it out for you. Anaxagoras was exiled for blasphemy. Polystratus was his pupil. You are charging Polystratus with blasphemy. Do you see the connection, now?

PISANDER

(*relieved*) Of course. Anaxagoras profaned the Mysteries, and —

ANDROCLES

No, stupid! The Mysteries have nothing to do with it! Anaxagoras said the earth eclipsed the moon.

PISANDER

Well — doesn't it?

ANDROCLES

Of course it does, you idiot! But this was eighteen years ago.

PISANDER

You're not being very logical, Androcles.

ANDROCLES

Stick to the record. The record has its own logic.

PISANDER

Yes, but what if he challenges me about the moon?

ANDROCLES

Forget the *moon*! Cut him to pieces with the facts.

PISANDER

What facts! I don't know any facts! I never heard of this man until a minute ago!

ANDROCLES

The facts are that Polystratus was the pupil of a convicted blasphemer. And he is now being charged with the same crime. Those are all the facts you need for our purposes.

PISANDER

No. It's too — flimsy. The Committee would laugh at me.

ANDROCLES

No, my boy. They won't laugh. They may be indignant. But they won't dare laugh.

PISANDER

(*doubtful — but impressed*) Well, but — how will I start? These are some pretty influential people.

ANDROCLES

(*eying him*) I — um — I have an idea. If you've the gall to try it.

PISANDER

What?

ANDROCLES

Suggest to the Committee — and the listening citizens — that the Mutilation may have been an aristocratic plot against the popular power.

PISANDER

That's already been suggested. About an hour ago. By a sour-faced grumbler named Cleobis. But he's a crackpot.

ANDROCLES

Not any longer, he isn't. Recall his testimony to the Committee. Then attack the regulars at Agathon's parties. Now among those regulars have been a number of exiles — (*His voice drops confidentially as he steers Pisander back to the Committee.*)

CRITIAS

Charicles. Pisander is returning. May I suggest we resume the Hearings. (*Charicles nods, and the Committee members take their places.*)

ANDROCLES

(*patting him*) Just jump in and swim, son. Good luck.

PISANDER

Clerk! May I have the testimony of Citizen Cleobis. (*softly, to Androcles*) Isn't Leogoras one of Agathon's regulars?

ANDROCLES

Forget Leogoras. Just concentrate on that list. (*The clerk hands Pisander the testimony.*)

PISANDER

Citizens! I want to recall to your minds this statement by a concerned and loyal citizen: Citizen Cleobis. (*Critias snorts. Pisander glances uncertainly to Androcles, then coldly stares Critias down.*) I quote: "In my opinion this crime was committed by some of those aristocrats." QUESTION: "Why do you say that?" CLEOBIS: "Well, everyone knows they don't like the popular government, and that they'll do anything to undermine the people's confidence in it. Well, this Mutilation undermines our confidence, all right, doesn't it?" (*He stares opaquely at them all.*) That is the end of the statement. I call to your attention that Citizen Cleobis volunteered this valuable information. (*There is a moment of blank amazement from the Committee.*)

CRITIAS

(*too stunned for indignation*) What do you mean "valuable information"? Are you proposing to indict a whole class of citizens because of the unsupported opinion —

PISANDER

(*quickly*) But *is* it unsupported, Critias? Take *your friend*, Agathon, for instance. (*As Critias wilts under this unexpected assault, Androcles, satisfied, leaves.*) Among Agathon's regular visitors have been Diagoras — who only yesterday left us as a convicted blasphemer; Aristophanes — whose open contempt for the common people has already been publicly censured; Euripides — whose *Melanippe* was shouted down by the people for doubting Zeus, himself. (*almost casually*) And then we have Leogoras.

LEOGORAS

(*on his feet*) Sirs. I protest!

PISANDER

For yourself, or for the others I have mentioned?

LEOGORAS

For myself, sir!

PISANDER

You are the one pure flower in Agathon's garden of weeds?

POLYSTRATUS

Pisander, your behavior is shocking.

PISANDER

The *crime* we are investigating is shocking! Citizens! I call to your attention the *fact* that the Herm belonging to Leogoras, *and* his son, Andocides, remained *untouched* last night. While yours — and mine — were desecrated. And I leave it to your imaginations to answer why this is so!

LEOGORAS

Why, you common dirt!

PISANDER

You aristocrats have always found us commoners "dirty" (*There is a cry or two of* "Yes!" *and* "That's so!" *He inflates with it.*) I am glad to appear so in your eyes, today — if to appear so is in the service of the people! (*a faint cheer or two*)

286

LEOGORAS

Charicles. Since you apparently cannot control your Committee, I am going to the Senate to demand that it remove you from office. (*He turns and goes.*)

CHARICLES

(*sternly*) Pisander, you will take your seat.

PISANDER

(*hesitates for only a moment*) Not until I finish what I have to say.

CHARICLES

You will sit, or I shall have you expelled from this Hearing.

PISANDER

(*waving his list*) Then you will force me to read this list to the people in the Market Place. I doubt that they will be pleased to hear that you have ignored testimony which concerns their welfare. (*He plays the spectators.*) Citizens! At this moment, the Senate is hearing the slave Andromachus denounce those who forced him to witness the profaning of the Mysteries at Pulytion's house. The Senate has sent me the names of all those so far denounced!

CHARICLES

Why wasn't the list sent to *me — I'm* the chairman.

PISANDER

(*making it an accusation*) I cannot say, Citizen Charicles. (*cries:* "Let us hear the names!") I shall now read the list: Pulytion — who is dead. Alcibiades. (*a gasp from the crowd*) Archippus. Oenius. Niciades. Panaetius. Archibiades.

CRITIAS

Great God — they're among the finest names in the city!

PISANDER

Exactly.

POLYSTRATUS

Pisander, it is contemptible of you to mention these names in this Hearing. We are here to find out who mutilated the Herms — and nothing else. These men you are naming had nothing to do with that crime.

PISANDER

Ah! But we don't know that, do we, Polystratus? They are — by this testimony — already accused of a related crime. A capital crime. The crime of sacrilege. (*An idea is forming.*) And since you are so concerned with the defense of criminals, suppose you summon these I've just named — (*waves the list to the crowd*) to this Hearing. To defend themselves against the charges we will raise this afternoon. Does that meet with the Committee's approval? (*His sudden, and dangerously personal, attack has un-nerved the Committee. They are aware, too, of the onlookers.*)

CHARICLES

I — I suppose so.

PISANDER

Good. (*to Polystratus*) I suggest you try to get them here alive, this time.

POLYSTRATUS

Do you seriously propose that I arrest my Commander-in-Chief — like a common thief — on the word of a slave?

PISANDER

I'm glad you mentioned that. I'll escort him here, myself. With a guard befitting his exalted rank. Captain Charmides! Assemble my honor guard and report back here. Immediately! (*Charmides — startled — salutes and goes.*)

MELETUS

Uh — Pisander. Why don't I take my platoon and help Polystratus?

PISANDER

Yes. That will — expedite matters. (*He grins and looks at his list.*) If you each take a name or two.

MELETUS

Lieutenant Euphiletus! (*He waves him to his side.*)

PISANDER

(*as Polystratus gets list copy from the clerk*) It is a solemn charge you carry. I remind you: Under the law, you are responsible for your prisoners — and each other — on pain of death. (*With satisfaction, he watches them start off.*)

MELETUS

(*pulling Euphiletus behind Polystratus*) You swore Andocides would take care of his Herm!

EUPHILETUS

He promised! I swear — he promised!

MELETUS

Well, we'll soon see. (*They are off.*)

PISANDER

Clerk. Let me have the schedule of witnesses. (*As he gets it, an angry, two-toned drumbeat — the quick march — approaches in the street below. There is a shout from the street:* "HAIL, ALCIBIADES! ALL HAIL!") What's that commotion — (*Charmides runs on and excitedly salutes.*) Captain Charmides?

CHARMIDES

(*handing him a dispatch*) Word just came that the fleet has voted to support Alcibiades. (*slyly*) That was your honor guard cheering. Sir.

CHARICLES

Oh, my — gentlemen, what shall we do?

MENIPPUS

With the fleet supporting him, to accuse him of a capital crime might force him to — take steps we might all regret.

PISANDER

(*stubbornly*) He is already Accused before the Senate.

MENIPPUS

But in *effect* he has already been tried and exonerated. The men of the fleet are all citizens. And in a majority.

CHARICLES

An *armed* majority. And, Pisander — even your personal guard seems to have gone over to him. (*Amid another cry of* "HAIL, ALCIBIADES!" *the Commander himself sweeps on, followed by a swirl of people — among whom is Androcles.*)

ALCIBIADES

Gentlemen! (*He surveys them contemptuously.*) I have just received word aboard my flagship of certain charges that have been made against me. So that it may be swiftly seen if I am guilty of the acts imputed to me, I demand an immediate trial.

PISANDER

Demand! You hold yourself too high, Alcibiades.

ALCIBIADES

(*with scarcely a glance at him*) It appears that way only to the untalented.

PISANDER

Take care how you anger me, Alcibiades.

ALCIBIADES

My dear fellow, if you knew the exquisite care and consideration I exert in *exactly* how I anger you, you'd be positively grateful. (*The onlookers laugh.*)

PISANDER

I see you don't care what enemies you make!

ALCIBIADES

On the contrary. I choose my enemies as carefully as I choose my sword.

PISANDER

Then count me among them, hereafter!

ALCIBIADES

I wish I could grant you that kindness, Pisander. But your ambition out-reaches itself: An enemy merits respect, if only for being large enough to oppose me. Hence, the best I can do for you is to number you among my minor enthusiasms. (*The laugh of the crowd confirms Pisander's defeat.*) Gentlemen. I repeat. I demand a trial.

CHARICLES

(*looking helplessly to the others*) I — I —

ANDROCLES

(*stepping into the vacuum*) General. In the heat of this fevered moment, I think you mistook the news you heard. There is no thought of a trial.

ALCIBIADES

I'm certain there isn't, Androcles. But charges have been made against me which may not be taken lightly — by anyone. I *demand* a trial. (*He plays the crowd.*) And if found guilty, I desire — as well as deserve — to be put to death. For to live with such an onus on me would be unthink-able. (*The people cheer.*) Citizens! If you believe me guilty, put me to death at once! For it is imprudent (*his eyes going to each of the Commit-tee*) to leave me in command of so great an Army, so vast a Navy, and in command of so many valiant allies, with so serious a charge hanging over me.

ANDROCLES

(*over the cheers: quickly*) General. *Please.* You do us all an injustice, to think that *we* should think ill of *you.* I know I can speak for this Commit-tee when I say that their intent here has been merely to sift all possible in-quiry into a grievous crime. Your name came into these proceedings — by merest chance. (*Pisander turns his back in disgust.*) It shall go out of these proceedings — with the gravest deliberation. (*a scattering of applause from the Committee*)

ALCIBIADES

Very clever. But I prefer exoneration. I insist upon it. I demand it.

ANDROCLES

Alcibiades need never *demand* anything of Athens — he has only to wish for it. (*cries of* "Hear, Hear!") Your reputation is your own best exonera-tion. I appeal to you citizens for the truth of that statement! (*There is a full-bodied cheer. Androcles smiles at Alcibiades.*) General, I can see no reason why you should not sail this afternoon, exactly as planned — with the best wishes of an admiring citizenry, ringing in your ears. (*again, a cheer*)

ALCIBIADES

(*bows, in grudging admiration*) Thank you, Citizen Androcles. (*He turns to the Committee.*) One final word, gentlemen. Do not, I beg of you, receive further slanders against me in my absence. I should not take that kindly. (*He makes a bow which is as much threat as salute, then goes — his cloak sweeping his followers behind him. As the Committee sits — deserted now, and robbed of all purpose — Alcibiades' quick march begins in the street below.*)

ANDROCLES

(*disdainfully*) Gentlemen, it has been a long and eventful morning. I suggest you resume your "deliberations" after lunch.

CHARICLES

(*with indecent haste*) Ah — yes. Gentlemen, we will adjourn. Two hours for lunch.

(*Dim to blackout.*)

MELETUS

(*in the blackout*) Where is your master!

POLYDOR

(*frightened*) In the women's quarters, sir, but —

MELETUS

Get out of my way, or I'll cut you down! (*calling*) Andocides! Andocides!

Scene 4

The women's quarters, Andocides' house, a few minutes later. Andocides, seated and attended by Adamantea, is confronted by the angry Meletus — sword drawn, and dragging the frightened Euphiletus with him as he enters. Polydor helplessly attends.

MELETUS

It won't do you any good to try to run, Andocides.

ADAMANTEA

(*stepping between them*) Please, sir, my master is very ill —

ANDOCIDES

(*as Meletus thrusts her aside*) It is all right, Adamantea. You may both go. (*The two slaves retire.*) Why should I run, Meletus — from a friend?

MELETUS

Why is your Herm undamaged!

ANDOCIDES
Should it be damaged?

MELETUS
(*his sword to Andocides' throat*) Now listen to me — you had better realize that your life is hanging on a proper answer.

EUPHILETUS
Threaten his life — now he's bound to lie! I tell you he said he'd take care of his Herm!

ANDOCIDES
When did I say all this, Euphiletus?

EUPHILETUS
(*brazenly*) Last night, that's when! When I carried you home!

MELETUS
Did he carry you home?

ANDOCIDES
So I'm told.

MELETUS
What do you mean?

ANDOCIDES
I was unconscious.

EUPHILETUS
He's lying — he's lying!

MELETUS
Get that slave in here!

EUPHILETUS
For the gods' sake — you can't believe *her*!

MELETUS
(*ignoring him, to Andocides*) Get that slave in here.

EUPHILETUS
You *can't* take her word against mine — she'll lie! To protect *him*!

MELETUS
(*coldly*) None of my slaves would lie to protect me.

EUPHILETUS
(*desperately reaching for something*) Well, but — none of your slaves is in love with you.

MELETUS
Is that true, Andocides?

EUPHILETUS
Of *course* it's true — everybody knows that!

MELETUS

I don't.

EUPHILETUS

You could tell — by the way she protected him from you. And she'll lie —

MELETUS

Then we'll torture her. (*to Andocides*) Get her in here.

ANDOCIDES

There is no need for torture, Meletus — she is from Melos.

MELETUS

(*as this sinks in*) Euphiletus — you're a dead man.

EUPHILETUS

(*Backing away, he gets Andocides between them.*) No! On my honor, Meletus — on my honor —

LEOGORAS

(*off*) Son! SON! Where ARE you? (*As he enters, Meletus — startled by the interruption — is directly before him.*) Meletus! Good god, man — what are you doing *here*? There's a warrant out for your arrest.

MELETUS

What — ?

LEOGORAS

You've been denounced for sacrilege. Before the Senate.

MELETUS

I don't — believe it —

LEOGORAS

You had better. I've just come from the Senate.

MELETUS

No!

LEOGORAS

And I must ask you to leave this house before you bring suspicion on it.

CHARMIDES

(*off*) DE-TAIL, HALT! REST!

MELETUS

My — god — they've sent a detail to — arrest me —

LEOGORAS

Well, they mustn't find you here.

MELETUS

I'll be — like Pulytion —

LEOGORAS

Meletus. Quickly. Through the alley — (*He points. The terror-stricken man just stares. He leads him, hurriedly, off.*) We'll get you to the Piraeus, and you can lose yourself in the fleet. (*They are gone. Euphiletus stands, uncertain what to do next.*)

ANDOCIDES

(*shocked at Meletus' sudden collapse*) What did he mean — "like Puly-tion"?

EUPHILETUS

He meant, the mob tore him apart! *That's* what he meant! With their barc hands! (*He now knows what has been holding him here, and his tone is deadly earnest.*) And let me tell you, friend: I will *do* anything, *say* any-thing, *swear* anything to keep out of those hands. Remember that when you think of me. *If* you think of me. Remember that.

ANDOCIDES

(*quietly*) I'll remember. And when they catch you — *if* they catch you — remember that you did this to them. Remember that. (*Their estranged leave-taking is interrupted by Charmides' voice.*)

CHARMIDES

(*off, exuberantly*) Hal-LO! Anybody home! Greetings, everyone! (*obviously talking to someone*) Hello, my love — my LOVE!

ANDOCIDES

(*measuredly*) Goodbye, Euphiletus. (*Euphiletus stares impassively. Then, gravely — to his comrade-in-arms — he touches his fist to his heart, and goes.*)

CHARMIDES

(*coming on, his arms about the Old Woman and Adamantea, teasing the girl*) D'you know — you're *almost* as pretty as your sister, Pamphylia. Greetings, cousin. Can you spare some food for my men? I promised them something special. To celebrate. (*He kicks his heels.*) To the short happy end of Pisander the Politician. *And* just in time, too. (*He cocks his head.*) You know — being your cousin is a career I just might want to give up.

ANDOCIDES

(*smiling at his cousin's gay mood*) Why?

CHARMIDES

This morning, it began to develop certain drawbacks — among them, brev-ity. (*pause*) Pisander attacked you and Uncle before the Committee.

ANDOCIDES

On what grounds!

CHARMIDES

Oh, he showed real imagination: He attacked you and Uncle for *not* mu-tilating your Herm. (*Not noticing Andocides' reaction, he blithely pro-*

ceeds.) In a horrible way, it was rather — fascinating. He does have a certain raw talent for slander.

ANDOCIDES

(*to himself*) Then he was *sent* — to arrest me —

CHARMIDES

Arrest you — who? What are you talking about?

ANDOCIDES

Meletus.

CHARMIDES

He was *here*?

ANDOCIDES

(*nodding; pause*) He's fleeing the city, you know.

CHARMIDES

He — *can't*!

ANDOCIDES

He is. He's been denounced.

CHARMIDES

I don't *care* — he's on prisoner detail with Polystratus. If he doesn't report back to the Committee — (*starting off*) Well, maybe my guards can catch him at the gates —

ANDOCIDES

He's going by sea, Charmides.

CHARMIDES

Oh, god — all those ships. (*He runs off. There is a silence — a waiting, throbbing silence the women can feel.*)

ANDOCIDES

(*between his teeth*) My skin is too tight!

OLD WOMAN

(*bringing a damp cloth for his head*) It is the fever.

ANDOCIDES

(*fighting for self-control*) No — it is — something else. (*pause*) My hands are tied! Not to each other, but *to* others!

OLD WOMAN

(*calmly, nodding her head*) Yes. We are all bound, one to another.

ANDOCIDES

You don't understand — violence passes through our door as though it weren't there. And I can do nothing to prevent it. (*trying to tell her, obliquely*) You knew Pulytion. (*pause*) He is dead. (*Her face remains unmoved.*) He is dead. He was torn to pieces in the street. (*She remains impassive.*) By his neighbors. (*She says nothing.*) You are not shocked.

OLD WOMAN

I am shocked, but not surprised. We have practiced the butchering of innocents and strangers. In time, that breaks down a certain nice restraint towards one's own neighbors.

ANDOCIDES

Oh, god! You are being moral when I am being concerned!

OLD WOMAN

In the long run, it is practical to be both.

ANDOCIDES

(*tries to articulate inchoate feeling*) I am trying to tell you! Twice today — I would have killed, if I could have. Something — is seeking us out. Something — implacable. It is thrusting us — in impotent — murdering rage — through our streets and houses, toward a — meeting, a confrontation with — itself.

OLD WOMAN

Is this "something" named Pisander?

ANDOCIDES

(*takes notice of the meaning behind her question*) No. When *I* meet it, it may wear Pisander's face — or someone else's. (*still trying to shape a "feeling"*) But behind that face — will be what guided Didymus' sword into his belly — what tore Pulytion apart — what is likely going to kill Polystratus this afternoon — no matter what.

OLD WOMAN

And you fear it.

ANDOCIDES

I — don't know. I will know — when it is ready to say — what it requires of me.

(*There is a sound: a dagger "thunking" into wood, as the lights dim to blackout. The dagger "thunks" again. Pause. Again.*)

Scene 5

A room off the Hearing Room, later that afternoon. Lights up on Pisander, alone, poised angrily to throw his dagger into the floor.

PISANDER

I am — a misbegotten *wretch*! (*He throws, talking as he retrieves, accenting the word on which he throws.*)
Bred on promises of *crumbs*!

A sparrow among *hawks*!
But I can hate like a *hawk*!
Like an eagle I can *hate*!
And I will hate, and eat my *crumbs*!
And wait — and *wait*!
And waiting I will hate —

ANDROCLES

(*off*) Pisander — Pisander!

PISANDER

(*poised to throw, growls*) The man who crawls —

ANDROCLES

(*coming on*) Pisander? Tch — aren't you a little old for mumblety-peg? (*Pisander resumes throwing.*) I've been looking for you. The people in the Market Place are demanding action. And I've promised them you'd give it to them.

PISANDER

Me! The whole Committee is against me. (*He throws his dagger again.*) And it will be worse when Polystratus and Meletus get back.

ANDROCLES

(*pause*) Meletus has fled the city. (*Pisander cocks his head in interest.*) So two of your opposition — are disposed of.

PISANDER

(*after considering a moment*) Aaah — it wouldn't matter if I disposed of the whole Committee. I haven't any — weapons.

ANDROCLES

What if I told you I've found a witness who will inform on the Mutilation of the Herms. (*Pisander turns to him. Androcles smiles.*) You won't have to run a diversion, this time.

PISANDER

Who is he?

ANDROCLES

His name is Teucer.

PISANDER

Teucer — what kind of name is that?

ANDROCLES

He's a Megarian.

PISANDER

(*disgusted*) A foreigner — what could he know about it.

ANDROCLES

Everything. He sent word from hiding that he was one of the actual Mutilators. (*pause*) He's also eager to inform on the profaning of the Mysteries.

PISANDER

(*already preoccupied with his climb back to power*) Well, don't worry about *that*. I'll steer him clear of the Mysteries.

ANDROCLES

You'll do nothing of the sort! I want Pulytion's party and the Mutilation coupled together in the public mind!

PISANDER

And get me involved with Alcibiades again — no, thank you.

ANDROCLES

You will do as I say!

PISANDER

Don't try to Hector me, Androcles. I watched you crawl on your belly to him. It was disgusting.

ANDROCLES

(*amazed, and with growing indignation*) Why you stupid ass —I smashed him! He wanted a trial, with his army about him — a travesty of a trial. But I smashed him! And he knew it! And now I'm going to put the seal to his ruin: I am going to hear charges against him, then order his arrest in the field. And *you* are going to do as I tell you, or by heaven, I'll drag you before the people as an incompetent — I'll break you back to the ranks!

PISANDER

(*pause*) Can this foreigner prove what he says?

ANDROCLES

He doesn't have to *prove* anything — he's going to admit to the crime. He's going to *confess*. He was in a club with Euphiletus.

PISANDER

A club with Euphiletus — Androcles, go and get your informer. (*As Androcles goes, Pisander begins to laugh — it is an exultation so pure it is almost innocent.*)

(*As the lights dim to blackout a slow, muffled roll of funeral drums begins, and grows louder as they approach in the street below.*)

Scene 6

The women's quarters, Andocides' house, a little later. Andocides watches the funeral cortege approach in the street below. The drums cease. A moment of silence. The drums resume, accompanied by the Lament for the Dead.

LEOGORAS

(*off*) Son — son?

ANDOCIDES

In here, Father. (*with real relief to see him*) I'm glad to see you home, Father.

LEOGORAS

(*preoccupied, he goes to the window*) Has Charmides returned?

ANDOCIDES

(*puzzled by his agitation*) No —

LEOGORAS

(*pacing*) Damn — I wonder what's keeping him. Well, if he doesn't come in time, he'll have to fend for himself. Our ship sails in an hour.

ANDOCIDES

Ship?

LEOGORAS

Yes, ship. I've arranged passage for us on a merchant ship. Well, don't stand about — pack your things. The captain won't wait, you know. (*He starts off to pack.*)

ANDOCIDES

Will the captain take the women?

LEOGORAS

(*as though answering his question*) We are going to flee this godforsaken city while we can.

ANDOCIDES

Yes, but what about the women?

LEOGORAS

They've arrested Philocrates. A member of the High Court. They're taking Polystratus away right now. To execute him!

ANDOCIDES

Yes, but —

LEOGORAS

When my country accepts the unsupported word of equivocal men to ruin her best citizens, then I am going elsewhere.

ANDOCIDES

Father —

LEOGORAS

What *are* you babbling about!

ANDOCIDES

The women — will the ship captain take the women? In time of war?

LEOGORAS

War — what's war got to do with it: he's a Phoenician. For enough money, he'll take anything.

ANDOCIDES

Good! (*He calls.*) Old Mother — Adamantea! Come in here, please. Quickly!

LEOGORAS

I'm going to pack. Now, don't stand dawdling, son. The ship sails in an hour. (*He is gone.*)

OLD WOMAN

(*coming on, assisted by Adamantea*) What is it, son? What is it?

ANDOCIDES

You must pack everything you'll need for a trip.

OLD WOMAN

What?

ANDOCIDES

You're leaving the city. On a ship.

OLD WOMAN

You've lost your mind. Women on the sea — in wartime!

ANDOCIDES

It's all right. The captain will take you — he's a — Phoenician.

OLD WOMAN

I've no doubt. Me, grudgingly. Adamantea with delight. And a nice purse he'd get for the pair of us.

ANDOCIDES

What are you talking about?

OLD WOMAN

Slavery. Why else do you think a ship captain would take us — He'd sell Adamantea to a Persian for a toy, and me for a blind freak — if he didn't cut me up for fish bait. We'll not budge.

ANDOCIDES

Old Woman, you are tying my hands. I need you out of the city — out of reach of the Committee's reprisal.

OLD WOMAN

You are free to do as you will. No one in Athens would dare touch an old crone like me.

ANDOCIDES

The Committee could humiliate you.

OLD WOMAN

It has taken eighty years to fashion me.
They are only the stuff of a bad moment.
You are free to act.

ANDOCIDES

(*pause*) Any slave in this house could be tortured. At least let us give *her* her freedom, and get her into the city. (*The Old Woman looks to the girl.*)

ADAMANTEA

And what should I do in the city — become a whore, like my sister, Pamphylia? Whose greatest lure is that she's the daughter of a conquered king? That novelty would wear off as soon as the next princess set up shop.

ANDOCIDES

(*kindly*) You might become a wife.

ADAMANTEA

An undowered foreigner, in a city that has contempt for foreigners? You are romantic, sir.

ANDOCIDES

(*simply, without flattery*) You have beauty to offer in place of wealth.

ADAMANTEA

A fool's dower, sir. Such an Athenian as I might get by beauty would be lost to me with beauty's loss.

ANDOCIDES

(*vexed; again without flattery*) That's nonsense. Your beauty will never grow less — only different.

ADAMANTEA

(*pause*) If freedom is to be truly freedom, sir, then should it not be at my option?

ANDOCIDES

I — suppose so.

ADAMANTEA

(*firmly*) Then I shall claim it at a later time. For the present, I will stay with my mistress. (*pause, levelly*) And you are free to — to do as you will.

LEOGORAS

(*bustling on*) Son, why haven't you packed? The ship won't wait for —

ANDOCIDES

(*with a look at the women*) I'm not going, Father.

LEOGORAS

Now, you listen to me —

ANDOCIDES

No, Father. *You* listen to me. There is something I must do. Something I could not do while you were within reach of Pisander.

CHARMIDES

(*off*) Uncle? Uncle?

LEOGORAS

In here, nephew! (*to Andocides, wary*) What is it?

ANDOCIDES

I am going before the Senate tomorrow. To denounce Euphiletus.

CHARMIDES

(*at the entrance*) Then you will denounce a dead man.

ANDOCIDES AND LEOGORAS

What!

CHARMIDES

(*grimly*) Eighteen members of your club have been denounced by an informer. Euphiletus is already executed. The others are being seized at this moment.

LEOGORAS

You see! Now will you hurry —

CHARMIDES

(*staying him*) Uncle. I've brought someone to see you.

LEOGORAS

No time, nephew. Not a moment to lose. The boat sails —

CHARMIDES

If you don't see this man — if he tells Pisander what he told me, Pisander's men will never let you set foot on that boat. (*He turns and calls.*) You may come in, now, Dioclides.

LEOGORAS

Dioclides — in my house!

DIOCLIDES

(*coming on, blandly*) Yes, well — we all have to accommodate ourselves, these days, Leogoras.

LEOGORAS

(*stiffly*) My nephew tells me you have something to say to me.

DIOCLIDES

(*affably*) Yes. You might say I have.

LEOGORAS

Well, what *is* it?

DIOCLIDES

Patience, friend — a thing like this takes telling. I'm just thinking how to begin. (*He is relishing the moment.*) Ah! You know I have a slave employed in the silver mines at Laurium? Well, this morning his wages for the month were due. It is a long trip, so I retired early last night. (*He chuckles.*) Too early, it would seem — for I awoke and, feeling refreshed, I thought it was morning. So I started on my journey by bright moonlight and — for a time — the torches of the revelers.

Well, gentlemen, it was very pleasant to be abroad in our festive city on a spring night. Until I got away from the crowds: then I began to feel an ominous chill. Isn't that strange? It was quite warm, really. But there it was — like a foreboding, so to speak.

Then coming to the Temple of Dionysius, I heard a low murmuring, and suddenly — I saw a great number of men descending the stairs from the Odeum into the Auditorium. They were conducting themselves in a manner to arouse my suspicions. Of what, I didn't know, of course — but there they were — like the chill: suspicions. So I retired quietly into the darkness and sat between the columns, under the statue of a general — Cimon, I think it was, but I can't be sure.

Well, gentlemen, there were — at least three hundred men, collected in little groups, whispering and talking in low tones. I couldn't hear exactly what they were saying — only a cryptic word or two. But I listened for some time, and then continued on my way to Laurium. I've only just now returned.

LEOGORAS

(*During this ominously innocent, and seemingly pointless recital, he has had to rein hard on his impatience.*) That's all very interesting. I fail to see what it has to do with me. (*He starts to leave.*)

ANDOCIDES

Why his point is perfectly clear, Father. Dioclides wants you to know that if the place is dark enough, and he is quiet enough, he can edge up to the company of men.

CHARMIDES

(*anxiously*) Please excuse him — he is ill.

DIOCLIDES

Oh, I would excuse a man like Andocides — for almost anything. Well,

303

to continue with my story: When I got back to the city, I heard about the Mutilation — and the ten thousand drachmae reward for information concerning the criminals. So I remembered those men I saw, and — well, I thought it would be friendlier if I told my story to someone in your family, before I told it to Pisander — to see what arrangements we could make.

ANDOCIDES

Arrangements for what.

DIOCLIDES

(*ignoring him*) As I said, Leogoras, I watched them for quite a while. And I recognized nearly all of them. I — uh — don't recall them all at once, but I *can* remember about fourteen or fifteen of your relatives. And *you*, of course.

ANDOCIDES

You — filthy — liar. You scum! (*He raises his hand as though to hit him.*) Get out of this house!

DIOCLIDES

(*ducking behind Charmides*) Oh, I wouldn't be too hasty, friend.

CHARMIDES

Wait, cousin, you don't understand —

ANDOCIDES

Get out! Get out, or by heaven, I'll kill you!

DIOCLIDES

I wouldn't do that, friend. I've left a letter with another friend, naming your father if anything happens to me. Now, you wouldn't want to cause your father's death like that poor boy in the story — would you? (*Andocides slowly lowers his arm.*) That's better — the soft answer is always better than the hard blow. Now. About my story.

ANDOCIDES

Oh, tell your story where you will. Last night my father dined at Agathon's house. In a company of distinguished men.

DIOCLIDES

I shouldn't rely on Agathon, if I were you — I hear he's left town. And all the men denounced so far have been distinguished men. Then, too, there's the point that — once someone is denounced — that cancels out his corroborative testimony, so to speak, doesn't it. I mean, he becomes equivocal then, doesn't he? Now — some of the men I saw might very well turn out to be Agathon's guests, mightn't they. And look at *you* — all bandages. Just the sort of thing that could have come from last night's esca-

pade. You can see — with all these considerations — why I came to you
first, rather than Pisander.

ANDOCIDES

Well, now you've told us. You may go.

LEOGORAS

How much do you want?

ANDOCIDES

Father. No one would believe that yarn for five minutes.

LEOGORAS

That would be quite long enough. I have no desire to have my innocence
affirmed posthumously. (*to Dioclides*) How much do you want?

DIOCLIDES

Oh — I'd say — two talents of silver.

LEOGORAS

Two talents!

DIOCLIDES

(*shrugging*) Yes, well — the cost of living is high, right now.

LEOGORAS

I haven't anything like that sum.

DIOCLIDES

Oh, but this is a family matter — I'm sure your relatives will want to share
the burden with you.

LEOGORAS

Even so, it will take time.

DIOCLIDES

Oh, come now, Leogoras, don't fret. We are all friendly here. Take all
the time you need. Take, say — a month. Is that agreeable? (*He takes
their silence as acceptance.*) Well, then. I'll leave you gentlemen to your
affairs — my dear wife will have dinner waiting for me. Good night, gentlemen. I'll let myself out. (*He goes.*)

CHARMIDES

The high cost of living —

LEOGORAS

"Look to your house," Diagoras said. "Look to your house." Great gods,
was that only yesterday — it seems another age ago.

OLD WOMAN

It was — its calendar ran out of days . . they are already legend . .
(*Though she seems to go far away in her mind, she holds their attention
hypnotically.*) I am an old woman . . yet I recall a day in that calendar,
and a man who made that day resound with his high call for valor . .

You boys were too young to remember that day, but you should recall it, grandson. You voted in his favor, that day. And came home full of exultation.

LEOGORAS

What day — who?

OLD WOMAN

Pericles — the day he gave answer to the Assembly's gravest question. How you made these halls ring with his words. (*She recites, in matter-of-fact tones.*) "It must be thoroughly understood that war is a necessity. And that out of the greatest dangers, nations and men acquire the greatest glory. This is an answer to Sparta agreeable to both the rights and the dignity of Athens." Do you remember that, grandson?

LEOGORAS

What on earth are you talking about?

OLD WOMAN

A calendar. It is now seventeen years since that great day, the calendar is run out: the men — the jury — to whom you might have trusted your honor lie wasted; and the only rights and dignity left to you now are at the mercy of an informer.

LEOGORAS

Oh, peace, woman — you're talking nonsense.

OLD WOMAN

Perhaps I am. Well, I am an old woman. I have outlived famine, earthquake, and plague. Perhaps I have outlived sense, too. (*She holds his eye for a moment.*) As you say, I talk nonsense. Well, I am an old woman, and I have outlived my time. (*She starts off, followed by Adamantea. At the door, she pauses.*) Perhaps, on that day, there *were* no other choices. And certainly Pericles is held in high opinion, still. Yet my son, your father, was called Andocides the Peacemaker, and the Spartans — when he made peace with them — were no better than they are now. But *we* were. (*She regards them all. It is a farewell.*) I will take my leave, now. (*With a slight bow of the head, she goes. The two young men look after her, then at each other, then at Leogoras.*)

CHARMIDES

So that was what he said. The day you voted. (*to Andocides*) Well, after all, it was — agreeable.

ANDOCIDES

Yes. We must not forget that it was — agreeable.

LEOGORAS

Boys — you mustn't — There *was* no other choice that day. We would have lost face —

ANDOCIDES

Yes. (*pause*) And one must never lose face. Must one.

CURTAIN

ACT THREE

Scene 1

Andocides' house, early morning, a month later. At the rise, Andocides is staring out over the city. His wounds are healed. A sleepy cock crows his morning herald. It is a desultory crowing — as though he is, perhaps, having second thoughts about it.

ANDOCIDES

That's right, old fellow — go back to sleep. There is no joy in announcing a day when men must answer to a Dioclides. (*Leogoras enters.*) You're up early, Father.

LEOGORAS

(*trying to cover agitation*) I've just come from Agathon's.

ANDOCIDES

(*surprised*) He's returned from Crete?

LEOGORAS

(*nodding*) He feels that Androcles will let the public hysteria die down, now that the commons have condemned Alcibiades for him.

ANDOCIDES

(*watching his father*) Was the party as brilliant as ever?

LEOGORAS

Party — I went like a beggar to ask him for eight thousand drachmae.

ANDOCIDES

And he refused.

LEOGORAS

No. (*Andocides is surprised, again.*) When I told him that in one month, all I had been able to scrape together in this godforsaken city was four thousand drachmae, he clucked his tongue, and wagged his head in that irritating way he has. "Well," he said, "with this dreadful little war dragging on so, people are inclined to hug their purses to their bosoms. But we are friends, and you shall have what you require."

307

ANDOCIDES

Eight thousand drachmae is a lot of money — does he know what you want it for?

LEOGORAS

Why else do you think he would give me such a sum! He sees the danger to himself, should Dioclides denounce *us*.

ANDOCIDES

(*still can't believe it*) You're really going to give Dioclides the money.

LEOGORAS

(*bitterly*) No.

ANDOCIDES

I'm relieved to hear it.

LEOGORAS

Because I can't! I haven't got it! Agathon came back, but he left his precious gold in Crete!

ANDOCIDES

What does it matter? No one will believe Dioclides, now — you, yourself, just said the hysteria will die down, now.

LEOGORAS

I said nothing of the kind — I said *Agathon* thinks so!

ANDOCIDES

And so do I. Androcles has his victim.

LEOGORAS

On *paper* — only madmen think they can kill on paper! In a few days that "dead man" will be outside our walls crying for vengeance. At the head of a very *live* Spartan army. The "dead man" has sold his sword.

ANDOCIDES

(*taking this in, calmly*) Well, our walls are as thick as our skins — they'll withstand Alcibiades.

LEOGORAS

Those same walls will lock us in! In the Market Place they are already guessing at the numbers in his army — each guess larger than the last. They are frightening themselves out of their wits. And Dioclides will accuse us before *them*.

ANDOCIDES

(*alarmed, now*) We must get you away.

LEOGORAS

There's no way out, son — the gates are closed against the Spartan patrols. I've been to the harbor — no ships for two days. There's no way out.

ANDOCIDES

(*putting an arm about his shoulders*) Well, then — you and I shall have to stand before our judges, together.

(*Dim to blackout. A processional of triumph — cymbals, flutes, triangles — swells up: a drunken, raffish march, with cheering crowds.*)

Scene 2

Androcles' house, just before noon. Menippus, with as much patience as he can muster, is watching Androcles at work over a paper. Androcles, with relish, writes a decisive signature, then looks up.

ANDROCLES

There! It's finished! Officially! All that remains of Alcibiades is his house, and this afternoon we'll start pulling that down. Sorry to have kept you waiting, Menippus. (*He cocks his head at a roar from the crowd in the processional.*) What's that — did we win a victory?

MENIPPUS

(*with venom*) The city is taking Dioclides to a hero's luncheon at the Prytaneum.

ANDROCLES

What are you talking about?

MENIPPUS

Dioclides — and your vicious protégé.

ANDROCLES

Oh, don't be so hard on the boy. He's just been carrying on a diversionary operation for me, so to speak.

MENIPPUS

He's a mad dog — while you've been killing a man on paper, he's been condemning innocent men out of hand!

ANDROCLES

Oh, perhaps a few innocents *have* been inconvenienced — had to flee the city, or had their purses taxed a bit. But you can't make an omelet without breaking eggs.

MENIPPUS

Breaking eggs — we are in mortal danger. Pisander rants at the mob and they sweep all law aside!

ANDROCLES

Keep calm, Menippus. Sidestepping the law in an emergency is a convenience, merely. When the emergency is past — as it is now — we return to our customary ways. And when we do, we find the law intact — waiting only for us to invoke it. Law, Menippus, is really nothing more than custom — canonized.

MENIPPUS

Well, it's become the custom to ignore the law. This morning, a very old custom was swept away completely — two Senators were seized on the floor of the Senate!

ANDROCLES

What — ?

MENIPPUS

Yes! Dioclides charged that the Mutilation was a massive plot against the democracy —

ANDROCLES

Don't be ridiculous.

MENIPPUS

(*grimly*) At least three hundred aristocrats are in the plot, he said. To start things off, he named fifty-two "conspirators" — beginning with Senators Mantitheus and Apsephion.

ANDROCLES

But everyone *knows* — it was those *boys*.

MENIPPUS

(*riding over him*) "Repeal the decree against torture," Pisander demanded. "So that Senators who have been informed against can be tortured — " (*He drives his imitation of Pisander, hard.*) "A single night must not pass without our discovering *all* the criminals in our midst!" *And the Senate cheered him!* It was horrible. The Accused grabbed the horns of the Senate altar, crying, "Sanctuary — Sanctuary — " They groveled on the floor, begging us all not to torture them. Myron and Phorbas couldn't stand it, and stepped forward to act as sureties for them. *They* are now dead.

ANDROCLES

Dead —

MENIPPUS

Yes! Dead! The Accused fled. Myron and Phorbas were killed in their place. There's your bloody omelet. (*He flings a roll of papers on Androcles' desk.*)

ANDROCLES

Oh, dear god —

MENIPPUS

Go on, read it. It's Dioclides' statement.

ANDROCLES

(*picks up the papers with an unsure hand; after only a moment*) This is a parcel of lies — from the first statement. There was no moon that night — it was overcast.

MENIPPUS

There's a moon, now. The overcast has been repealed.

ANDROCLES

We'll see about that. (*He calls.*) LYSIPPUS! (*to Menippus*) I can't undo what Pisander's done, Menippus. But I can, and will, stop him from doing any further damage.

MENIPPUS

Then you had better hurry. Leogoras and his whole family are already in prison. In chains.

ANDROCLES

In chains — they're citizens!

MENIPPUS

Pisander ordered chains. The Committee does just as he says. (*Lysippus enters.*)

ANDROCLES

Well, he'll do as I say. Lysippus, go to the Prytaneum and tell General Pisander I want to see him here. Immediately. (*Lysippus goes.*) Will you stay to lunch?

MENIPPUS

I don't think it would be wise for me to be here when he comes. If he comes.

ANDROCLES

He'll come. If he knows what's good for him, he'll come.
(*Dim to blackout. The processional march fades up.*)

Scene 3

A prison cell, same time. A shaft of light from the high cell-window pierces the dark. Andocides stares at his shackled wrists.

ANDOCIDES

In chains — in chains — that he could bring me here, in chains, stands me before the civil justice, in fact, condemned. And with me all my House — (*He thrusts his face to heaven.*) O Great Zeus, Who guards the Brave and Free, how may the Helpless pray to you? I stand before you suppliant, with courage useless to me — (*Aware of a presence at the edge of the light, he breaks off. Warily, he turns.*) Who is there . . Pisander? . . Who is there?

ADAMANTEA

It is Adamantea. (*She steps into the light, with a grave dignity.*) Of Melos.

ANDOCIDES

(*Her manner arrests, and puzzles, him.*) *Not* Adamantea of the House of Leogoras —

ADAMANTEA

No. She would not have come. *I* come of my own will.

ANDOCIDES

I see. (*To match her demeanor, he bows, gravely.*) Then, welcome — Adamantea of Melos.

ADAMANTEA

I have brought you food.

ANDOCIDES

Thank you. (*pause*) Will you rest? (*She accepts a place, on the tier, as though she were at court.*) How did you get in?

ADAMANTEA

(*as a commonplace*) I bribed the guards. (*pause*) It is damp here.

ANDOCIDES

I doubt it will matter much. I shan't be here long.

ADAMANTEA

(*considers how to begin*) I overheard your prayer.

ANDOCIDES

(*nettled by her intent stare*) Yes?

ADAMANTEA

It was a foolish prayer, I think.

ANDOCIDES

Do you, indeed.

ADAMANTEA

(*ignoring his cold tone, simply*) Yes. I have learned that one cannot pray the gods for help against the gods. One must pray for the attainable.

ANDOCIDES

(*nonplused*) Really . . And what would *you* pray for? In my condition.

ADAMANTEA

(*gravely sincere, devoid of pity*) I think — strength to endure what must be endured. Or a quick death.

ANDOCIDES

(*at a loss*) I see. And you came here — to tell me that, child?

ADAMANTEA

(*a fact: for the record*) I am not a child. I have been betrothed.

ANDOCIDES

I see.

ADAMANTEA

I might now be carrying a king beneath my heart, had you — had Athens not come to Melos.

ANDOCIDES

(*jarred, flatly*) I see.

ADAMANTEA

Do you? *What* do you see?

ANDOCIDES

Adamantea. Avenger of her House.

ADAMANTEA

You are sentimental.

ANDOCIDES

How do you mean?

ADAMANTEA

Revenge is for children. Or weaklings.

ANDOCIDES

Then — why have you come?

ADAMANTEA

(*pause*) To bring you this. (*The jeweled scabbard of the dagger she takes from her cloak glitters in the light. She offers it as though it explains itself.*) It is called "The King's Messenger" — my father's dagger.

ANDOCIDES

(*As he takes it, he looks sharply at her.*) You have heard that — they will torture me.

ADAMANTEA

(*startled*) No.

ANDOCIDES

(*watching her face closely*) This is not — a mercy, then.

ADAMANTEA

No.

ANDOCIDES

(*baffled*) Then what is it?

ADAMANTEA

My dowry.

ANDOCIDES

(*thinks he sees now, smiles*) Well . . (*One must say "something."*) It — it is a very rich one.

ADAMANTEA

I am the daughter of a king.

ANDOCIDES

I see. (*briskly*) Well, while my name still has life to it, give me something to write on.

ADAMANTEA

Write?

ANDOCIDES

(*Isn't this what it is all about?*) You have to have a document to claim your freedom.

ADAMANTEA

Freedom — what freedom is there for me here!

ANDOCIDES

Well, but — then freedom to leave.

ADAMANTEA

What ship would take *me* in time of war?

ANDOCIDES

Well, what then, child?

ADAMANTEA

Am I a child? (*She frankly demands his inspection.*) Regard me closely. Don't be embarrassed. I have stood naked in the Market Place. Am I a child?

ANDOCIDES

(*pause*) No.

ADAMANTEA

(*choosing her words carefully*) Then by what you see, tell me what I am.

ANDOCIDES

A woman.

ADAMANTEA

Then I will tell you that by everything you cannot see, I am not. (*pointedly*) And yet I would be.

ANDOCIDES

(*pause*) You'd invite *me* . . to woo?

ADAMANTEA

And to sire my sons.

ANDOCIDES

(*pause*) No.

314

ADAMANTEA

(*confronting him eye to eye*) You said once, that I was beautiful. Am I less so, now?

ANDOCIDES

No.

ADAMANTEA

Then why?

ANDOCIDES

I'm the destroyer of your House.

ADAMANTEA

Who better to restore that House?

ANDOCIDES

No. I am — have been — your enemy.

ADAMANTEA

If the wooer is accepted, he's not enemy, but friend. And you have mercy in you. I would have mercy in my sons.

ANDOCIDES

Adamantea — I'll be dead, tomorrow.

ADAMANTEA

(*relentlessly*) You are alive, now.

ANDOCIDES

I am dishonored.

ADAMANTEA

(*pressing him*) And you will die so. I will teach your son to honor your name. (*She has made a point. More gentle, now.*) Before she died, my mistress and I talked of this — though in a different context. We spoke of what would happen when you were fit to fight again: "How sad," she said, "that he will have no chance to raise up sons. He will likely fall, contesting some inch of alien soil with a stranger, and leave no record of his ever having been."

ANDOCIDES

(*He has been reached, but . .*) Adamantea — I — I am in chains.

ADAMANTEA

Andocides — *I* had thought to be courted. (*With level gaze, she urges.*) If you will raise your chains a little — (*He raises his arms slowly, and she slips under them, to straighten up within their chained circle.*) There. You see — we will manage. (*As he regards her, for the first time a shyness comes over her. It is not coyness — merely innocence.*)

ANDOCIDES

Yes. I see.

ADAMANTEA

(*softly, prompting*) And — do you love me, now?

ANDOCIDES

(*pause*) Yes. I do. And will. And shall — (*remembering her words*) my — friend.

(*As the lights dim on them there is a low rumble of timpani.*)

Scene 4

The Committee Hearing Room, about the same time. Pisander — holding a large scroll before him as though it were a scepter — is staring at it, trancelike, as though it were power, itself.

ANDROCLES

(*striding on*) Pisander!

PISANDER

(*calmly turning; he has acquired an Androclesian polish — with a difference*) Ah! Citizen Androcles.

ANDROCLES

Don't you "ah" and "citizen" me, you insolent puppy. Where have you been?

PISANDER

Why, where I should have been — discharging the sovereign people's business.

ANDROCLES

I sent for you, Pisander.

PISANDER

I could not come.

ANDROCLES

I understand you've accepted Dioclides' statement that the conspiracy numbers three hundred citizens.

PISANDER

You're well informed.

ANDROCLES

To govern, one must be informed, Pisander.

PISANDER

Citizen Androcles. Let me remind you: only the people govern.

ANDROCLES

Do not instruct *me* in what I taught *you* — I gave you power!

316

PISANDER

The people gave me power — you merely showed me where to find it.

ANDROCLES

Pisander, let's not quarrel. I came to ask you not to accept Dioclides' statement.

PISANDER

(*smiles at the change in tactic*) It has already been accepted. And broadcast to the people. (*Behind them, the Committee and Dioclides are coming on, from lunch.*)

ANDROCLES

It could as easily be set aside. Dioclides is a known liar.

PISANDER

Not on the record. On the record — at your vouching — Dioclides is a creditable and accepted witness. (*As he speaks, Dioclides, with laurel on his brow, is being seated.*)

ANDROCLES

I used Dioclides to say only what was substantially the truth! He was a convenience.

PISANDER

And so he is now.

ANDROCLES

His testimony is a palpable fraud!

PISANDER

(*a note of threat*) Is it?

ANDROCLES

All the evidence you've heard points to a little band of young men. Men — most of them were boys. And they have all been punished. Why perpetuate this atmosphere of crisis?

PISANDER

I sorrow to hear that note of timidity in your voice, Androcles. Crisis is the tempered word for opportunity: the sharp-edged sword with which I shall cut my way to absolute power. And do not get in the way of my sword's length — Dioclides has so far remembered only fifty-two of those he saw plotting the Mutilation. He might remember others.

ANDROCLES

You wouldn't dare!

PISANDER

I might not — but Dioclides may: The servitor acquires a natural distaste for the master's arrogance at being master. Think well, my friend, the things you say in future. And to whom. (*Rudely, he turns from An-*

317

drocles.) Charicles. A word with you. (*Pisander joins Charicles. Menippus, who has been watching, now comes to Androcles.*)

MENIPPUS

I take it things did not go as you expected.

ANDROCLES

You were right, and I was wrong. Oh, heaven, how wrong.

MENIPPUS

What do you propose to do now?

ANDROCLES

I'll have to think.

MENIPPUS

There's little time to think. By morning, fifty men will have been condemned and executed.

PISANDER

(*turns from Charicles*) Guard. Call Citizen Andocides. (*The guard goes. He turns to the Committee.*) Gentlemen, I have reason to believe that Citizen Andocides will prove to be one of the principal criminals — if not the organizer of this conspiracy.

CRITIAS

Why? This is the first time Andocides has been mentioned in the case.

PISANDER

Not the first time, Critias. *I* mentioned him on the very first day we convened this Committee. Since then, just observe how often we have encountered him. First, he admits in the Assembly that he belongs to the conspirators' club. (*He looks maliciously at Androcles.*) I believe you will recall that, Androcles. Then, those club members take part in a sacrilegious rite at Pulytion's house. Next, more of his club's members are implicated in the Mutilation, itself. It was Andocides' Herm which was the only one left untouched by the Mutilators —

CRITIAS

(*impatient at such chop-logic*) So far you have implicated only Andocides' friends — not Andocides.

PISANDER

Yes, Critias. But remember: this is a *secret* conspiracy. Yet in spite of its secrecy, Citizen Dioclides (*this next a threat to Critias*) — in recalling some of the three hundred he actually saw plotting the crime — has named not only Andocides, but his whole family. (*as Andocides is pushed on rudely*) Indeed, Critias, it seems that everywhere we turn, we find Andocides.

ANDOCIDES

(*with quiet dignity*) Gentlemen.

PISANDER

Citizen Andocides, son of Leogoras, you are before this Committee of Inquiry, to answer to the charge of secretly conspiring against the State, in time of war. Have you prepared a statement?

ANDOCIDES

I have.

PISANDER

We are prepared to hear it.

ANDOCIDES

(*bypassing him*) Gentlemen, like you, I am a free citizen. (*He thrusts his wrists at them.*) Why am I in chains?

PISANDER

You are charged with conspiracy, in time of war.

ANDOCIDES

Am I then convicted? (*to the others*) Why am I in chains!

CHARICLES

The — uh — Committee thought it best — to — (*He is embarrassed by Andocides' unrelenting stare.*) As a — uh — precautionary measure.

ANDOCIDES

The laws of the State notwithstanding!

PISANDER

We are at war, citizen. The laws of the State were not designed to protect criminals who would aid the enemy.

ANDOCIDES

I am not yet even indicted!

PISANDER

Don't be impatient, citizen. You will be. But we are here to give you an impartial hearing, first.

ANDOCIDES

Then I fear that I am doomed.

PISANDER

(*surprised*) You are going to admit your guilt?

ANDOCIDES

I cannot admit to what I did not do. (*bypassing him, again*) But, gentlemen, I must ask you to be more than impartial. My accuser — on no more evidence than just his word — has obtained enough of your confidence for you to bring me here before you, chained. You must already believe it possible for me to have conspired as charged — or you would not have brought me here in this fashion. My accuser, therefore, has the advantage of me: He has your partly pledged belief, while I must plead with suspicion hanging about me like a deadly pall. And so — because my words must be filtered to you, through this fog of perjured inference — I must ask you, please, for more than impartiality. I must ask you to believe in my innocence.

PISANDER

A clever plea, Andocides. And one to be expected from so skilled an orator.

ANDOCIDES

(*with only a glance at him*) You, too, are clever, Pisander. For how am I charged, gentlemen? I am charged with a *secret* conspiracy. In heaven's name, was there ever a conspiracy that wasn't secret? Yet this word has been insinuated into the charge over and over again. For a purpose: I am charged, in such a fashion, and in such an atmosphere, that if I say, "It is not so," Pisander will say, "You see, gentlemen. He is still a conspirator." The only course of action he would leave open to me is to say that I am guilty. Then Pisander would inflate his chest and say, "You see. It is as I told you."

PISANDER

(*nettled*) Andocides, on the night of the Mutilation you were seen in the company of three hundred other conspirators.

ANDOCIDES

(*as though he weren't there*) Gentlemen, on the night of the Mutilation, I was seen by several people in quite another place. I was confined to my bed with a fractured skull and a fractured collarbone. My horse fell with me that day at Cynosarges.

PISANDER

Wasn't that the same day you attacked our country's war policies in the Assembly!

ANDOCIDES

(*taken aback*) No!

PISANDER

Oh, citizen! Didn't you say that we were wrong at Melos?

ANDOCIDES

Yes! But I did not attack our country's war policies! I *accused* Alcibiades — I accused *him*, of stampeding our people into an action which violated all that we stand for among the Greek nations.

PISANDER

An interesting distinction. You also charged that the Assembly was defiled.

ANDOCIDES

I was speaking figuratively.

PISANDER

A "figurative" defilement. And that night, all the *figures* of our city's Guardian were defiled. Very interesting. But you were saying you fell from a horse — somewhere.

ANDOCIDES

At Cynosarges. Practicing hurdles.

PISANDER

You can prove this, of course.

ANDOCIDES

Harponicus the Physician treated me at my house.

PISANDER

I'm afraid that won't do, citizen. Harponicus has fled — along with the other proven blasphemers.

ANDOCIDES

How proven?

PISANDER

Their flight was a confession of their guilt.

ANDOCIDES

Or their fear.

PISANDER

No innocent man need fear us.

ANDOCIDES

I am innocent. And I fear you.

PISANDER

I am gratified to hear it. But your innocence remains to be proved.

ANDOCIDES

Gentlemen, the hardest thing in the world to prove is innocence. Guilt is easy, both to imply and to admit to. But who was ever criminally charged with innocence?

PISANDER

We're wasting time. Who else saw you bedridden?

ANDOCIDES

Euphiletus.

PISANDER

Who was executed for treason.

ANDOCIDES

Meletus.

PISANDER

Who will be executed if he ever returns to Athens.

ANDOCIDES

My father.

PISANDER

Who is here in prison with you.

ANDOCIDES

Charmides.

PISANDER

Who is similarly charged. Have you no — unequivocal person?

ANDOCIDES

Would you call yourself unequivocal.

PISANDER

Were I a witness in your behalf, certainly. Have you such a person?

ANDOCIDES

(*pause*) One of my slaves.

PISANDER

You offer her for torture, of course.

ANDOCIDES

The slave I refer to is a man. What led you to say "her"?

PISANDER

(*flushing*) You said — you were injured. I assumed you meant a woman.

ANDOCIDES

You assume too much, Pisander.

PISANDER

Then do you offer *him* for torture?

ANDOCIDES

You have condemned some of the best men in Athens, on the testimony
of a slave, given without torture. If you can condemn without torture, you
can exonerate without torture!

PISANDER

And violate the law? Oh, citizen —

ANDOCIDES

You were not so scrupulous when you accepted the testimony of the slave
Andromachus!

PISANDER

We only try to comply with the will of the people, here. Or don't you ap-
prove of the will of the people?

ANDOCIDES

Not when they are being stampeded into rash decisions!

PISANDER

And who is to be the judge of when a decision is rash — you?

ANDOCIDES

If need be, yes!

PISANDER

And if the people make enough rash decisions, your disapproval might take the form of an overt act against them?

ANDOCIDES

No! I believe in government by law. My disapproval is directed against those men who would make Athens into a government by men.

PISANDER

But the people are the law. And the people are men.

ANDOCIDES

And as such are fallible.

PISANDER

Then you regard the people as mere cattle.

ANDOCIDES

I did not say that — ever!

PISANDER

You used the word "stampeded." To me, "stampeded" has always applied only to cattle. Have you any other opinions regarding the people that you wish to air? (*He smiles benignly at Andocides.*) We do want to be fair — if not impartial.

ANDOCIDES

(*pause*) No, gentlemen. I have nothing further to say.

PISANDER

Guard. Take Citizen Andocides to his cell. And bring us his brother-in-law, Citizen Callias. (*as the guard escorts Andocides off*) Gentlemen, I suggest we take a brief recess. We've a long day's work ahead.

CHARICLES

Ten minutes' recess. (*Pisander, in passing, gloats at Androcles — who watches him nearly off, then calls out.*)

ANDROCLES

Charicles — Critias: a word with you.

MENIPPUS

(*scurrying to his side: excitedly*) You've thought of something!

ANDROCLES

I think so.

MENIPPUS

Well, what!

ANDROCLES

(*his eye on the approaching Charicles*) Patience.

CRITIAS

What is it.

ANDROCLES

(*his attention undiverted from Charicles — on whom it remains no matter who is addressed*) I want you three to do something for us all. (*crisply, to Menippus*) You said Pisander told the Senate: "Not one night must pass without our catching all the criminals." (*as Menippus nods*) Good. Then it's on the record. (*to Charicles*) I want you, as chairman — and you two, as the majority of the Committee — to take that record to the people in the Market Place. I want you to recall to their attention that, by Pisander's own count, two hundred and forty-eight of those "criminals" are still at large amongst us.

CRITIAS

You've lost your mind —

CHARICLES

That would be suicide!

ANDROCLES

(*riding over them*) I want you to play up the fact that while the fifty Accused have been occupying our investigations, the *majority* of the numbered "criminals" are free amongst us to do us harm. I want the mob in the Market Place clamoring at your backs *demanding* that you produce the rest of the "criminals" immediately — or give them *other* relief.

CHARICLES

No!

CRITIAS

It's too ridiculous even to consider. (*He turns away.*)

ANDROCLES

(*His cold growl stays them.*) Now you *listen*. (*indicating Menippus*) An hour ago *you* sent this sniveler to me, crying for help. "Stop him," you cried, "or he'll destroy us." And so he shall. Unless you use the Committee. Now. While you can.

CHARICLES

Committee! Pisander *is* the Committee!

ANDROCLES

Only because you've had no weapons with which to fight him. You have one, *now* — he has laid it before your very eyes. You have only to find the will to pick it up and use it. But you must do it *now*. *Now*, and no other time. By this afternoon, it will be dulled and useless: by tomorrow — gone.

But *now* — *now* it is keen and sharp. With it you can cut him off from his power. But you must use it *now*.

CRITIAS

(*irritably*) Why do you keep saying "now," "now" — what is different "now" from "before"!

ANDROCLES

(*quiet amazement*) Have you been too frightened of him even to *listen* to him — he's finally made a mistake. A public mistake — *two* mistakes, as a matter of fact. He's created a Supreme Criminal Expert — with a reserve potential for blackmail by "memory," and —

CHARICLES

And death, too. Don't forget that.

ANDROCLES

(*eying him*) Yes. Death, too. And — let us say — *your* death. If he chooses.

CHARICLES

I intend to give him no reason for choosing so.

ANDROCLES

Andocides gave him no reason — save to stand above him by birth. And who among us does not stand above him by *rank*. (*His eyes bore in on Charicles.*) But you are missing my main point.

CHARICLES

(*uneasily*) How do you mean?

ANDROCLES

The "Supreme Expert" is subornable. Given a little time — a little incentive — he can be used against anyone. *By* anyone — with will enough to use him. (*His eyes go over each of them.*) I have such a will. And you, gentlemen, will be kind enough not to afford me an incentive.

CHARICLES

I — see.

CRITIAS

(*stiffly*) You spoke of two "mistakes." What is the other?

ANDROCLES

(*straight — not sarcastic*) My god — how have such as you dared to play with power? Let me read you what he said — right here, in your presence — not five minutes ago. (*reads from notes*) "Gentlemen, I have reason to believe that Citizen Andocides will prove to be one of the *principal* criminals — if not the *organizer* of this conspiracy."

CRITIAS

(*testily*) And what does *that* mean?

325

ANDROCLES

(*with an edge*) It *means* that he has publicly characterized Andocides. *And* been stupid enough to commit his power to that characterization. He has just used his "Supreme Expert" to create a "Supreme Criminal." (*making certain, now, that they are following him*) We are now going to use that characterization to cut him off from his power —

CHARICLES

(*trying desperately to understand*) How?

ANDROCLES

I'll spell it out for you again: You are going to go before the people in the Market Place to demand that *Pisander's own will* — as expressed before the Senate — be carried out immediately: "Not one night must pass without our catching *all* the criminals in our midst." And — in aid of carrying out Pisander's will — you will ask the people for use of his Chief Criminal: you will demand that they give Andocides an Immunity. So that *he* — and only *he* — can tell us who are the real criminals.

CHARICLES

No! Pisander would — would —

ANDROCLES

What can he do — repudiate his own witness? What are you frightened of! You'll be acting *publicly* — in pursuit of *his* publicly expressed desires, man! And you have his own words, here, to stop his mouth if he objects. (*He holds out his notes.*)

CHARICLES

N-no — you don't know him —

ANDROCLES

It's *because* I know him that I'm telling you what you have to do!

CHARICLES

Then *you* do it!

ANDROCLES

I haven't time! Fifty men will die if I can't persuade Andocides to cooperate while *you* are persuading the people.

CHARICLES

Oh, god — god —

ANDROCLES

Stop blubbering! Just face him down and he'll *yield*. He *will* yield. He has no choice but to *yield*. But only if you face him down.

CHARICLES

Wh-what if I d-do it — and Andocides won't accept?

326

ANDROCLES

(*He is already urging him off.*) There's no time to worry about that. You must go to the people *now*. This *minute*. Before Pisander gets back. (*He motions to the guard.*) Take your guard with you. Use the herald to summon the people. Stand there flanked by all the authority you can summon. And when Pisander gets there — if he gets there — face him down. Make him yield once, and he'll soon get the habit. Now — go! (*They are off. Alone now, he speaks to himself, as he crosses to leave the other way.*) You may even find yourself enjoying it. (*He is off. The Hearing Room is empty for a moment. Then Pisander enters.*)

PISANDER

(*stopping abruptly as he realizes the Committee is gone*) Where is — everyone — ?
(*As the lights dim on him, he freezes and holds. Androcles — followed by the shackled Charmides — peers into the shaft of light from Andocides' cell window.*)

ANDROCLES

Andocides — ?

ANDOCIDES

(*stepping into the light*) Well. Androcles. Has the contagion spread to you? Suspicion is a disease easily caught, these days. Greetings, cousin.

ANDROCLES

I — I hope I'm welcome, too, Andocides.

ANDOCIDES

You are, indeed. I cannot think of anyone in all the city more welcome to share my fate. Or more deserving.

ANDROCLES

I must confess to that. I've created a monster.

ANDOCIDES

Only that? You are too modest —

ANDROCLES

Andocides, please — we've no time for recriminations, though I accept them. I've come to beg of you.

ANDOCIDES

What would you have that I could give?

ANDROCLES

Athens.

ANDOCIDES

(*holding up his shackles*) You are welcome to that part of her I own.

327

ANDROCLES

Listen to me. You hold the city in those shackled hands. You can give her back to reasonable men — or pull her with you into your grave. As you choose.

ANDOCIDES

(*matter of fact*) You're mad. Absolutely mad.

ANDROCLES

I wish I were — it would make a maddening logic easier to bear. For what's our case? You are innocent, yet charged with guilt. The man who charged you knows that you are innocent, yet feels secure, believing that you must die with your innocence wrapped about you for a shroud.

ANDOCIDES

And how has that become "our case"?

ANDROCLES

I offer you an Immunity — if you will use it.

ANDOCIDES

I do not follow you.

ANDROCLES

If you confess to guilt in the Mutilation, you can then speak as an expert witness. You can say — where Dioclides cannot — what all considered men now know — and will *accept* — to be the truth: that this "conspiracy" was nothing more than the escapade of twenty-five or thirty young men.

ANDOCIDES

You *are* mad —

ANDROCLES

No. Merely corrupt enough to know what must be done to save the city.

ANDOCIDES

Corrupt, yes — but corruptly mad, to think that I might perjure all my family's name, and mark "Informer" on my House's door.

ANDROCLES

If you die tomorrow, the next day there will be no house. Nor door. And all posterity will know your tribe as "Traitor."

ANDOCIDES

Yes, but let me die in innocence, and posterity will one day find me out to restore my name.

ANDROCLES

What innocence will you take with you in such a prideful death? What name can be restored to you when posterity — someone else's posterity — counts the worth of all those men you'll drag behind you in a bloody train.

328

For I mean to tell the world that you had a choice. Will all that blood not sully your white innocence?

ANDOCIDES

Why do you ask *me* — why this "choice" for *me*?

ANDROCLES

There is a certain logic to events and men: You can best say what must be said.

CHARMIDES

Cousin. You were going to denounce Euphiletus when you thought he was alive. What harm when he is dead? And all your friends are likewise dead — or fled to safety.

ANDOCIDES

I would have denounced Euphiletus as a free agent, and spoken truth. This is — vile.

CHARMIDES

But is it better to die, convicted of a crime, when you might now live it down — and living, let us all live with you?

ANDOCIDES

(*his face a mask; to Androcles*) You mentioned twenty-five men. Eighteen have been named.

ANDROCLES

Yes.

ANDOCIDES

There were not twenty-five.

ANDROCLES

There must be more than eighteen. (*Charmides reacts sharply to this.*)

ANDOCIDES

Are you suggesting that I sacrifice some innocent men?

ANDROCLES

No. I am saying that fifty innocent men will certainly die if there are not more than eighteen. (*He stares insistently at Andocides.*) It is a heavier burden than innocence. And you haven't much time to consider it.

ANDOCIDES

I would that I had less.

CHARMIDES

(*pause*) Would you leave my cousin and me alone for a moment? (*Surprised, Androcles goes to one side.*) I see his point, cousin. The "reasonable men" will want an earnest of your sincerity — some sacrificial "evidence." Perhaps such a city is not worth living in. (*diffidently*) Cousin, you may name me.

ANDOCIDES

I go free and let you die — never think that I could love you so little, cousin. (*He half-turns — with a growl of frustrated rage.*) Oh — come all you gods of vengeance! Confound my enemies. Let me be your sundering arm. And I will make the gutters run with villains' blood, for I can name a hundred villains! (*As he turns to call, Charmides watches with deep concern.*) Androcles! (*Androcles hurries to him.*) I will inform. Upon condition.

ANDROCLES

Son, you're not in a position to impose conditions upon the Committee.

ANDOCIDES

I am in a position to impose conditions upon you. I shall want a promise from you.

ANDROCLES

If I can grant it.

ANDOCIDES

I shall name four men. Before I name them, I shall want you to bring them a pass to get them out of the city.

ANDROCLES

It would be better if I sent Lysippus. I might be needed here.

ANDOCIDES

However you do it, *will* you do it.

ANDROCLES

Yes. (*pause*) Did they really do the Mutilation?

ANDOCIDES

Yes.

ANDROCLES

Then, why — ?

ANDOCIDES

I am not the law. Nor would I be.
(*The lights begin to cross fade.*)

PISANDER

I will not permit this! You will rescind the Immunity!

CHARICLES

(*blandly baiting him*) We can't, Pisander. It has already been announced to the people.
(*The lights are up full, on the embattled Pisander, raging before the Committee.*)

PISANDER

Then unannounce it!

CHARICLES

The people would think we are confused.

PISANDER

They'll think you have regained your senses!

CHARICLES

With two hundred and fifty dangerous conspirators running loose in our midst — oh, citizen.

PISANDER

They've "run loose," as you put it, for a month with no discernible harm to us!

CHARICLES

Then this Committee is no longer necessary — is that what you are trying to tell us, Pisander?

PISANDER

That's not what I meant, and you know it!
I demand that you rescind this Immunity!

CHARICLES

Demand, Citizen Pisander? May I remind you that this Committee is empowered by the people to act as it sees best, in the wisdom of its *collective* judgment. (*Andocides is being escorted on behind Pisander.*) Now, you will please be seated. The prisoner is here for interrogation.

PISANDER

He's *my* prisoner! *I'll* interrogate him.

CHARICLES

He is the people's prisoner, citizen. And you will be seated. Or I shall instruct the guard to remove you for obstructing the people's business. (*The threat is real, and Pisander yields to it. Unused to sitting, he is uncertain where to take his place. Charicles smiles faintly.*) Citizen Andocides. (*Andocides steps forward.*) You have been granted an Immunity from punishment for any part you may have played in the criminal conspiracy which has come to be known as the Mutilation of the Hermae. Do you accept that Immunity?

ANDOCIDES

I do, sir.

CHARICLES

Then you are prepared to admit your guilt.

ANDOCIDES

Yes. I do, sir.

PISANDER

(*jumping up*) There! You see! And now he goes free!

331

CHARICLES

(*with crushing logic*) Of course. One does not grant an Immunity to the innocent. (*to Andocides*) Perhaps it would expedite matters if you made a statement. Are you prepared to do so?

ANDOCIDES

I am.

CHARICLES

(*with point*) You realize the gravity of what you are about to say.

ANDOCIDES

I do, sir. Fully.

CHARICLES

Then, proceed.

ANDOCIDES

Citizens. It is with the deepest sense of shame that I now say — what I must. (*pause*) I was one of a group of young men who made a fearful attack upon the Sacred Guardian of our nation.

MENIPPUS

(*quickly*) How many were in this group?

ANDOCIDES

Twenty-two, sir, besides myself.

MENIPPUS

(*to clerk*) Make certain that is noted.

PISANDER

He lies! Dioclides said there were three hundred. Are you going to take the word of an admitted criminal, against that of an honest citizen?

ANDOCIDES

You will have to take the word of one or the other of us. And Pisander, himself, has pointed out that I was one of the organizers of the crime. (*Andocides stares at Pisander opaquely. Menippus snickers.*)

PISANDER

This is no laughing matter, Menippus! (*Pointing at Andocides, he resumes his old position before them all.*) Citizens! This criminal has stood before you and solemnly told you lie after lie. He swore — under sacred oath — that he was innocent. By his own admission, now, everything he said earlier was a lie. He is therefore a *proven* liar. If because of his Immunity we cannot now punish him for his admitted crime, then let us send him out among our people, clearly labeled for what he is — a self-confessed liar! In that way, we may yet serve the people and our honored office.

ANDOCIDES

(*addressing the Committee, but directly engaging Pisander*) Gentlemen. It is true that I have lied. And I ask you to believe that I lied as much from horror at publicly admitting what I had done, as from fear of punishment. But now both reasons for lying have been removed:

Gentlemen, if I committed this crime – and I have admitted to it – then you must believe that I know more about its planning, its perpetrators, its execution – than a man who alleges merely to have *seen* what he calls "a suspicious-looking" group of men. Did he overhear their plotting? *Would* they have plotted so serious a crime in the open air? Can he suggest to you – even by hearsay – what their exact intent was in committing this crime? Gentlemen, I can, and will, do all these things. And I think that even Pisander will have to admit that I speak with more authority in this matter than Dioclides.

PISANDER

I admit nothing. You lie. To protect your unapprehended accomplices.

ANDOCIDES

I concede that that might be a possible way of regarding my testimony. (*He turns to the others.*) But, gentlemen, you *must* have thought of that before you granted me my Immunity. You must have thought of that – and of the terrible weapon which you have placed in my hands.

CHARICLES

(*startled*) What weapon is that?

ANDOCIDES

The people are waiting to hear who my confederates were. (*He looks pointedly at each of them.*) So many people are fled. I doubt any of you could prove – at this moment – where you were on that night, one month ago. And like Dioclides, I could as easily name three hundred as twenty-two. You must pray that I use my weapon wisely – and truthfully.

PISANDER

What would an admitted perjurer know of truth! I say that –

CHARICLES

You have said a very great deal, Citizen Pisander! I suggest that you sit down and let some of us say something for a change. (*Pisander glares intimidatingly.*) YOU MAY BE SEATED, CITIZEN! (*Pisander, reluctantly, sits.*) Citizen Andocides, that was a very serious thing for you to say.

ANDOCIDES

I was aware of that when I said it. Might I point out to you that Dioclides has had that same weapon in his hands for a long day, now. With the result that two Senators have fled in disgrace – men who, I can tell you, had nothing to do with this crime — and two other Senators have been put to death, merely for being brave enough to stand as sureties for men who had been frightened out of their wits. Gentlemen, I ask you to observe the demeanor of Dioclides. See him as he sits, uneasy in his unaccustomed seat of honor. Watch him closely as I tell you of a visit he paid my house on the night of the Mutilation — to ask for money, in return for silence. (*Dioclides' fixed gaze, as the Committee turns inquiringly to him, is that of a bird, enchanted by the snake which will soon devour him.*)

CHARICLES

Is that true, Dioclides?

DIOCLIDES

(*This is all unreal.*) N-no — no. He's lying, lying. L-like Pisander said, he's lying. Like he lied before — he — he's a liar, liar — and he's — lying — (*He seems to run down.*)

ANDOCIDES

Might I ask the witness a direct question?

PISANDER

No! We are the prosecutors here!

CHARICLES

Citizen Pisander, the question was addressed to me. And I remind you that we are empowered only as a Committee of Inquiry. The courts will take care of the prosecution. (*to Andocides*) You may ask your question.

ANDOCIDES

Dioclides, why did you wait one month before giving your information to this Committee?

DIOCLIDES

(*same feeling of "This can't be happening"*) Why because — you see, gentlemen, I — I —

ANDOCIDES

I say that he waited a month because he extorted from my father a promise to pay two talents of silver in exchange for his silence. That is the price of a king's ransom, gentlemen, and Dioclides gave my father one month in which to try to raise it.

CHARICLES

(*shocked*) Are you now implicating your father in this crime?

ANDOCIDES

No — only in terror, sir. That was a day of terror. As all the days since have been days of terror. And when Dioclides threatened to tell his fabrication to your Committee, my father was afraid. He had just seen Polystratus led away to be executed, and he was afraid that he, too, might be executed before his innocence could be found out.

CHARICLES

(*with an awesome sternness*) Be careful where your Immunity leads you, young man! You are implying that this Committee ordered the death of an innocent man.

ANDOCIDES

(*eye to eye*) Sir, we are all of us guilty of many things — but not always of what we are charged with. (*Charicles begins to deflate.*) Polystratus was an honorable man. Because he was honorable, he trusted a man who was not. My father saw him taken away to be executed for that trust. In panic that such a thing could happen, he was preparing to flee the city when Dioclides came. And so, in terror — but in the midst of this city's terror — my father agreed to extortion. (*The Committee accepts this answer. Slowly, with a terrible dignity, the members turn to Dioclides.*)

CHARICLES

Citizen Dioclides. Have you a better reason to offer for your delay in coming before this Committee? (*Dioclides — still lost in his shattered dream of riches and glory — puts out a weak hand, as if to fend off their stares.*)

DIOCLIDES

N-no — it wasn't to be that way — (*He looks helplessly about him.*) Pisander — help me. (*He throws himself at Pisander's feet.*)

PISANDER

(*drawing back in angry contempt*) I do not protect perjurers. I can only apologize for this witness, gentlemen. (*His eyes now go to each of the Committee members, and there is a threat under each word.*) But I was misled by him, as completely as the rest of *you*.

CHARICLES

Ah — yes. Under the — ah — circumstances, that is — ah — yes. (*Pisander smiles faintly, and sits.*)

DIOCLIDES

No! That isn't the way it was to be! (*Their faces are closed against him. With a desperate charm*) Gentlemen! If you will grant me an Immunity, I — I'll tell you who bribed me — you see? It wasn't *me* — I was *bribed* — b-bribed. And if you'll just grant me — (*reasonably*) I mean, I was only doing what the others did — I didn't mean any *harm* — I mean, you gave me a banquet, you put this laurel — on — my — head . . (*Their demeanor bears in on him.*) Oh! *You're* going to kill me — aren't you — But there were others, too! I mean, all that money —

(*It is not proper to hear such a sad threnody to greed and weakness in the light, so the lights dim down discreetly, and Dioclides' last words are heard in merciful darkness. There is a moment of silence. From the streets come the sounds of the city celebrating its release from fear — shouts, laughter, the music of street musicians.)*

Scene 5

Andocides' house, just before sundown. Adamantea is standing expectantly at the window. Androcles is sitting, waiting.

LEOGORAS

(*off*) Home! My god, boys, we're home!

ADAMANTEA

They're here! (*As Androcles jumps to his feet, Leogoras — followed by Charmides, then Polydor — enters.*)

LEOGORAS

I can't believe it! Alive! Home! Free! (*He turns and calls.*) Come on, son — what are you doing out there? Here we are at home, and he dawdles about in a gloomy hall. By the gods, Androcles, what do you think of it — we're here! Alive! (*Andocides comes on behind him, holds out his hand to Adamantea, and she goes to him.*) Adamantea, fetch us some wine — we must celebrate! Get the Samian wine — the best!

ANDOCIDES

Polydor will get the wine, Father.

LEOGORAS

(*bubbling*) I don't care who gets it, so long as somebody gets it! Well, Polydor, run! Get the wine! Bring great jars of it!

ANDROCLES

Son, you were magnificent, today. Truly magnificent.

ANDOCIDES

(*dryly*) Was I?

ANDROCLES

Yes, you were. Cool — sharp as a knife. You should be proud of him, Leogoras.

ANDOCIDES

Yes. He should be very proud.

ANDROCLES

Yes, he should. And so should you. You handed those demagogues a beating today that they'll never forget.

336

ANDOCIDES

I didn't beat them, I outmaneuvered them. And there's a bitter difference in the word.

ANDROCLES

Why, what's the matter, lad?

ANDOCIDES

I'll tell you what's the matter. You stood me and my family in the shadow of the executioner today, and I am not grateful for what you had me do to get us out of that shadow.

ANDROCLES

(*sympathetic*) I know. But it was politics, son —

ANDOCIDES

I had to lie. But I did something worse than merely lie. By my very presence before that liar's bench, I willed to the city's children — to my own sons — the legacy that those public frauds you foisted on us are men of virtue — with title to respect instead of to contempt.

ANDROCLES

(*pacifying*) Well, but —

ANDOCIDES

I endorsed the streets through which I was driven, stumbling over the rubble of once-proud houses. I endorsed the ruins that bore the marker "Traitor." And the marble dust that blew into our eyes as they drove me — chained like an animal — to prison. The dust of houses even then being pulled down. The dust that choked us all, captive and captor, alike. And yet, I lied. And as I lied, I canonized the monstrous lie that pulled those houses down, and put chains on me.

ANDROCLES

(*sincerely concerned*) It's been hard for you, son. But we've learned our lesson. I say that as an old — but repentant — *ex*-demagogue. (*He smiles encouragingly.*) And just to show you that I mean what I say, tomorrow — as first order of business — we'll dissolve the Committee.

ANDOCIDES

(*pause*) And its record — that will stand, as written?

ANDROCLES

(*genial, now*) Perhaps we can change even that — at a more convenient time.

CHARMIDES

(*very "relieved"*) I'll send that word to Polystratus' son, cousin. It will brighten his exile to know that some day his family's honor may be restored — when it is convenient.

ANDROCLES

(*placating*) Oh, don't be unreasonable, boys. We have a war on our hands. A very messy war. At a time like this, you can't expect politics to be — neat.

ANDOCIDES

Oh, yours are very neat. For every public question you have an orthodox answer. It's required to be a lie, of course — one just can't use truth to serve an orthodoxy built on equivocation.

CHARMIDES

Yes, but, cousin — when you're the High Priest, the lie *does* have the virtue of being An Orthodox Lie.

ANDROCLES

That's quite funny — orthodoxy — how I wish I had one. But on any given day, boys, I can depend on as many opinions being shouted in the Assembly as there are voters present.

ANDOCIDES

Only on means — never on ends. You will fight each other to the death over *how* to gain dominion over others, but not over *whether*, or *why*, or *if* we should do so. And that is *orthodoxy*! (*He rides over Androcles' attempt at reply.*) For seventeen years, you have held up to the world a shield of brazen myth: that we are free men bearing freedom to others — by the force of our arms. And behind that shield, with the cry of "blasphemy," you have silenced every voice with courage enough even to doubt that myth. And *that* is orthodoxy!

ANDROCLES

(*affably*) Oh, I don't know — as I recall, *you* had quite a say in the Assembly on just that subject. (*He grins tolerantly at Leogoras.*)

ANDOCIDES

Yes, I did. And I ended up in chains for having done so.

ANDROCLES

(*astounded*) Oh — that's — ridiculous, son.

ANDOCIDES

You — don't — see — that — do you. To force our will on the world, you have had to force your will on the Assembly — you, and Alcibiades, and Critias, and the others. But we have refused the name of conqueror, so you could not enforce that will in open debate. And threat by threat, intimidation by intimidation, you have turned that Assembly into a pit of confusion — where men congress together only to keep a fearful eye on each other. And — you — don't — see — it. *Do* you!

CHARMIDES

"The Master of Geometry cannot do simple sums."

ANDROCLES

(*indulgently*) I felt the way you do, once — when the world was young. And I can do simple sums, Charmides. This is the first year of the Ninety-First Olympiad. That tells me the year is 361. The world is no longer young. And in that no-longer-young world, we have responsibilities. And commitments to our allies. And a place in the world to keep. I serve those responsibilities and commitments as best I can. (*He has impressed Charmides.*)

LEOGORAS

Yes, well — a cup of wine is what we all need.

ANDROCLES

(*genial, once more*) Yes. A cup of wine will make you both see things in a different light. Get good and drunk tonight, sleep late tomorrow, and by the next day, everything will be back to normal.

LEOGORAS

(*passing the wine*) Yes. The important thing is that we're all home. Back among familiar things.

ANDOCIDES

(*to Charmides*) Here's to normalcy.

CHARMIDES

To normalcy!

ANDROCLES

That's the spirit. (*They all drink. Androcles puts his cup down.*) Well, I must be going. (*putting an arm about Leogoras as he goes*) Your son deserves the city's gratitude for what he's done, Leogoras. And I'll see to it that they express their gratitude in some substantial way — or make every mother's son of them regret the day he was born. (*turning back to wave farewell*) Drink hearty, lads. (*He and Leogoras go. Charmides — looking into his cup — thinks deeply for a moment, drinks to the bottom, sets his cup down firmly, then looks jauntily at the other two.*)

CHARMIDES

Well. Goodbye, cousin. (*He holds out his hand.*)

ANDOCIDES

Goodbye — ? (*Taking his cousin's hand in the soldier's handshake, he studies his face.*) You'll be going to Syracuse?

CHARMIDES

(*nodding, mock-solemn*) I *had* thought of drinking my way back to normalcy — but then I remembered what normalcy was. (*pause*) You know

339

—between wars, this is a nice place to visit. But I wouldn't want to live here. (*With a grin and a wave, he is gone. Alone, now, with Andocides, Adamantea is reserved, withdrawn. Andocides studies her for a moment.*)

ANDOCIDES

Well. How are you, Adamantea of Melos?

ADAMANTEA

I have been thinking — (*Pause. She is shy, but frank.*) How shall we live, now — you and I?

ANDOCIDES

(*lightly*) Why — I shall come home from a day at the Market Place, you will wipe the spittle off me, and we shall sit down to dinner.

ADAMANTEA

(*not knowing how to take this*) Why — why would they — spit on you?

ANDOCIDES

Because they are reasonable men. And I have collaborated with them. And I think that they will not love me for it. (*He is looking out the window, and a resolve is taking shape in him.*) Come, look at them — so you can report them, and me, to our son.

ADAMANTEA

(*pause; flatly*) You will go to fight at Syracuse, too.

ANDOCIDES

No. I have confessed to sacrilege. (*He smiles at her.*) I am no longer eligible to perform such sacred rites.

ADAMANTEA

Then why will you not be here?

ANDOCIDES

(*feeling his way*) There is a — logic — to events. And men. (*He takes her hands in his.*) Let me try to tell you. You were born of a Spartan people. Had you been a boy, from birth you would have been taught to be valiant. And you would have been. I have fought the Spartans, and they *are* valiant. But in this house, where *I* was born, there is an altar that says: "To Zeus — Who guards the Brave and Free." And I was taught that to be one without the other was to be — merely valiant. To be both was to be an Athenian. I was born an Athenian. I will die an Athenian. And I have learned today that in between birth and death, it is better if I choose — of my own will — to *be* an Athenian. (*He kisses her lightly; his tone is wry.*) But I am a man, and I live among men, and we are responsible, each to the other. So you must tell our son what I will tell the Assembly, tomorrow: That we must find other means to gain our ends from our adversaries than those which destroy what we are, as we use them. That only means

340

which strengthen what we are, are worth the using. (*He smiles gravely at her.*) Do you agree, Adamantea of Melos? (*Equally grave, she nods.*) Then that is what I shall say to the Assembly.

ADAMANTEA

(*considering*) And they will banish you for it —

ANDOCIDES

I think so. But it will have been said.

ADAMANTEA

(*pursuing the logic of why she is to be left alone*) And no ship will take a woman in time of war.

ANDOCIDES

No.

ADAMANTEA

Perhaps we could find another — Phoenician captain?

ANDOCIDES

The places I will be free to go to will be Athenian. I think that I will not be very — popular — there, either.

ADAMANTEA

I see. (*Polydor enters with a dispatch.*)

ANDOCIDES

What is it, Polydor?

POLYDOR

This just came for you, sir.

ANDOCIDES

(*taking it*) Very official-looking.

POLYDOR

It is from the Senate, sir. (*He goes.*)

ANDOCIDES

No doubt an invitation to the Prytaneum — they'll have to dine me at least as well as Dioclides. (*As he reads, his smile fades into a mask.*)

ADAMANTEA

What — is it?

ANDOCIDES

Nothing. (*impersonally*) Would you say that "all" is singular, or plural?

ADAMANTEA

Plural — why?

ANDOCIDES

Because this decree reads in part: ". . and *all* who have desecrated Sacred Objects are hereby denied the use of the Market Place, the Assembly, the Senate, and the Temples, on pain of death." And there is no one

341

left alive in Athens who fits that description, save only Andocides the Informer. (*pause*) Like an emperor, I gave Athens back to the reasonable men. It is only reasonable, therefore, that henceforth I must be imperially Plural. (*He takes her in his arms and holds her tightly.*)

ADAMANTEA

It is as though they knew. And would not hear what you would tell them.

ANDOCIDES

(*grimly*) Oh, they will hear. I inform you that they *will* hear. And I am Andocides the Informer, who informs you that. From the first Market Place I reach, I shall inform them.

ADAMANTEA

(*concerned*) If you do, they will then call you "Traitor."

ANDOCIDES

(*smiling to reassure her*) Then I will know that they are listening.

ADAMANTEA

(*levelly*) They will say that you aid the enemy —

ANDOCIDES

Then I shall inform them that there is no enemy abroad so dangerous to us as our blind belief in our own virtue.

ADAMANTEA

(*gravely*) They will send men, to hunt you from island to island —

ANDOCIDES

(*lightly*) I think it more likely that they will hear me with indifference. (*He kisses her.*) But if you are right — then from island to island, I shall send back the word, that to fail our better selves is to shame ourselves before ourselves, as no mere conqueror ever could.

ADAMANTEA

I — I shall teach our son — to be proud.

ANDOCIDES

(*simply*) No. Teach him only that every man owes his gods one death. Teach him that how he pays that debt — if he would be a free man — must be a very personal transaction. (*He smiles, and with an echo of the prison-cell courtliness, holds out his hand.*) Come, Adamantea of Melos — you must help me pack. (*She moves to join him.*)

CURTAIN

The Long War (under the title *Three Days before Yester-day*) by Kevin O'Morrison was presented on July 14–16, 21–23, 1966, at Scott Hall Auditorium, University of Minnesota, Minneapolis. It was directed by Michael S. Lessac.

Cast of Characters

DIAGORAS	Stephen Benson
CHARM VENDOR	Richard Ramos
POLYDOR	Morley Frantzick
LEOGORAS	David Morgan
ALCIBIADES	Robert Lanchester
CHARICLES	Joseph Karioth
MENIPPUS	Paul Nickolatos
CRITIAS	Russell Walsh
ANDROCLES	James Horswill
METON	Richard Lippke
PISANDER	Donald Seay
CHARMIDES	Mark Donicht
ANDOCIDES	John Ney
ADAMANTEA	Karen Stenback
OLD WOMAN	Flo Castner
EUPHILETUS	John Sherman
POLYSTRATUS	Jack Starr
PULYTION	Richard Ramos
MELETUS	Mark Stromwall
DIOCLIDES	Richard Lippke
HOPLITE GUARD	John Gunderson
CITIZENS	James Kieffer
	James Steiner
	Michael Tazla